PURSUING A JUST
AND DURABLE PEACE

Recent Titles in
Contributions in Political Science
Series Editor: Bernard K. Johnpoll

Revolution and Rescue in Grenada: An Account of the U.S.-Caribbean Invasion
Reynold A. Burrowes

The Merit System and Municipal Civil Service: A Fostering of Social Inequality
Frances Gottfried

White House Ethics: The History of the Politics of Conflict of Interest Regulation
Robert N. Roberts

John F. Kennedy: The Promise Revisited
Paul Harper and Joann P. Krieg, editors

The American Founding: Essays on the Formation of the Constitution
J. Jackson Barlow, Leonard W. Levy, and Ken Masugi, editors

Japan's Civil Service System
Paul S. Kim

Franklin D. Roosevelt's Rhetorical Presidency
Halford R. Ryan

''Jimmy Higgins'': The Mental World of the American Rank-and-File Communist, 1930-1958
Aileen S. Kraditor

Urban Housing and Neighborhood Revitalization: Turning a Federal Program into Local Projects
Donald B. Rosenthal

Perforated Sovereignties and International Relations: Trans-Sovereign Contacts of Subnational Governments
Ivo D. Duchacek, Daniel Latouche, and Garth Stevenson, editors

New Approaches to International Mediation
C. R. Mitchell and K. Webb, editors

Israeli National Security Policy: Political Actors and Perspectives
Bernard Reich and Gershon R. Kieval, editors

More Than a Game: Sports and Politics
Martin Barry Vinokur

PURSUING A JUST AND DURABLE PEACE

John Foster Dulles and
International Organization

Anthony Clark Arend

Contributions in Political Science, Number 212

Greenwood Press
New York • Westport, Connecticut • London

Library of Congress Cataloging-in-Publication Data

Arend, Anthony C.
  Pursuing a just and durable peace : John Foster Dulles and
international organization / Anthony Clark Arend.
     p.   cm.—(Contributions in political science, ISSN 0147-1066;
no. 212)
  Bibliography: p.
  Includes index.
  ISBN 0-313-25637-3 (lib. bdg. : alk. paper)
  1. Dulles, John Foster, 1888-1959—Views on international
relations. 2. Dulles, John Foster, 1888-1959—Views on peace.
3. International organization. 4. Peace. I. Title. II. Series.
E748.D868A74   1988
973.921'092'4—dc19   87-37552

British Library Cataloguing in Publication Data is available.

Library of Congress Catalog Card Number: 87-37552
ISBN: 0-313-25637-3
ISSN: 0147-1066

First published in 1988

Greenwood Press, Inc.
88 Post Road West, Westport, Connecticut 06881

Printed in the United States of America

The paper used in this book complies with the
Permanent Paper Standard issued by the National
Information Standards Organization (Z39.48-1984).

10 9 8 7 6 5 4 3 2 1

This work is dedicated to
Dr. Paul Joseph Arend
(1930-1983)
teacher, writer and loving father

Contents

x   Contents

Acknowledgments

I would like to thank several individuals who contributed in one way or another to this study. First, I am indebted to Inis L. Claude, Jr., who is the Edward R. Stettinius, Jr. Professor of Government and Foreign Affairs at the University of Virginia. His encouragement, insight, and patience were of immeasurable help to me. I only hope that I can live up to his scholarly example. Professor William V. O'Brien of the Department of Government at Georgetown University deserves a special word of thanks for his advice over the years. He has been a constant source of support and encouragement in my work in international law. I am also grateful to John Norton Moore, Walter L. Brown Professor of Law at the University of Virginia Law School and Director of the Center for Law and National Security for his encouragement and financial support.

In addition to these individuals, I would like to thank Donna Packard and Charles McGraw who typed this work. Mr. McGraw, who also served as my teaching assistant, was invaluable during the final stages of preparation of the manuscript. Their dedication was beyond the call of duty. Of course, this study would not have been possible without the support of my parents, Paul and Cora Arend. My father did not live to see this work completed; it is thus to him that it is dedicated. Finally, I wish to thank Him without whom nothing is possible.

1

Introduction

John Foster Dulles may have been one of America's most controversial secretaries of state. He has been associated with dramatic phrases such as "liberation," "roll back," "massive retaliation," "positive loyalty," and "agonizing reappraisal." He has been called a "peacemaker,"[1] a "statesman,"[2] a "champion of freedom,"[3] a "cocksure man,"[4] a "complex amalgam"[5] and a "tactician who operated on fixed moral and religious premises."[6] While many studies have been made of Dulles and his role as a cold-war policy maker, few works have concentrated on another important aspect of his life -- international organization. Relatively speaking, however, much more of his life was devoted to thinking about and working with international organization than to high-level policy making.

While still a very young man, Dulles had unique opportunities to attend international conferences that helped further international organization. During the interwar period, he wrote prolifically on international organization and served as chairman of the Commission to Study the Bases of a Just and Durable Peace, which worked for the creation of a new international organization. As the Second World War was coming to an end, he advised the United States delegation to the founding conference of the United Nations and later served as a delegate to that organization. Even after he became secretary of state in 1953, he continued to have an acute interest in international organization.

This study will focus specifically on Dulles's thoughts about and involvement with international organization. In the course of this examination, this work will reveal two major things about Dulles. First, the popular conception of Dulles as a cold warrior ignores the early period of his thought. His early conception of the nature of the international system was vastly different than the cold-war image would suggest, and, in consequence, his early formulation of the roles of international organization was also quite different. Second, during the mid 1940s, his early understanding of the international system underwent a drastic change which, in turn, altered his perception of the functions of international organization and his policies toward international organization.   In short, this study will show that Dulles was a much more complex individual than he is often perceived to be.

NOTES

1. M. Comfort, *John Foster Dulles: Peacemaker*.
2. M. Guhin, *John Foster Dulles: A Statesman and His Times*.
3. D. Eisenhower, address at Gettysburg, Pennsylvania, May 24, 1959, reprinted in H. Van Dusen, ed., *The Spiritual Legacy of John Foster Dulles*, (1960) vii.
4. H. Finer, *Dulles over Suez*, 11.
5. R. Pruessen, *John Foster Dulles: The Road to Power*, xii.
6. T. Hoopes, *The Devil and John Foster Dulles*, 488.

PART ONE

THE EARLY DULLES
(1919–1945)

2

The International System
(1919–1945)

By the time John Foster Dulles was thirty-one, he had already had a tremendous amount of exposure to international affairs. In 1907, he attended the Hague Peace Conference at the invitation of his grandfather, John Watson Foster, who had been President Harrison's secretary of state and was at the time an advisor to the Chinese delegation to the conference. Later, during the First World War, Dulles worked with the U.S. War Trade Board and eventually served as a legal advisor to the U.S. delegation to the Paris Peace Conference. Most of Dulles's activities relating to international organization, however, came after Paris, as he began systematically developing his thought on the nature of the international system[1] and the roles of international organization. In 1939 he published his first book, *War, Peace and Change*, to address many of these areas. This chapter will discuss Dulles's early thought on the nature of the international system, while subsequent chapters will explore his early thought on the roles of international organization.

WAR, PEACE AND CHANGE: THE DYNAMIC VERSUS THE STATIC, THE PROBLEM OF SOVEREIGNTY, AND INTERNATIONAL CONFLICT

In *War, Peace and Change*, Dulles began his discussion of international conflict by looking first at human nature. According to Dulles, at the heart of human nature was selfishness:

> Whenever life assumes a form which involves consciousness there is an awareness of needs and a desire to satisfy them. Selfishness in this sense is a basic human

instinct. These needs are in part material. Man seeks the
food, clothing and shelter necessary to perpetuate his life
and the lives of those upon whom he is dependent for
emotional or material values. There are also needs which
are non-material. "Man does not live by bread alone." He
reaches out for imponderables, such as love and beauty and
intellectual stimulus. Aware of his own finite character,
and his inadequacies, man seeks self-exaltation by
identification with some external Cause or Being which
appears more noble and more enduring than is he himself.[2]

But, these needs, material and nonmaterial, could only be fulfilled in
cooperation with others. Hence, "we have gregariousness as a
derivative or supplemental tendency."[3] The combination of this desire
to fulfill individual needs and this gregariousness leads to conflict:
"[T]he fact that human beings, all selfish, are in contact with each
other inevitably brings dissatisfaction."[4] As Dulles explained, "[t]his
is due in part to desires which are inherently irreconcilable and in
part to a material shortage of resources wherewith to satisfy all
desires."[5] In general, individuals fell into one of two categories:
those who were essentially satisfied and desired to keep
circumstances as they were, and those who were not satisfied with
existing conditions and desired to obtain something from others.[6]

In prehistoric days, conflicts between competing individuals were
resolved "by force or the threat of force,"[7] but as time passed,
individuals became aware of the undesirability of such a system.
Consequently, "[t]here inevitably grew up a demand for a social
mechanism which would permit human beings to derive the advantages
of association without incurring the acute disadvantages incident to
force being the only method of resolving the conflicts which were
the inevitable incidents of association."[8]

According to Dulles, efforts to establish alternatives to the
force system fell into two broad and interrelated categories: the
"ethical" solution and the "political" or "authoritarian" solution.[9] The
ethical solution sought to orient human thinking away from selfish
desires and incline it to compromise and self-sacrifice. But since
such efforts, while partially successful, were not able by themselves
to eliminate conflict entirely, the "political" or "authoritarian"
solution was also needed. Dulles explained that "[h]uman beings who
sought the benefit of association together have through conscious
decision or unconscious evolution organized themselves into a polity,
usually with some governing authority."[10] The function of this
authority was

to familiarize itself with the various desires and needs of
its group, to appraise the possibility of their being
satisfied and reconciled, and to proscribe rules of conduct,
consonant with the *mores* of the community, which would

be calculated to permit the maximum of satisfaction, or the minimum of dissatisfaction. Once such rules are promulgated, the alternative procedure of violence can be, and is banned. The political authority is given by the group the right and the means to enforce rules and to compel, in lieu of individual resort to violence, the utilization of the peaceful procedures laid down by the authority.[11]

A state thus evolved as a collection of individuals where some central authority was recognized. This authority would promulgate rules to govern the community and would balance the competing desires for changing the status quo against those for maintaining it. Force was effectively eliminated since the inhabitants of the territory acknowledged the legitimacy of the authority to make these decisions and would, therefore, willingly abide by them. Force was also mitigated by the application of the ethical principle to create an atmosphere of self-sacrifice.

On the international level, however, Dulles argued, neither the ethical nor the political solutions had been successful in preventing major conflict. The ethical principle was limited for several reasons. First, it was very difficult to generate feelings of self-sacrifice for individuals who are geographically removed: "Self-satisfaction is apt to be derived from satisfying others only if the others be those whom, through personal contact, we have come to love, or at least to know and like, and only if we can see for ourselves the gratification which we cause."[12] The problem was compounded since religions that could instill a sense of duty to others were often limited in their applicability. According to Dulles, "[f]ew religions conceive of their deity as concerned with the welfare of all mankind."[13] Moreover, there was a tendency for religions "to become identified with human authorities."[14] The religions tended to be associated with the "secular order" and lose their effectiveness in transcending national borders.[15]

The second problem limiting the effectiveness of the ethical solution on the international level was the corporate nature of states and other groups that engage in economic relations on the international plane. Self-sacrifice could be made by individuals who were convinced that some activity in the interest of others was really in their own best moral interests, but the authorities of corporate beings -- businesses and states -- were expressly charged with the duty to act solely in the interest of their stockholders or members. Dulles explained, "the political affairs of the nations and their relations with each other are administered by persons acting in a representative capacity and who, in such capacity, are not deemed to have any mandate to sacrifice for the general welfare the specific interests of the group which has placed them in a position of authority."[16] Furthermore, unlike individuals, corporations and states had no mortal souls that could be condemned for ignoring other entities; consequently, "bodies corporate are immune from any moral law."[17]

Dulles also recognized limitations on imposing the "political" or "authoritarian" solution on international politics. The first problem was that as the body to be governed increased in size, it became more difficult to manage. In small societies, on the other hand, it was easier for an authority to arbitrate disputes and secure property, and it was also relatively easy to see the effects of particular decisions. Once the membership in the community increased, however, "many acts, seemingly innocent, [might] have the indirect and unintended effect of causing great suffering for many without comparable satisfaction for the few."[18] It was thus increasingly difficult to be certain that the actions of the authority would not have deleterious effects.

Another major problem of governing international society was that "its component elements are in constant flux."[19] One of the major themes of Dulles's thought was the pervasiveness of change. In any system, as noted earlier, there were static and dynamic elements. The static elements were essentially the "haves"[20]: those who were satisfied with the status quo and had a vested interest in maintaining it. The dynamic elements, or "have-nots,"[21] were those who felt that the status quo was unfair. With these elements, a government had a difficult task: "It is necessary that the rules be such as to maintain a reasonable balance between those opposing and partially irreconcilable desires."[22] To do this, the authority needed to establish enough "collective security"[23] to satisfy the static powers that their persons and property would be protected. The government also needed, however, to achieve enough "insecurity"[24] for the dynamic forces to have the potential to make inroads into the status quo. If there were too much security, the dynamic forces would be frustrated and take recourse to force. Conversely, if there were too much insecurity, nothing would be accomplished in society and the static elements would perhaps resort to force. This balancing act, Dulles argued, was difficult enough on the nation-state level; consequently, with other problems, "[t]he difficulties which inherently beset the successful operation of a polity which has grown to national dimensions suggest why the political solution has not yet been extended to the world of nations."[25]

A final problem associated with the ineffectiveness of the political solution on the international plane was a feeling on the part of nations that other groups were hostile competitors.[26] This resulted from the tendency of national authorities to portray other states as "bad" in order to enhance their own power and the tendency of individuals in a state "to personify the group authority and to identify themselves therewith to such an extent that they derive vicarious pride from the power and pomp displayed by their group authority, from its prestige in relation to that of other group authorities and from the deference seemingly accorded it by such others."[27]

In light of these problems of securing international order, no alternative had been successfully instituted to replace war as the means of resolving international disputes. Consequently, the international system was a "war system", whereby force was "sanctioned as a legitimate and indeed primary method of settling international differences and determining changes in the domains of the sovereign states."[28]   For years, Dulles contended, the force system had been tolerated;[29] professional armies had been able, for the most part, to keep the conflict to the battlefield. As technology developed, however, war had become more destructive and civilian populations had become increasingly involved in armed conflict. With the advent of World War I, it became clear that war had taken on a "totalitarian" character,[30] in which the entire population was mobilized against the perceived enemy.

Mobilizing the population for a totalitarian war involved a number of the elements that contribute generally to friction among states.   First, the people needed to be persuaded to overcome the inherent selfishness that would tend to inhibit their involvement in a war for reasons other than self defense.[31]   This normally was achieved by stimulating the people to personify their state as the ideal hero, the "nation-hero personality."[32]   In essence, the state was practically deified and portrayed as the people's ultimate benefactor. Furthermore, as noted earlier, the people also experienced vicarious achievement when their state succeeded.   Second, there must also be the personification of another state or states as a "villain." According to Dulles, "[o]nce a nation personification has been achieved it provides the ideology which readily lends to mass sacrifices."[33]   The people were thus ready to die for their beloved nation and ready to fight the villain that was "threatening" them.

As Dulles viewed the international system in the 1930s, he saw the demonstration of his theory: a concrete struggle between the dynamic and the static. Germany, Japan, and Italy were all dynamic, energetic states that desired a change in the status quo. However, the powers that preferred the status quo, like Britain and France, held them back. Germany felt stultified and relegated to an inferior position; the war guilt clause of the Treaty of Versailles, forced disarmament, and ethnic loyalties were major problems.[34]   But "no mechanism functioned for remedial action."[35]   Finally, Germany acted unilaterally; it rearmed, annexed Austria, and was eventually given the Sudetenland.

The case of Japan was somewhat analogous. A dynamic state, Japan primarily desired "an enhanced moral and social status,"[36] and secondarily sought territorial augmentation.   Dulles argued that if Japan had received increased status, "the pressure for further change would have been greatly allayed."[37]   However, "[a]s dynamic pressure grew with the closing of the outlet first desired, Japan intensified her efforts to enlarge otherwise her domain"[38] and moved into Manchuria.

Italy was also denied a "change of moral and social status."[39] Dulles explained that Italy "became insistent that she should now be recognized as a major power and she particularly sought such recognition in relation to Mediterranean affairs."[40] When Britain and France did not look favorably upon this new status, "Ethiopia became a victim, not because of its intrinsic worth -- which is problematic-- but because its conquest would be symbolic of Italy's new stature and would tend to compel acceptance of Italy as a major factor in the Mediterranean area."[41]

While condoning none of these activities, Dulles argued that the rigid status quo powers were largely responsible by not allowing the timely expression of the dynamic elements. Moreover, no formal means existed to handle the dynamic forces. The Treaty of Versailles became a straitjacket and the League of Nations failed to act effectively. Simply put, "[t]he world [was] too rigid in its structure and thinking to accommodate itself properly to such demands."[42] Indeed, the Munich Agreement seemed to be a prime example of this. Because the international system could not afford timely and orderly change to Germany, it eventually forced a radical change that Dulles felt was both heinous and potentially destructive of world peace.

FURTHER ELABORATIONS ON THE PROBLEM OF SOVEREIGNTY: ECONOMIC ARROGANCE

In *War, Peace and Change*, Dulles's thesis seemed to be that conflict results from the inability of the international system to balance the static and dynamic elements, coupled with the "nation-hero" and "nation-villain" ideology that mobilizes the population for a totalitarian war. A system consisting of independent sovereign states provided no relief from this problem, since there was no effective authority above the individual sovereignties. Dulles continued to examine the problems of sovereignty in his other early writings, especially in terms of the economic irresponsibility of states in what he perceived to be an independent world.

From his early involvement with the reparations and debt issues following World War I, Dulles became aware of the interconnectedness of the international economy. He began to see clearly how European economic problems were hurting the United States. In 1922, he believed that both decreasing buying power in Europe and European inflation were producing grave effects within America.[43] On the problem, he observed:

As foreign currencies depreciate, the financial ability of the rest of the world to purchase these [U.S.] commodities declines. Until this decline is checked, the continually increasing burden is thrown on American producers and American bankers, and ultimately we may have to curtail our production to the strict needs of our domestic market, with consequent unemployment and loss of invested capital.[44]

In Dulles's view, nations did not operate in economic vacuums, but greatly influenced the rest of the world with their actions.

Dulles also demonstrated his awareness of the interdependent nature of the international economy by illustrating the effects that economic interference could produce when used as a weapon by one state against another.   In an article written in 1929 entitled "Conceptions and Misconceptions Regarding Intervention," he emphasized how economic sanctions could be far more damaging to the internal affairs of a state than even direct military intervention.[45]   He also recognized the economic vulnerability of states in articles relating to his work with the Committee on Economic Sanctions of the Twentieth Century Fund.

In the early 1940s, Dulles became chairman of the Federal Council of Churches' Commission to Study the Bases of a Just and Durable Peace (later called the Commission to Study a Just and Durable Peace), which sought to translate Christian ideals into concrete principles for organizing the postwar world.   By the time Dulles became involved with the commission, his appreciation of economic interdependence and his concern for its implications were quite prominent in his thought.   In a major address entitled "The Church's Role in Developing the Bases of a Just and Durable Peace," delivered on May 28, 1941, Dulles contended: "[A]s science and invention have overcome the separations which geography formerly imposed, what is done in one part of the world has repercussions which extend far beyond the national frontier.   The world has become an independent economic machine."[46]

With the fact of economic interdependence, Dulles saw an economic irresponsibility on the part of states that was contributing to international conflict and thus needed to be restrained.   Even before becoming chairman of the commission in December 1940, Dulles had applied to the economic realm the proposition that "[p]olitical power should be accompanied by a responsibility coextensive with power."[47]   He explained that "[t]his means in the economic sphere that those governments whose trade and monetary policies vitally affect millions beyond their border should only exercise such power with [a] sense of responsibility toward these others."[48]

In his May 1941 speech, Dulles illustrated other deleterious aspects of a laissez-faire economic system operating within the context of sovereign states.   He explained that during "the past century and a half the world has counted upon short-range material profit to arouse the effort required to drive our economic machine, to discover and develop natural resources, to market and manufacture them and to get them into consumption."[49]   This functioned fairly well "so long as the world was one of open and constantly expanding opportunity,"[50] but as time passed, this system began to break down: "We have seen during recent years extended periods during which millions of men were idle and facing misery and privation in the midst of potential plenty."[51]   Indeed, Dulles contended, "a solution of the problem of unemployment has been found only in armament programs."[52]

This general dependence on the profit motive to run the international economy caused problems far beyond those caused in a capitalist domestic environment.   As Dulles stated, "[t]he evil of dependence upon self-centered motivation is particularly acute in the field of international relations."[53]   The problem is largely due to the fact that, unlike a scheme with checks on competition such as taxation and anti-trust laws, the international system is essentially unregulated.   He explained that "[t]here is no recognition of the principle that power involves a decent respect for all who are subject to that power.   There exists no political mechanism to carry out the principle, even if it should be recognized."[54]

This lack of regulation is the direct result of an international system based on the principle of sovereignty.   Dulles argued that "'[s]overeignty' means, by very definition (Webster) 'independent of, and unlimited by, any other.'   It implies the right to do what one pleases, irrespective of the effect elsewhere."[55]   Consequently, a sovereign state can lawfully undertake any number of actions that could harm another state or states:

> Our nation can, if it pleases, arbitrarily cut off access to
> our markets and products.   It is irrelevant that that may
> bring unemployment and privation to millions elsewhere.
> We can arbitrarily alter the value we place on monetary
> metals, like gold and silver, even though this may dislocate
> the trade and business of the world and the domestic
> economies of other nations.   The political leaders of each
> nation have, in law, a duty only to their own people.   The
> welfare of others in no ways restricts what they may do.[56]

According to Dulles, this sovereignty system, which permitted such economic responsibility, was "as obsolete as the unregulated public utility."[57]

The ability to alter the economic well-being of other states had grave consequences since, in Dulles's mind, economic discontent was a major cause of war.   In fact, he advanced economic conditions as a major cause of World War II, augmenting somewhat his analysis in *War, Peace and Change*.   Rejecting the "popular view" that "four great nations of the world . . . happened at the same time to fall under the domination of a few evil men,"[58] Dulles argued that economic distress provided the basis for conflict.   He explained that "at times, particularly times of prolonged economic depression, large sections of a community become disheartened and despondent. They seem to face a future without opportunity and with constantly diminishing security. The young in particular become resentful and revolutionary in spirit."[59]   Under these circumstances "violent and ruthless men" are able to gain power; "[t]hey promise the disaffected that, if they will but organize for forcible action, the existing order can be overthrown and a new order installed which will provide the opportunity and security they crave,"[60] and "[t]hereby is started a chain of events which moves readily to war, perhaps civil war, perhaps foreign war.[61]

While Dulles would not apply these causes to all wars, he did feel that "a sequence of events such as I have outlined explains the rise to power in Germany, Italy, Japan and Russia, of ruthless military dictators and it explains the willingness of these peoples to sacrifice to dictatorship their personal freedoms."[62]   Dulles was, however, able to generalize that "given the present industrial and economic state of the world, wars of destructive magnitude are most apt to spring from causes such as those I have outlined."[63]

SPIRITUAL INADEQUACIES

During Dulles's work with the commission, he also became very vocal on what he perceived to be "spiritual inadequacies" in the international system.   While these ideas were most thoroughly developed in the 1940s, they were present in embryonic form in *War, Peace and Change.*

As noted earlier, one of the causes of totalitarian war, in Dulles's mind, was the tendency to personify the state as the "hero-nation;" essentially to deify this image and portray it in constant struggle with the "villain-nation."   Part of the reason for this development, Dulles suggested, was the degeneration of traditional religion:

> There have been many times when religious concepts dominated human emotion and the action that springs therefrom.   This has primarily been at times when such concepts involved the dramatic contrasting of God and Devil, of Heaven and Hell, of Believer and Infidel.   But such ideology, doubtless beneficent at its inception, became exaggerated to a degree that led to widespread destruction and suffering, as during the period of religious wars.   A reaction and dilution occurred.   But such dilution involved religion becoming more universal and abstract. When this occurred, religion became less gripping and vital. It became inadequate to satisfy the mass need of a clear-cut, vivid object of adoration and sacrifice.[64]

In other words, as religions became less *real* in the eyes of individuals, they began to lose some of their potency to promote devotion and loyalty. But as religions began to lose their potency, the personified state stepped in to fill the gap. As Dulles said, "[a]t this point the gods of nationalism were imagined to fill the want which most men feel."[65]   Consequently, people began rendering devotion fit only for a divine being to the very human, but now deified, state -- as Dulles put it, "[w]e have been rendering unto Caesar that which is God's."[66]   The problem is that "[t]he finest qualities of human nature are at once too delicate and too powerful to be put blindly at the disposal of other humans who are primarily concerned with their own kingdom -- not the bringing into being of the Kingdom of God."[67]

This theme of spiritual inadequacies continued throughout Dulles's early writings. During the course of World War II, Dulles argued, spiritual inadequacies developed on both sides. On the one hand, what initially sprang from deprived economic conditions was soon compounded by spiritual problems. He explained in his May 1941 address:

> Germany and Russia today pose problems which are more than economic. Their designs are broadly revolutionary and they seek to overthrow not merely the old economic order, but also its political and moral ideologies. Just as the French Revolution, which grew out of economic distress, became atheistic, so the German and Russian revolutions are atheistic. Undoubtedly the world is now faced not merely with economic issues, but with moral and political issues of the utmost gravity.[68]

He continued to explain that this moral or spiritual problem on Germany's part would eventually contribute to its downfall. He explained that Germany "can never gain her peace so long as she idealizes the method of violence, so long as she rejects the Christian concept that every human being has value as a person, irrespective of nationalities, color or class."[69]   In sum, "[t]he failure of Germany's leaders will be due to disregard of precisely those Christian virtues which Hitler so likes to hold up to ridicule and contempt."[70]

But Dulles also saw spiritual weakness on the other side. In his May 1941 address he cautioned that "[w]e also will never achieve our peace if we seek to perpetuate a world system which we believe to be to our immediate economic advantage because it legalizes the irresponsible use of our power. That, too, is immoral and un-Christian and bound to fail."[71]   He thus concluded that "[o]ur great national weakness today is not physical, but spiritual," explaining that "[w]e lack a constructive power which is inspiring and contagious.

We appear to be purely on the defensive and to be supporting the *status quo* of a national sovereignty system which has become vitally defective and which is inevitably productive of just such convulsions as the present World War."[72] It is interesting to note that here the economic irresponsibility on the part of America took on, in Dulles's eyes, the nature of a spiritual weakness.

Dulles also voiced this concern for spiritual problems in the West in subsequent writings. In an address delivered at the National Study Conference on March 3, 1942, Dulles cautioned against building up hatred against the Axis powers. He explained that "we realize that to attain our end [in the war] requires a national purpose forged by hearts and minds that are comprehending and free from the evil emotions which Christ condemned."[73] He explicitly rejected the notion that victory required "hatred, vengefulness and self-gratification."[74] While these emotions may seem to stimulate one to fight, they end up by "fouling his mind and soul."[75] These evil emotions "burn up the moral fiber of a people; they do not produce a type of will which is persistent; they build up external resistances which make victory more difficult to obtain, and they render victory illusory if it is finally achieved."[76] As support for his proposition that hate should not be generated, Dulles cited the injunctions of Christ and the attitudes of Abraham Lincoln in support of forgiveness and healing.

Dulles also argued that the victors should not merely be satisfied with the "negative task"[77] of defeating the enemy on the battlefield. He explained that "[v]ictory is not itself the end. It is a means to an end, namely the organizing of a better world."[78] Consequently, the United States needed a sense of mission besides ending the war. It needed a "national purpose which conforms to great human needs, a purpose," Dulles explained, "that is responsive to the insistent demand of suffering humanity that a way be found to save them and their children and their children's children from the misery, the starvation of body and soul, the violent death, which economic disorder and recurrent war now wreak upon man."[79] It was the purpose of Christians, such as those assembled when Dulles spoke, to help show the world how to accomplish these positive tasks.

DULLES'S EARLY THOUGHT AND THE WORK OF THE COMMISSION TO STUDY THE BASES OF A JUST AND DURABLE PEACE

From the above discussion of Dulles's early thought on the nature of the international system, three basic elements can be identified. First, Dulles believed that the international system was composed of two types of states -- those that were essentially static and supported the status quo and those that were dynamic and supported change. Second, Dulles believed that the sovereignty system supported a form of economic arrogance through which states, by virtue of their juridical independence, disregarded the deleterious effects that their behavior could have on the world economy. Third, Dulles felt that the international system was rifted by spiritual inadequacies. Indeed, it seems that these spiritual failings may have been the cause of the economic arrogance. Not surprisingly, all those elements of Dulles's thought were reflected in the publications of the Commission to Study the Bases of a Just and Durable Peace.

In December of 1942, the Federal Council of Churches adopted a set of "Guiding Principles," which had been prepared by the commission. These principles continued all three aspects of Dulles's thought. Principle Six recognized that the world is "living and therefore changing."[80] Consequently, the dynamic must be allowed to express itself: "Any attempt to freeze an order of society by inflexible treaty specifications is bound, in the long run, to jeopardize the peace of mankind."[81] The principle continues: "Nor must it be forgotten that refusal to assent to needed change must be as immoral as the attempt by violent means to force such change."[82]

Similarly, Dulles's concepts of interdependence and the problem of state arrogance are reflected in Principle Four, which refers to the "interdependent life of nations."[83] It advocates the institution of a system of cooperation, as opposed to one based on absolute state sovereignty, stating that "[a] world of irresponsible, competing and unrestrained national sovereignties whether acting alone or in alliance or in coalition, is a world of international anarchy."[84] Principle Five explicitly cautions against economic arrogance, contending that "the possession of such natural resources should not be looked upon as an opportunity to promote national advantage or to enhance the prosperity of some at the expense of others."[85]

Since the commission was most concerned with spiritual problems, these are discussed at the beginning of the Guiding Principles. Principle One proclaims that there was, in fact, a "moral law" that "undergirds the world."[86] According to Principle Two, "the sickness and suffering which afflict our present society are proof of indifference to, as well as direct violation of, the moral law."[87] Furthermore, "[a]ll share in responsibility for the present evils. There is none who does not need forgiveness. A mood of genuine penitence is therefore demanded of us -- individuals and nations alike."[88] Principle Three echoes Dulles's injunction against hatred of the enemy, arguing "that it is contrary to the moral order that nations should be motivated by a spirit of revenge and retaliation."[89] This approach would only be self-defeating, since "[s]uch attitudes will lead, as they always have led, to renewed conflict."[90]

These Guiding Principles, based, as can clearly be seen, largely on Dulles's thought, underlay the more specific proposals that the commission developed for the establishment of a new international order. These specific proposals will be examined in more detail in the next chapters, which look at Dulles's thought on several specific roles that international organization can play in world politics.

NOTES

1. Dulles was quite concerned about the prospects of another war. See Dulles, "The Road to Peace," 492; R. Pruessen, *John Foster Dulles: The Road to Power*, 154–177.
2. J. F. Dulles, *War, Peace and Change*, 6.
3. Ibid.
4. Ibid., 7.
5. Ibid.
6. Ibid.
7. Ibid.
8. Ibid., 8.
9. Ibid., 9.
10. Ibid., 11.
11. Ibid.
12. Ibid., 17.
13. Ibid., 19.
14. Ibid.
15. Ibid., 19–20.
16. Ibid., 26.
17. Ibid., 23.
18. Ibid., 29.
19. Ibid., 30.
20. Ibid., 30 n.2. Dulles, however, prefers the terms "static" and "dynamic" to "haves" and "have-nots."
21. Ibid.
22. Ibid., 30.
23. Ibid., 31.
24. Ibid.
25. Ibid., 33–34.
26. Ibid., 34.
27. Ibid.
28. Ibid., 1.
29. Ibid.
30. Ibid., 3.
31. Ibid., 67.
32. Ibid., 58.
33. Ibid., 63.
34. Ibid., 147–148.
35. Ibid., 147.
36. Ibid., 144.
37. Ibid.
38. Ibid.
39. Ibid., 146.
40. Ibid.

41. Ibid.

42. Ibid., 149.

43. Pruessen, *John Foster Dulles*, 90-91.

44. Dulles, "America's Part in An Economic Conference," Jan. 19, 1922, quoted in Pruessen, *John Foster Dulles*, 91.

45. Dulles, "Conceptions and Misconceptions Regarding Intervention," 102-104.

46. Dulles, "The Church's Role in Developing the Bases of a Just and Durable Peace," May 28, 1941, *JFD Papers*, 17.

47. Letter from JFD to Professor Eugene Staley, Jan. 3, 1940, in *JFD Papers*.

48. Ibid.

49. Dulles, "The Church's Role in Developing the Bases of a Just and Durable Peace," 13.

50. Ibid.

51. Ibid.

52. Ibid.

53. Ibid., 14.

54. Ibid., 15.

55. Ibid.

56. Ibid., 15-16.

57. Ibid., 16.

58. Ibid., 8.

59. Ibid., 10.

60. Ibid.

61. Ibid.

62. Ibid., 11.

63. Ibid.

64. Dulles, *War, Peace and Change*, 115-116.

65. Ibid., 116.

66. Ibid., 117.

67. Ibid.

68. Dulles, "The Church's Role in Developing the Bases of a Just and Durable Peace," 11-12.

69. Ibid., 25.

70. Ibid.

71. Ibid.

72. Ibid., 25-26.

73. Dulles, "Opening Address Delivered at the National Study Conference," Mar. 3, 1942, *JFD Papers*, 1.

74. Ibid., 3.

75. Ibid.

76. Ibid., 5.

77. Ibid.

78. Ibid., 1.

79. Ibid, 5.

80. Federal Council of Churches, "A Just and Durable Peace, Statement of Guiding Principles," Dec. 11, 1942, *JFD Papers*, 4, (hereinafter cited as "Statement of Guiding Principles").

81. Ibid.

82. Ibid.

83. Ibid., 3.

84. Ibid.

85. Ibid., 4.

86. Ibid., 3.

87. Ibid.

88. Ibid.

89. Ibid.

90. Ibid.

3

Peaceful Change

Dulles believed that a major source of international conflict was the lack of an international authority to adequately balance the dynamic and static elements in the international system. With no workable mechanism to provide for change, war became the only realistic way for dynamic states to gain their desired change in the status quo. For Dulles, establishing procedures for peaceful change was *the* central function of international organization. Not surprisingly, one of Dulles's main concerns during this period of his thought was to criticize unsuccessful efforts to establish mechanisms for peaceful change, and to make recommendations to ensure that future international organization would perform this function.

THE FUNCTION OF PEACEFUL CHANGE AND THE FAILURE OF THE PRE-LEAGUE ERA AND THE LEAGUE

According to Dulles, any adequate proposal for international peace must recognize the need for change and provide peaceful mechanisms to obtain it. In "The Road to Peace," published in 1935, Dulles argued that "[p]eace plans, if they are to be effective, must be constructed so as to take into account these two fundamental facts-- namely, the inevitability of change and the present lack of an adequate substitute for force as an inducement to change."[1] In *War, Peace and Change*, he went even further and prescribed the specific elements that the rules of an international (or domestic) authority must possess "to secure permanent peace within the group."[2] First, the rules "must be formulated by a central authority which owes and feels a duty to the group as a whole and to all of its constituent parts."[3] Second, the rules "must create a condition of flexibility, which will give qualified and balanced satisfaction to both the dynamic and static elements."[4]   Third, the rules that are formulated "must always be changeable and in fact be changed when they fail to provide the desired balance.   Underlying conditions are constantly in flux and only through adaptation of the rules of conduct can a reasonable balance be preserved."[5]

When Dulles applied these three requirements for international organization to the pre-League and League regimes, he found the situation   quite   unsatisfactory.   First,   he   examined   general international law as a preorganizational attempt to regulate relations among   states.   On   this   effort   Dulles   noted   that   "[s]o-called international law, which is principally embodied in treaties, largely lacks each of these three characteristics indispensable to municipal law if it is to preserve peace within the group."[6]   The first problem was that the norms of international law were not formulated by a central   authority   with   a   duty   to   all   states.   There   was   no international organization.   Furthermore, the norms did not seek to establish a mechanism to secure peaceful change and, hence, did not fulfill Dulles's second and third requirements for international peace. He explained that

> Political treaties, with minor exceptions, are not designed
> to provide a status of reasonable flux between the static
> and dynamic forces of the world.   In the main they
> consecrate a specific act of taking by one nation away
> from another nation.   When initially made they may reflect
> the existing power between desires.   More often, they
> merely reflect the fact that, at this moment, there *is* a
> preponderance of power in a certain nation or group of
> nations.   A very small superiority of power can be and
> often is utilized, through "peace" treaties, to create a
> result quite disproportionate to the relative power of the
> parties.   In any event, most political treaties do not seek
> to create a condition of elasticity, which will be adaptable
> to changes in the balance of power initially existing.
> Rather, such treaties tend to perpetuate the results
> obtainable from possession of an initial command of
> power.[7]

In essence, such treaties froze a given status quo.   They did not provide for change when the underlying conditions of the status quo changed.   Furthermore, "they themselves are not normally changeable except through force or the threat of force."[8]   Even though there was   a   "vague   doctrine   of   *rebus   sic   stantibus*,"   the   customary international   law   doctrine   whereby   a   fundamental   change   in circumstances can allow the altering of treaty obligations, "political treaties   are   in   the   main   of   perpetual   or   indefinite   duration,   not subject to change to meet changes in the underlying conditions."[9]   A number of specific treaties illustrated Dulles's point. For example, the Kellogg-Briand Pact, which Dulles had initially favored, soon became in his view "the most futile of all peace efforts"[10] because it called for the renunciation of the use of force for change without providing a peaceful alternative.

According to Dulles, the League of Nations Covenant represented the first major effort to institutionalize procedures for peaceful change. Article 19 of the Covenant, which had been advocated by Woodrow Wilson and the U. S. delegation, provided that "[t]he Assembly may from time to time advise the reconsideration by Members of the League of treaties which have become inapplicable and the consideration of international conditions whose continuance might endanger the peace of the world."[11] While recognizing that the League could only "advise," Dulles observed that "there is here found for the first time in history the germ of an international group authority with power to give or withhold moral sanction in respect of treaties and under injunction to exercise this authority in the general interest, with a view of preserving the world from international violence."[12] Thus, even though the article lacked the "teeth" to compel change, the possible use of moral suasion in this respect was a very forward-looking development. This provision had, according to Dulles, great potential; it "was the 'heart' of the League, the genesis of an international authority responsible for the welfare of the whole, able to give to the treaty structure of the world that flexibility which is the indispensable complement to sanctity [of treaties] and the renunciation of force."[13]

Unfortunately, the potential of article 19 was never realized.[14] Although the allies had agreed to this provision, "it was formal acceptance without intellectual understanding."[15] When the U. S., the advocate of the article, refused to join the League, the states that had just fought World War I to preserve order clung "to those provisions of the League Covenant which were primarily designed to preserve the existing order."[16] Hence, "the entire weight of League authority was placed behind Articles 10 and 16, designed to prevent 'aggression.' No thought was given to setting up machinery to effect changes from time to time in those treaties and in those international conditions 'whose continuance might endanger the peace of the world.'"[17] Without universality and an effort to implement peaceful change, the League became "an alliance of the satisfied nations to maintain the *status quo*."[18] As a consequence, "[i]t was left to force to effect changes more farreaching and more ominous than those which would have sufficed if freely and promptly accorded."[19]

DULLES'S PROPOSALS FOR PEACEFUL CHANGE

War, Peace and Change

Given the inevitability of change, the preeminent goal of an international authority must be to ensure that change is *timely*. According to Dulles, if the dynamic forces were detected at an "early stage,"[20] provisions could be made to accommodate them gradually and, hence, forestall an explosive change later on. Demands for change on the international level involved several forms. First, there was a change that "relates to moral and social standing of a nation and its nationals."[21] Second, there was the form of change that "relates to political and economic influence beyond the confines of the national territory,"[22] and finally, there was the desire for change that "relates to the national territory itself" and involves "a transfer of territory from one sovereign to another."[23] If dynamic forces were caught early, Dulles argued, change might be limited to the first and second types.[24] Nevertheless, "it should at all times be borne in mind that the objective sought is not necessarily the total elimination of territorial change."[25] Boundaries were not, contended Dulles, meant to be written in stone.

Before making any recommendations for mechanisms of peaceful change, Dulles recognized that peaceful change would be difficult to institutionalize. On the domestic level, the power of an authority to provide for change would mean a major challenge to individual freedom.

> The endowment of an authority with these prerogatives involves a large measure of abdication of individual freedom. Those who desire perpetuation of the *status quo* and indefinite retention of what they have must largely subordinate their desires to the dictates of the authority, contenting themselves with the fact that at least the *status quo* will change only gradually and then not by violence. Those who desire a change in the *status quo* and to acquire what both have, must accept the peaceful and sometimes slow procedures established by the authority and renounce the quick and direct methods of force. In both cases individual freedom is sharply curtailed.[26]

On the international level, in the world of sovereign states, this "would mean a substantial abandonment of 'sovereignty' as now conceived."[27] States would no longer be able to behave as they wished. Consequently, Dulles realized that the implementation of peaceful change on the international plane would come very slowly. Nevertheless, that fact did not obviate the necessity of beginning to move forward.[28]

Understanding the difficulty of the task, Dulles developed suggestions for establishing an international mechanism for peaceful change.   He began by noting, once again, that article 19 of the League Covenant was an important "first Step."[29]   Any international authority must possess all the elements that were present in article 19:

> There are inherent in Article 19 the elements essential to an effectively functioning authority, namely: (a) the objective -- avoidance of violence; (b) the means -- a periodic but measured alteration of the *status quo*, designed to strike an acceptable balance between the dynamic and static desires of the national groups; and (c) the placing of responsibility for achieving this balance in the hands of an impartial and continuous body owing responsibility to all. By another Article, sanctions were provided.[30]

To move toward the implementation of these elements, Dulles advocated an evolutionary approach.   First, the attitudes of the people of the world must be moved away from the "nation-hero" and "nation-villain" imagery.   The "ethical solution," as well as the "authoritarian solution," must be utilized.   This could be done by encouraging cooperation with other nations, whereby there could be a dilution of the "nation-benefactor concept."[31]   The significance of national boundaries could also be lessened with a freer flow of people across them.   States must also begin to recognize the importance of change, realizing that it was not, "*per se*, something abnormal and strange and to be avoided except as a matter of dire necessity."[32] This attitude toward change would be possible "if we could develop in international affairs a viewpoint corresponding to that which is epitomized by the common law."[33]

To develop this concept, Dulles drew the analogy of the United States and the British Commonwealth.   Both the American colonies and the Commonwealth nations developed in the common law tradition.   In this tradition the law was very fluid, permitting incremental change.

> No one knows with precision what the common law is.   No one can tell at what precise moment it changes, and the many changes which have occurred have not, in detail, been spectacular.   We find here conformity with the criterion we suggested, namely, that change should preferably be almost imperceptible except in retrospect.   When legal rulings showed signs of undue rigidity, then there was implanted upon it "equity" -- the Chancellor's conscience.   The basic conception was that human rights are changing things which could not with advantage be made the subject of meticulous and permanent definition.[34]

This common-law background, Dulles argued, allowed the American states, once disjointed colonies, to merge "into a single nation."[35] They were unified initially by a treaty, the Constitution, but it "prescribed a regime so elastic and was itself an instrument of such general terms that it has proved possible thereunder for momentous evolutions gradually to occur."[36]   The nations of the British Commonwealth, also under this common-law influence, were similarly able to grow together. Consequently, Dulles concluded that:

> The history of the United States and the British Empire suggests that powerful and non-disturbing evolution could occur in the world as a whole if we had fewer treaties, and if those which we had were less permanent and more conducive to the development of a flexible body of international practice which might ultimately become so grounded in the *mores* of the world community as to attain the status of law.[37]

For Dulles, it was essentially a regime of adaptable and fluid customary international law that could serve as a beginning of the evolutionary process toward the establishment of an international authority for peaceful change.

As for "the constitution of those bodies which we suggest might serve as the germ of an international authority," Dulles was not very specific.[38]   Writing in 1939 in *War, Peace and Change*, Dulles suggested that perhaps the League would serve in this capacity, since "it is an existing organization and already contains within its constitution provisions which are appropriate to the end which we have in mind."[39] Dulles did not, however, have great hopes for the League, and realized that it "may now be unacceptable as a medium for dealing with the problem in its totality."[40]   More appropriate perhaps would have been a form of regional organization. Argued Dulles, "[i]f the initial effort is to divide the task in accordance with geographic areas, as heretofore suggested, then there may be an arrangement appropriate to each such area and such arrangements might differ as between themselves."[41]   In any case, it was "obviously desirable that there should be a formality which gives assurance of continuity and that the status accorded those persons who have a duty of study and report should be, so far as practicable, independent and divorced from the exigencies of national politics."[42]

In *War, Peace and Change*, Dulles thus went no further toward a detailed proposal, admitting that there was "no occasion to deal with all the intricacies of implementing our concept."[43]   Before any concrete step could be made, the public must understand and want such an organization.[44]   He explained that it was "generally easy to find ways to do that which we want to do, whereas the most perfect machinery in the world will not be used if it is not understood or if its product is not wanted."[45]   The initiative for this new authority remained with the states themselves. It would be a slow, halting evolution. It might thus take some time to establish an international authority; "until there is an effectively functioning international authority, the various states must anticipate and voluntarily do that which an authority would presumably propose and at a time when an authority would presumable propose it."[46] The achievement of this would be extremely difficult, since large measures of cooperation were required, but it "becomes possible with public education as to the true nature of peace."[47] Ideally, when the public of the world realized that true peace involved a condition that allows for change and for the balance between the dynamic and static elements, they would be receptive to an international arrangement to institutionalize this procedure.

Other Proposals

Dulles continued to develop his thought on peaceful change during the 1940s. On January 23, 1940, he prepared a draft on "Peaceful Change" that was published the following year, with minor revisions.[48] In this draft, Dulles reiterated his general advocacy of peaceful change mechanisms and discussed "three different kinds of a world order which permits [sic] peaceful change."[49] These three types were the league system, the federal system and the "voluntary" system.

The league system was essentially what was already designed in article 19 of the League Covenant. Sovereignty is not eliminated; each state is still allowed "exclusive power within its domain."[50] But "we seek by treaty or covenant to bind each state, in advance, to accept such changes in its domain as may from time to time seem necessary for peace."[51] While the state is in control of its "domain," it may find that its domain will change: "the unit is the sovereign and its domain is made subject to change."[52] The federal system is different in that it "treats the individual as the unit and seeks for him a system under which he can, through availing of opportunities elsewhere, change his own status to his advantage."[53] The system "does this by taking certain powers away from existing sovereigns, and vesting them in a body which derives its authority from, and has responsibility toward, all of those affected."[54] The final system, the "voluntary system," "relies upon the nations which are dominant in the world to exercise their power with a sense of moral responsibility and with intelligence."[55] It relies upon the willing acceptance of the equality of all people and the notion that power must be exercised with responsibility. It also recognizes "that attempts at arbitrary restraint and the monopolization of natural advantages in the long run defeat themselves and are self-destructive" and thus this system "relies upon nations following a course upon which both morality and expediency coincide."[56]

Writing during the midst of World War II, Dulles was unable to say which method of world order would be likely to succeed. The league system had not worked for long because "[s]overeign states, even though bound by covenant, are seldom willing to shrink their domains because others think this necessary for the cause of world peace.[57] Nevertheless, Dulles did not reject the system out of hand. The federal system also had difficulties; "it may be that the federal system will not operate successfully unless based upon a population which is homogeneous."[58] According to Dulles, "[i]f this limitation be accepted the federal system may merely develop the world into groups which, while larger then any present nation, will still, as between themselves, be exclusive and resistant to change."[59] The problem of sovereignty would still exist, only on a larger scale. Finally, the "voluntary system" may not work, especially since in a democratic system that "tends to exaggerate short-range planning" leaders will be unable to implement successfully long-range goals.[60] In any case, Dulles concluded that these problems must be studied and, echoing previous injunctions, he explained that there must be a clearer public understanding of the principles involved.

PLANNING FOR THE POSTWAR ORGANIZATION

As Dulles became involved in formal efforts to plan for a postwar international organization, his support for peaceful change was reflected in his activities with the Commission on a Just and Durable Peace. As noted earlier, the official publications of the commission tended to mirror Dulles's conception of the nature of the international system; similarly, they reflected his views on peaceful change. In the 1942 "Statement of Guiding Principles," the commission recognized the importance of change, and proclaimed in Principle Six "that international machinery is required to facilitate the easing of such economic and political tensions as are inevitably recurrent in a world which is living and therefore changing."[62] The commission's 1943 statement, called the "Six Pillars of Peace," also supported peaceful change. Pillar III explained that the postwar "peace must make provision for an organization to adapt the treaty structure of the world to changing underlying conditions."[63]

In light of these views, Dulles and his commission responded to all efforts at international organization with a special concern for peaceful change. Even before issuing the above statements, in September 1941 the commission had published a pamphlet entitled "Long Range Peace Objectives," which contained an analysis by Dulles of the "Roosevelt-Churchill Eight Point Declaration," the Atlantic Charter. In these comments, one of Dulles's fears was that the principles of the charter were aimed at preventing change. Seemingly innocuous provisions were disturbing to Dulles. For instance, Great Britain and the United States pledged in Point One to "seek no aggrandizement, territorial or otherwise."[64]   While recognizing the positive side of this pledge, Dulles feared that it would prevent beneficial growth.

> It is well that we should disavow "aggrandizement" with its implied disregard of the welfare of others. We must remember, however, that growth, in itself, is not something inherently evil. It is, indeed, the peculiar genius of the Constitution of the United States that it could and did operate as an open end instrument, bringing more territory and more peoples into federal union. That conception should not now be renounced.[65]

Similarly, Point Six bothered Dulles. It too seemed innocent, expressing "the hope that peace 'will afford to all nations the means of dwelling in safety within their own boundaries.'"[66]   Dulles feared, however, that this statement could have led to an overemphasis on the sanctity of boundaries. While hoping for safety, he felt it necessary to

> recognize that such hope cannot be realized merely by seeking to make sacrosanct, for all times, the boundary advantages which now enure to some. The extent to which boundaries will be free from physical inroads depends on the nature of the restraints which the boundaries create. As frequently pointed out by Secretary of State Hull, if boundaries are unnatural barriers to the movement of men, trade and investment, their maintenance inevitably become subject to attack.[67]

Finally, Point Eight, which dealt with the ultimate renunciation of force and the immediate disarmament of nations that threaten the peace, caused problems. Despite the ultimate desire for the renunciation of force by all, the statement seemed to Dulles to imply disarmament of the vanquished states and a freeze in the status quo. In fact, however, "there will be no acquiescence in unilateral disarmament, and no permanent renunciation of efforts to develop national power, until the world is made organically flexible, with mechanisms to assure a peaceful political response to the constant fluctuations of underlying conditions."[68]

In an effort to correct the flaws in the Charter, Dulles proposed several steps that the Allies should take. For the purpose of this discussion, his proposal for "an international federation for peace"[69] is the most important. This organization would have been composed of all states. They would have resolved to recognize the principle of interdependence and cooperate toward common ends. Indeed, if a given action threatened to produce deleterious effects within another nation, they would have been bound to obtain "the judgement of the federation as to the effect thereof upon the peace of the world."[70]

The federation would have been run "through an executive organ made up of outstanding personalities who would be solemnly pledged to place the peace and welfare of humanity as a whole above the advantage of any particular nation, race or class."[71] This executive organ would have been charged with pursuing peaceful change:

> The executive organ would keep the international situation constantly under review in order to detect, at their incipiency, any conditions the continuance of which might endanger the peace of the world. It would report to the members on any such conditions and would propose measures which in its judgement would be calculated to prevent such conditions ripening into international violence. The nature of such measures would be determined by the executive organ. They might call for a revision of international conditions designed to ameliorate the economic or political lot of certain peoples. They might call for measures to repress sporadic threats of violence.[72]

This organ would thus essentially have implemented the provision of article 19 of the League Covenant. States would have been obligated to follow the recommendations of this authority.

Following his negative reaction to the Atlantic Charter, Dulles reacted more positively to the Moscow Declarations of October 1943. In November of that year he issued a statement on the new declarations. Although the declarations did not explicitly mention peaceful change, their advocacy of "a general international organization" implied that it would deal with change. Dulles felt that peaceful change "would presumably be the ultimate responsibility of the 'general international organization' which was proposed. By implication the Moscow decisions recognized that political order, if it is to promote peace, must be flexible."[73] Furthermore, Dulles believed that the European Advisory Council, established at the time of the Moscow Declarations, indicated the Allies' desire for peaceful change. This commission illustrated "the kind of expert standing body that is needed to study and advise on the need for adapting, from time to time, the political order of Europe to changing underlying conditions."[74] Consequently, "[i]f such a body is made a permanent part of the 'general international organization' and if similar expert standing bodies are set up in relation to other areas, then good progress will have been made in creating machinery for detecting and curing future maladjustments before they develop consequences that menace the world."[75]

Dulles's reactions to a subsequent proposal for international organization were not so optimistic. The July 18. 1944, "United States Tentative Proposal for a General International Organization" raised some difficulties with respect to peaceful change. Article V, section 5, provided: "Any member state should have the right to bring to the attention of the general assembly or the executive council any condition, situation, or controversy the continuance of which the member deems likely to endanger international security or peace."[76] Dulles found this proposal too weak. First, he believed that any state, not just members of the organization, should be allowed to bring the condition to the attention of the Assembly or Council. Second, he believed that the document should specify that treaty conditions may be among those conditions that could be brought up; this would be similar to article 19 of the League Covenant. Third, he felt that the phrase "the continuance of which the member deems likely to endanger international security or peace" was too restrictive. This would mean that the issue would have to be nearly explosive before it could be brought to the international organization; "a state petitioning for revision would in effect have to put itself in the position of threatening to breach the peace in violation of its covenant."[77]

Dulles's preferred version would have read: "5. Any state should have the right to bring to the attention of the General Assembly or the Executive Council any condition or situation (including those created by treaty) or controversy, the continuance of which the state considers may cause international friction."[78] This would have broadened the provision to include nonmember states, specify treaties as a possible condition, and lessen the level of conflict necessary for the issue to be brought to the organization.

The Dumbarton Oaks Proposal of October 1944 dealt with many of the concerns that Dulles had expressed about earlier drafts. The two provisions that related to peaceful change read:

1. The Security Council should be empowered to investigate any dispute, or any situation which may lead to international friction or give rise to a dispute, in order to determine whether its continuance is likely to endanger the maintenance of international peace and security.

2. Any state, whether a member of the Organization or not, may bring any such dispute or situation to the attention of the General Assembly or of the Security Council.[79]

Read together these provisions seem to respond to most of Dulles's concerns. The right to bring the issue to the organization was expanded to cover "a situation which may lead to international friction or give rise to a dispute." This particular addition may have, in fact, been due directly to Dulles's memorandum on the subject. According to Ruth Russell and Jeanette Muther, this addition "reflected in part a suggestion made by Governor [Thomas] Dewey, that situations that could be brought before the Assembly or

Council should include those that might lead to 'friction.'"[80]   Since
Dulles was Dewey's foreign policy adviser and since the word
"friction" was the exact word used by Dulles, it is reasonable to
assume that Dewey had relayed Dulles's suggestion to the U. S.
Delegation to the Dumbarton Oaks talks.

The only addition suggested by Dulles that was not included in
the Dumbarton Oaks proposals was the proposal that treaties be
specifically mentioned.   Apparently, Dewey had requested "that the
text should clearly show that any situation or controversy arising
from treaty provisions was among such matters" that could lead to
friction, but "[t]he American Group felt the general power to
consider, investigate, and recommend on any situation likely to
endanger peace or security would cover any needed recommendations
on existing treaties."[81]   They feared that "the specific enumeration
of treaty situations, without listing all other factors, would risk the
exclusion of unlisted ones by subsequent interpretation."[82]

Despite these favorable additions to the Dumbarton Oaks
Proposals, Dulles found other problems relating to peaceful change in
the document.   Although the General Assembly had the right to take
actions to correct international situations that could become
dangerous, the Council was not given such power.   Dulles explained:

> Once the Security Council assumes jurisdiction, the General
> Assembly must be mute.   The Security Council itself is
> confined to a mechanistic role.   It can act only after there
> is a dispute likely to threaten the peace.   Then it can call
> for sanctions, but only "to maintain or restore."   It has no
> mandate to seek to remedy conditions which unnecessarily
> repress human aspirations or to seek the revision of
> treaties or prior international decisions which will seem
> unjust.[83]

This presented, according to Dulles, a major problem.   The Security
Council was intended to be "the dominant organ of the new world
organization."[84]   Furthermore, "[i]t is given 'primary responsibility'
for the maintenance of peace.   It is designed to 'function
continuously.'   It is compact enough to be effective.   Its membership
will permit the great nations there to exercise a responsibility
comparable to their power."[85]   Consequently, the "Council ought to
be endued with an active principle.   It should judge the merits of
situations which may give rise to friction and neither it nor member
states should be required to use force to sustain a condition found to
be unjust."[86]   Hence, the Council should be able to respond early to
alleviate conditions that could give rise to a breach of the peace and
should thus not have to be in a position where it was enforcing an
unjust status quo.   In the same address, Dulles also urged that
amendment provisions for the Charter be "liberalized,"[87] lest the
organization become too rigid.   Specifically, he hypothesized that in

the future, as conditions changed, the permanent members should perhaps be changed as well. Without such liberalization, the U. N., he feared, would go the way of the League.

AN EVALUATION OF DULLES'S DISCUSSION OF PEACEFUL CHANGE

Before proceeding to a discussion of Dulles's thought on other possible roles of international organization, it is important to examine several interesting aspects of Dulles's conception of peaceful change. First, it is noteworthy that one important element of peaceful change is not developed very explicitly in Dulles's writings. Under the theory of peaceful change, an international organization exists not only to ensure change *per se*, but to establish a mechanism by which entities are given the opportunity to present their desires for change. The organization will then act on the basis of what it believes is best for the entire system; it may or may not institute the desired change. But if it does not, its rules will be followed by the losing state because the institution itself, and its procedures, are seen as legitimate. This is not unlike the attitudes during a domestic civil suit, when the parties pledge to abide by the decision of the court whether or not it is in their favor, and resolve not to resort to force. In Dulles's writings, he seems to put the emphasis on the institution functioning *to allow for change* and does not stress the fact that change may not always be granted.

Nevertheless, even though Dulles does not pay very much attention to this aspect of peaceful change, he seems to understand its importance. In *War, Peace and Change*, he explained:

If a philosophy of non-change is unsound and provocative, a philosophy of pure change is equally so. Change in itself is no cure-all. In *some* form, elasticity is an essential ingredient of any condition of non-violence. This fact needs to be brought home to those peoples which, satisfied with their international position, tend to equate peace with rigidity. It is on that account that the emphasis of this study primarily stresses the inevitability of change. But it must not be forgotten that the objective of a regime of flexibility is to assure a qualified conservation of the existing status. The so-called static peoples have rights which must be protected and conserved and which rank equally with those of the dynamic peoples. Insecurity, of a kind, must be accepted as the price of a security which is more highly prized. But if the latter security is not achieved, then the insecurity has been accorded in vain. Change should be formulated in the light of this dual role. It should serve to protect, as well

as to accord. This means, as we have seen, that change
ought to be adapted to building up static influence within
the dynamic states.[88]

Given this statement, and Dulles's earlier comment that states must
willingly submit their desires to the authority,[89] there would seem to
be an indication that he recognized certain caveats about peaceful
change. He felt, however, that it was necessary to place more stress
on the role of the authority *to* institute change, since this was often
neglected.

A second noteworthy element of Dulles's analysis is his belief
that it would be easy to determine when circumstances required
change. In *War, Peace and Change*, he said that "[d]ynamic forces
are usually detectable at an early stage."[90] According to him, "[m]an
has had centuries of experience and experimentation which permit
him to identify forces of a kind which become more powerful if they
are sought to be resisted and contained."[91] Conditions that required
change would thus seem to be able to be identified objectively. This
seems to accord with Dulles's suggestion, noted above, that the
executive organ of the international federation be "made up of
outstanding personalities who would be solemnly pledged to place the
peace and welfare of humanity as a whole above the advantage of
any particular nation, race or class,"[92] and would also be consistent
with his praise for the European Advisory Commission and "similar
expert standing bodies."[93] It seems fair to infer that since Dulles
believed that conditions giving rise to change could be objectively
identified, a body of individual experts would be sufficient. It
appeared to be more of a technical task than a political task to
determine what change was needed. On this point Dulles was perhaps
overly optimistic, first, in believing that conditions could be so easily
identified, and second, in believing that this function could be so
depoliticized.

Dulles's optimism was also reflected in a third aspect of his
thought on peaceful change; his belief that state acceptance of
peaceful change would be facilitated through "public education."[94] He
believed that if people throughout the world became aware of the
"true" nature of peace, they would eventually realize the need for
mechanisms for peaceful change. While the effects of education are
indeed often great, this contention reflects an excessive faith in the
perfectability of human beings. It assumes that if people only knew
what true peace was, they would immediately desire it. It also
assumes that in all states public education could easily affect
government activities. Clearly, in a strong totalitarian or
authoritarian state, such "public education," if at all possible, would
have to contend with an intransigent government that was conducting
its own "education program."

Finally, from this discussion of peaceful change, it should be
obvious that Dulles believed that peaceful change was the most

important aspect of international organization. Other functions seemed to be only of secondary importance. Thus, in his critique of the Atlantic Charter, he generally objects to what, on their face, appeared to be quite noble aspirations, especially in the middle of a war begun by overt aggression -- provisions such as the renunciation of territorial aggrandizement or those calling for the establishment of security. But in Dulles's mind, provisions of this nature could lead to another Versailles-like status quo settlement; something he fervently wished to avoid. In the following discussions of other functions of international organization, this preeminent emphasis on peaceful change will become even clearer.

NOTES

1. Dulles, "The Road to Peace," 492, 493.
2. Dulles, *War Peace and Change*, 40.
3. Ibid.
4. Ibid.
5. Ibid.
6. Ibid.
7. Ibid., 40-41.
8. Ibid., 41.
9. Ibid.
10. Dulles, "The Road to Peace," 494.
11. Dulles, *War, Peace and Change*, 48-49.
12. Ibid., 49.
13. Ibid., 50.
14. Ibid.
15. Ibid.
16. Ibid., 50-51.
17. Ibid., 82.
18. Ibid., 84.
19. Ibid., 51.
20. Ibid., 138.
21. Ibid., 140.
22. Ibid., 140-141.
23. Ibid., 141.
24. Ibid.
25. Ibid., 154-155.
26. Ibid., 135-136.
27. Ibid., 136.
28. Ibid.
29. Ibid., 137.
30. Ibid.
31. Ibid., 152.
32. Ibid, 156.
33. Ibid.

34. Ibid., 156-157.
35. Ibid., 157.
36. Ibid.
37. Ibid., 158.
38. Ibid., 158-159.
39. Ibid., 159.
40. Ibid.
41. Ibid.
42. Ibid.
43. Ibid.
44. Ibid.
45. Ibid.
46. Ibid., 165.
47. Ibid.
48. Dulles, "Peaceful Change," 369 *International Conciliation*, 1941, 493.
49. Dulles, "Peaceful Change," draft of Jan. 23, 1940, *JFD Papers*, 6.
50. Ibid., 7.
51. Ibid.
52. Ibid.
53. Ibid.
54. Ibid.
55. Ibid., 8.
56. Ibid. Preussen emphasizes the coincidence of morality and expediency in Dulles. See Preussen, *John Foster Dulles*.
57. Dulles, "Peaceful Change," *JFD Papers*, 8.
58. Ibid., 9.
59. Ibid.
60. Ibid.
61. Ibid.
62. Federal Council of Churches, "Statement of Guiding Principles," 4.
63. Commission on a Just and Durable Peace, "A Just and Durable Peace, Statement of Political Propositions," Mar. 12, 1943, *JFD Papers*, 7 (hereafter cited as "Six Pillars of Peace").
64. Quoted in Commission on a Just and Durable Peace, "Long Range Peace Objectives," Sept. 18, 1941, *JFD Papers*, 2.
65. Ibid.
66. Ibid., 6.
67. Ibid.
68. Ibid., 8.
69. Ibid., 15.
70. Ibid.
71. Ibid., 16.
72. Ibid.
73. Dulles, "Analysis of Moscow Declarations in Light of the Six Pillars of Peace," Nov. 16, 1943, *JFD Papers*, 3.

74. Ibid.

75. Ibid.

76. "United States Tentative Proposals for General International Organization," reprinted in R. Russell and J. Muther, *A History of the United Nations Charter: The Role of the United States 1940-1945*, 995, 1000.

77. Dulles, "Memorandum Re Article V," section 5, 1944, *JFD Papers*, 2.

78. Ibid.

79. "Dumbarton Oaks Proposals for the Establishment of a General International Organization," reprinted in Russell and Muther, *A History of the United Nations Charter*, 1019, 1023-1024.

80. Russell and Muther, *A History of the United Nations Charter*, 459.

81. Ibid.

82. Ibid., 459-460 (footnote omitted).

83. Dulles, "From Yalta to San Francisco," Address of Mar. 17, 1945, *JFD Papers*, 7.

84. Ibid.

85. Ibid.

86. Ibid., 7-8.

87. Ibid., 8.

88. Dulles, *War, Peace and Change*, 164.

89. Ibid., 135-136.

90. Ibid., 138.

91. Ibid., 138-139.

92. Dulles, "Long Range Peace Objectives," 16, (emphasis added).

93. Dulles, "Analysis of Moscow Declarations," 3.

94. Dulles, *War, Peace and Change*, 165.

4

Collective Security

Collective security is one of several possible systems of international conflict management. Under this system, force is renounced by states as a means of settling international disputes. Any state that takes recourse to force, except in self-defense, is deemed to have committed an act of aggression. In order to prevent such aggression, all members of the system formally pledge in advance to unite through an international organization in collective action to repress the aggressor. The particular form of collective action will vary, depending on what was necessary to end aggression in the given case. It could include economic sanctions, whereby the severance of economic ties is aimed at crippling the offending state, but it could also involve collective military action. Under the theory of collective security, it is hoped that by states promising to act to end aggression, any potential aggressor would be deterred, realizing that if he uses force, the overwhelming power of all the other nations would confront him.

For a collective security system to work, there must be an absolute commitment of all states. They must be willing to combat aggression, wherever and whenever it may occur. Although a conflict may seem quite removed, the theory of collective security holds that if an act of aggression anywhere goes unchallenged, the security of all states is threatened. They must also be willing to act no matter who the perpetrator may be. Special relationships or alliances are not allowed to interfere with the duty of states to confront aggression. Moreover, states must also be willing to act no matter how "just" the cause of aggression may seem to be. In this system, the international community has determined that the highest goal of the system is the preservation of peace; even "just causes" do not justify aggression. Without this total commitment to act, regardless of circumstances, the collective security method of conflict management loses its deterrent effect.

THE ALTERNATIVE TO FORCE: THE KELLOGG-BRIAND PACT, MORAL FORCE AND ECONOMIC SANCTIONS

During the early period, Dulles's thought on collective security passed through at least three different phases. In the first phase, he took an essentially nonjudgmental stand on the issue, but, in light of the U. S. rejection of the League Covenant, he attempted to develop alternatives to the military aspect of collective security, while judiciously avoiding specific criticisms of the League.

In a 1928 manuscript entitled "The Renunciation of War," Dulles described the opposing schools of thought on collective security during and after the formulation of the League Covenant. On the one side, there were those who supported collective security, "those who believed that peace can be assured only if the nations unite in some legal relationship designed to assure the application of collective force to any wrongdoing nation."[1] The other school was composed of "those who believe that any such organization implies the sanctioning of war, whereas permanent peace can be obtained only through a state of mind which regards all war as both abhorrent and illegitimate."[2] According to Dulles, France had been in the first school, proposing "a confederation of the principal nations of the world under an arrangement which would create an international body functioning to maintain peace through disposing of an army and navy acting as an international police force."[3] Although the American delegation "opposed any such super-government, . . . Wilson decided . . . that it was wise to accept a plan whereby the principal nations of the world would be legally confederated with a view to coercing any nation which threatened to breach the peace."[4] But "[i]nstead . . . of any international police force, there were substituted the provisions of Articles 10 and 16 of the Covenant requiring member states to preserve each other against external aggression and to blockade any covenant-breaking state."[5] Unfortunately, Wilson had misread the desires of the American people, who refused to commit themselves to collective security. The Treaty of Versailles was not ratified by the United States "primarily because the American people were unwilling to enter into any international confederation, however laudable its objective, which permitted the conception that war was proper and necessary to maintain peace and which put the United States under a legal or moral obligation to go to war in certain contingencies."[6]

Having failed to ratify the League Covenant, the United States did not propose an alternative method of securing peace until the signing of the Kellogg-Briand Pact in 1928. With this treaty, said Dulles, "[t]he United States no longer occupie[d] a merely negative attitude on the subject of world peace."[7] Instead, the United States took a positive step that entirely changed the status of war. Prior to the treaty, "[i]nternational law and practice . . . [had] admitted war as a wholly legitimate and appropriate method of advancing national aims and settling international disputes."[8] With the Kellogg-Briand Pact, "[t]he peoples of the world, acting through their respective governments, condemn war as an institution and agree not to resort to it as a means of settling their disputes."[9] Interestingly enough, Dulles here seems to deny any legal significance to the use of force provisions of the League of Nations Covenant, which, even though they did not entirely prohibit recourse to force, did severely limit the circumstances under which it could be used. Although the Covenant was not universally ratified, it was binding on the parties and did create international law as far as they were concerned. Consequently, it really could not be argued that prior to the Kellogg-Briand Pact international law had left war totally unregulated.

Dulles was uncertain as to how soon the treaty would "have practical effect,"[10] but he was very optimistic about its ultimate effectiveness. He explained that it was "certain . . . that sooner or later so profound and formidable a change in the status of war must operate to minimize resort thereto."[11] Indeed, the Kellogg-Briand Pact gave "a new standing to those throughout the world who are opposed to war and [put] in their hands a new instrument which can be used with powerful effect to prevent war."[12] But since the treaty carried no sanctions with it, "its effectiveness must, in the last analysis, depend upon the extent to which it reflects and crystallizes and reinvigorates the public opinion of the world."[13] Some may doubt the ability of public opinion to underwrite the treaty; "[t]hey believe that no treaty will be respected unless there exists some physical force with which to threaten its violators."[14] Yet this attitude, argued Dulles, "would appear to misjudge completely the efficacy of public opinion, which, as repeatedly demonstrated both in domestic and international affairs, has always proved not only the most potent, but the essential, support of any law."[15]

In this manuscript, Dulles was careful to indicate that he did not believe the Kellogg-Briand Pact was incompatible with "the system of the League whereby covenant breakers are threatened with the application of some international force,"[16] and did not preclude the possibility of the United States joining the League. Nevertheless, despite the compatibility of League sanctions, Dulles demonstrated a tremendous amount of hope for the "moral sanctions" serving to uphold the Kellogg-Briand Pact.

As time went by, however, Dulles became convinced that moral force alone would not be enough to deter aggression and began to examine the feasibility of economic sanctions, still avoiding the advocacy of military enforcement measures. In the early 1930s,

Dulles wrote several articles that supported economic sanctions while still recognizing the many pitfalls that accompany their use. In these pieces, he generally prefaced his remarks by pointing out that neither moral force alone nor military force was a workable way to enforce the Kellogg-Briand Pact. On the question of moral force, Dulles continued to believe that it was necessary, but recognized that "moral pressure alone does not suffice."[17] This was true for two reasons. First, moral pressure tended to be diluted by the public opinion that had already been generated in the state supporting the proposition that force was justified.[18] Second, "the moral sense of the rest of the world, even though it is aroused, does not work with sufficient rapidity and does not become solidified unless it is directed into concrete measures adopted by the governments themselves."[19] Simply put, moral force was, in Dulles's mind, a necessary but not a sufficient condition. Military force, on the other hand, was, as in Dulles's previous works, assumed to be excluded from consideration because the United States was unwilling to commit itself to such action.[20] With these prefatory remarks, Dulles concluded that "any constructive thought of sanctions must turn to the conception of economic sanctions."[21]

While economic sanctions were, for Dulles, the only alternative, the structure the League had set up to implement those sanctions presented many problems. These procedures were established in article 16 of the League Covenant, which provided in part that:

1. Should any member of the League resort to war in disregard of its covenants under Articles 12, 13 or 15, it shall, *ipso facto*, be deemed to have committed an act of war against all other members of the League, which hereby undertake immediately to subject it to the severance of all trade or financial relations, the prohibition of all intercourse between their nationals and the nationals of the Covenant-breaking State, and the prevention of all financial, commercial or personal intercourse between the nationals of the Covenant-breaking State and nationals of any other State, whether a Member of the League or not.[22]

This general framework was, according to Dulles, unworkable.[23] Article 16 was too impractical to be a credible deterrent. Argued Dulles, "any system of sanctions, if it is to be practicable, must be susceptible of being readily carried out by the nations who are called upon to enforce it."[24] He continued: "It does no good to write on paper penalties which on their face are very severe, if, either through excessive severity or through throwing excessive burdens on those who are expected to enforce the penalties, they become unworkable."[25] If sanctions are not workable and are thus not likely to be used, they lose any potential deterrent effect.

The unworkability of Article 16 manifested itself in several ways. First, there was the problem of a complete blockade. While it may seem that this measure would have been most damaging to the recalcitrant state, it also had a tendency to injure the sanctioning state. As Dulles explained:

> [t]o interrupt that [the flow of commerce and goods] arbitrarily costs one nation as much as it does another, the receiving nation as much as the selling nation, and many nations are so tied together economically that it is utterly impossible for them to contemplate a complete and abrupt breaking off of all relations with another state of economic importance.[26]

Because of this problem, not all states would necessarily participate in the sanctions. A second problem, argued Dulles, was "that economic sanctions bear very unequally upon the different nations who are called upon to enforce them."[27] Some states would be hurt greatly, some not at all. Third, while sanctions are aimed at the bellicose *government*, they actually hurt the *people* of the state. Explained Dulles, "I do not believe that the public opinion of the world today would support a system of economic sanctions which, in effect, would involve the wholesale starvation of a civilian population."[28] With all these problems, it would be unlikely that a total blockade would be imposed, and with such an expectation the bellicose state would probably not be deterred.

In light of these difficulties, Dulles proposed a different approach to sanctions, which was also suggested by the "Committee on Economic Sanctions of the Twentieth Century Fund," of which Dulles was a member. Examining both Dulles's work and the committee's proposal, this approach becomes clear. To implement this proposal, the states that are parties to the Kellogg-Briand Pact should adopt "an appropriate protocol or agreement supplemental from the Pact."[30] In this agreement, the signatories would pledge several things. First, "[i]t should be agreed in advance that if there is a breach or a threatened breach of the Pact of Paris, economic sanctions shall be applied."[31] Second, it should be agreed that the first, automatic step "would be the cessation of any shipment of arms or absolute contraband to the nation or nations which are held to have violated or threatened to violate their obligations."[32] Further sanctions would be determined at the time, and adapted to the particular case: "those should be determined by the enforcing nations at the time, after analyzing the situation and picking out the economic weakness, the point of vulnerability, of the particular nation or nations to whom the sanctions are to be applied."[33] These provisions, Dulles believed, would prevent many of the problems associated with a total cessation of intercourse. He felt that this would be a workable compromise, containing "some conception of justice," but not "ignoring all considerations of self-interest."[34]

In sum, during the first phase of Dulles's thought he seemed to have understood quite clearly why the United States rejected collective security -- out of an unwillingness to live up to its rigorous requirements on the use of force -- and thus endorsed alternative means of conflict management. He seized the Kellogg-Briand Pact as this alternative, first advocating moral force as a means of ensuring its implementation, and then moving to a modified, more realistic use of economic sanctions. Yet he seemed to have avoided explicit criticism of collective security, accepting the goal of collective security, the prevention and suppression of aggression, but, due to the U. S. rejection of the League, proposing nonmilitary means of achieving it.

COLLECTIVE SECURITY AND PEACEFUL CHANGE

During the next phase of Dulles's thought, he became less concerned with devising alternative sanctions to the use of force (accepting its necessity at times), than with advocating the preeminent importance of first establishing a political order worthy of defense. Collective security was, in essence, putting the cart before the horse. A collective security enforcement mechanism could not be substituted for a political mechanism to balance competing static and dynamic elements, nor could it be substituted for the general public moral support that must underlie a functioning political arrangement. In *War, Peace and Change*, Dulles explained how a democratic system maintains order:

> Within the state a police force exists, but it is effective only to control a tendency towards violence which may be manifested by a small minority of the group members. Laws depend for their enforcement primarily upon the force of public opinion. No police force can be organized which will serve permanently to control the disposition toward violence of a substantial part of the group. The reduction to small dimension of those disposed to violence is effected by other means, and the achievement of this result is, as we have seen, a principal task of the group authority. It is charged with the duty of creating a form of society which will provide powerful means for resolving those omnipresent clashes of desire which are primarily represented by those, on the one hand, who would retain and those, on the other hand, who would acquire -- the static and the dynamic.[35]

In the democratic system, peace is maintained not primarily by the threat of sanctions, but by an established political system that satisfies the vast majority of the people by reconciling the activist, dynamic forces with the status quo, static force. As Dulles succinctly put it: "[A] police force cannot serve and is not designed to serve as a substitute for the creation of a healthy balance between dynamic and static forces."[36]

Taking this principle for the functioning of an adequate domestic system, Dulles drew the same conclusion for the international system. He explained:

> We must in the international field look upon sanctions as adapted only to play a comparable role. They are not themselves a primary method of avoiding violence. The task is one to be achieved by the creation of a flexible and balanced form of world society. Until this is achieved it is premature to consider sanctions. When it is achieved, the role of sanctions will have shrunk to small dimensions and the problem of their form will be one of manageable proportions.[37]

Consequently, a collective security mode of conflict management would not work until an effective mechanism of peaceful change first had been established. Without peaceful change, collective security becomes, according to Dulles, merely a straitjacket on the status quo. In March 1938, he wrote that "'Collective Security' represents essentially an alliance of satisfied nations to preserve their existing advantages intact."[38]

As the world began planning for a new international organization, it was not surprising that Dulles placed little emphasis on collective security and, as a consequence, had to defend himself against criticism that he was paying too little attention to enforcing peace. After sending a copy of his 1940 "Draft on Peaceful Change" to noted international relations theorist Quincy Wright, Dulles received the following comments:

> Could there not somewhere be a suggestion of the essential relationship between peaceful change and collective security? That is, while a system of collective security which merely preserves the status quo can never be permanent, on the other hand a system of peaceful change, no matter how perfect, can never preserve peace unless it is accompanied by a system adequate to prevent changes by violence. It is possible that if the states had lived more perfectly up to their obligations to prevent aggression, the dynamic states would have become convinced of the impossibility of change through aggression and would have labored, perhaps succesively [sic], to make Article XIX [of the League Covenant] work. And perhaps in such a situation the less dynamic states, being assured

that any concessions they might make would not be the opening of the dam for further demands, would have been less resistant.[39]

To this Dulles responded:

> As I have already said, I agree to the inter-relation of collective security and peaceful change, although I think the emphasis should be on the latter rather than the former. As I say in my book, the amount of force required is very little if society is well organized. Broadly speaking, I would say that the degree of force required is a measure of the defect of the social system, and if the social system is very defective no amount of force will serve to keep the peace.[40]

In effect, Dulles did not believe that sanctions would be totally unnecessary, but rather that generally too much emphasis was paid to maintaining the existing peace rather than securing a real peace, where states would be sufficiently satisfied and resorts to force would be rarer. But despite Dulles's emphasis on peaceful change, some of Wright's criticisms may have had some effect. In a 1941 article in *International Conciliation*, Dulles explained:

> On paper, at least, the Covenant [of the League] provided the two essentials for a stable world order: peaceful change and collective security. Article 10 contemplated the "reconsideration . . . of treaties which have become inapplicable and the consideration of international conditions, whose continuation might endanger the peace of the world." Thereby might have been prevented the occurrence of widespread popular discontent attributable to unequal international conditions. It is such popular unrest which leads to revolt which is formidable both because of the massed power which it represents and because of a certain moral justification to which it can lay claim. No repressive measures will, in the long run, subdue it. *On the other hand, it is necessary to provide collective security against the aggression of ambitious and unscrupulous leaders.* This was envisaged by Article 16, providing for collective economic sanctions.[41]

Here he acknowledged *both* peaceful change *and* collective security as essential for "a stable world order," and explicitly discussed the need for sanctions. Nevertheless, peaceful change was still first. In 1942, he told James Pope that he did "not believe that any force can be created sufficient to repress violence unless we have a kind of world which eliminates those sore spots of mass discontent and despair, which give to violent and unscrupulous men the opportunity to assume a leadership which becomes formidable."[42]   Here, consistent with his thought on the nature of the international system, Dulles recognized the need to ameliorate poor economic and social conditions, which also give rise to war, before collective security can be implemented.

As the postwar planning progressed, Dulles continued to express concern that the role of force was overemphasized.[43]   He also had problems with another aspect of collective security -- defining aggression.   Under the theory of collective security, when an act of aggression occurs it must be fought by the collective forces of the members of the international system.   This tenet of collective security presupposes that it will be possible objectively to identify an act of aggression.   Dulles, however, had doubts about this possibility. In a letter to Richard S. Childs, on February 29, 1944, he explained:

> I have considerable question whether it will prove practical to adopt a definition of "aggression" which will make this matter a justiciable question.   A great deal of thinking of a high order was given to this matter in the early years following the last war without any positive result.   "Aggression" is a subtle thing.   Does it include economic aggression?   Some nations are in a position by economic pressures to coerce others.   We have not infrequently done this over the past.   And does it include political interference in another country which brings about revolutionary change of government from which a foreign nation is a beneficiary, as, for example, Texas, Panama, and perhaps now, Poland?   Will nations which may be subject to aggression be satisfied with a system whereby aid to them must wait until there can be a court determination?"[44]

One bar, therefore, to the effective functioning of a collective security system, argued Dulles, was being able to identify subtle forms of aggression.

Within the Commission on a Just and Durable Peace, the issue of collective security was very controversial.   In response to portions of the September 1941 paper on "Long Range Peace Objectives," in which Dulles expressly omits a discussion of sanctions because "they are at the present time highly disputable and I do not consider them essential to inaugurating an era of peace,"[45] the members of the commission fell into several camps.   Some individuals felt that sanctions were necessary to any peace plan.[46]   Others agreed with Dulles's emphasis on first securing a stable political order.   Finally, some seemed to have believed that sanctions, under any conditions, were incompatible with Christian ethics.[47]

In December 1942, when the commission issued the "Statement

of Guiding Principles,"[48] there was no mention of sanctions; but by March 1943, when "Six Pillars of Peace" was published, mention was made of collective enforcement. Pillar Six provided that "[t]he peace must establish procedures for controlling military establishments everywhere."[48]   In the related comment, it was explained that this principle meant two things. First, and most obvious, it meant that procedures for general arms control should be established; but second, it meant that there must be a system of collective security:

> A positive purpose of control is to bring such military establishments as remain into the affirmative service of international order. International agencies, such as those we contemplate, will primarily need to depend upon the moral support of the great body of mankind. That is their only reliable source of permanent power and unless they can commend such moral backing they are not entitled to other forms of power. But any society will produce minority elements who are not subject to moral suasion and who, if they feel able, may defy the general interest to advance their own. Therefore, the economic and military power of the world community should be subject to mobilization to support international agencies which are designed to, and do in fact, serve the general welfare.[50]

This statement is very much in keeping with Dulles's thought. Moral support must first be built to establish an international community, but, in order to protect the great majority of society from those few that would not respect political authority, an enforcement system is needed. Collective security plays a role, but only a subsequent one.[51]

THE DUMBARTON OAKS PROPOSAL AND "LIMITED" COLLECTIVE SECURITY

In the last phase of Dulles's thought on collective security, he became less troubled about overemphasis on force as he saw the international community implementing something different from a pure collective security system. Although the Dumbarton Oaks Proposals contained provisions that emphasized the role of force in maintaining peace, Dulles reacted in a very restrained manner. He recognized that despite appearances to the contrary, the Dumbarton Oaks proposals would not have established a true collective security system. Hence, the provisions dealing with the collective use of force were "little more than security."[52]

Collective security, as discussed above, requires a quick, virtually automatic, reaction of aggression. As Dulles explained, "if such a police force is to be effective, it must be under a commanding executive who can surely and quickly bring it into action."[53]   But if the procedure becomes politicized, then the system will not work. Dulles said: "If the use of force becomes highly problematic and contingent on the outcome of debate and negotiation, actuated by conflicting considerations of expediency, then it ceases to be an effective instrument -- either for good or evil."[54]   This, argued Dulles, was the nature of the procedure worked out at Dumbarton Oaks.   An enforcement action would occur only after very political debates in the Security Council.   He explained:

> The national force quotas can be brought into action only by the vote of a council of representatives of 11 nations and, while the matter is not yet explicit, we can assume that the majority of 6 must always include the representative of China, France, Great Britain, the Soviet Union and the United States of America.   Further, these representatives are not bound to any principle of action or rule of conduct.   Their vote is wholly discretionary and will be directed primarily by national considerations.[55]

Consequently, this procedure lacked the objectivity and automaticity required for a true system of collective security.

The failure to establish a collective security system was not "a deficiency of draftsmanship,"[56] but rather a necessity dictated by "the present state of the world."[57]   According to Dulles, what was needed before any collective security system could be instituted was either despotism or a clear, legal definition of unlawful behavior that would require international sanction.   Under such an arrangement, "[t]he Executive has no discretion, but it is bound to use force he controls without fear or favor, and against great and small."[58]   But, as Dulles noted earlier, there was not even an agreed-upon definition of aggression.   Until there was a "moral consensus of the community"[59] on the definition of acceptable and unacceptable state behavior, and behind the law-making procedure and the executive, there could be no collective security.[60]

AN EVALUATION OF DULLES'S CONCEPTION OF COLLECTIVE SECURITY

To someone familiar with only the popular impression of Dulles as the cold-war advocate of "massive retaliation," his early views on collective security may seem surprising.   In light of the times and Dulles's background and experiences, however, his attitude toward collective security was not so unusual.   With the failure of the "war to end all wars," there grew a general disillusionment with collective security, which had not even managed to get off the ground, let alone function successfully to prevent aggression.   Pacifist and world federalist movements grew in intellectual circles as alternatives to a system that advocated war as a means of preventing war. Although Dulles rejected as idealistic the immediate implementation of such plans, he nevertheless shared some of the skepticism regarding the use of force. Himself a liberal internationalist, he endeavored to downplay the role of military force. In the absence of some underlying political community, the amount of force required to establish peace would be impossibly great. First, states must reach agreement upon the type of order they wish to enforce. This order must be sufficiently flexible that change will be facilitated and a rigid status quo will not be maintained; second, with a sense of community, there must also be a common definition of what constitutes an international transgression. Not until these prerequisites are met can a collective security system work.

NOTES

1. Dulles, "The Renunciation of War," undated, *JFD Papers*, 1.
2. Ibid.
3. Ibid., 1–2.
4. Ibid., 2.
5. Ibid.
6. Ibid.
7. Ibid.
8. Ibid., 3.
9. Ibid.
10. Ibid.
11. Ibid.
12. Ibid.
13. Ibid.
14. Ibid., 5.
15. Ibid.
16. Ibid.
17. Dulles, "Should Economic Sanctions Be Applied in International Disputes?," 103.
18. Ibid.
19. Ibid.
20. Ibid., 104.
21. Ibid.
22. *Covenant of the League of Nations*, June 28, 1919, 225 Parry's Treaty Series, art. 16, para. 1.
23. Dulles, "Should Economic Sanctions Be Applied in International Disputes?," 104.
24. Ibid., 105.
25. Ibid.
26. Ibid.
27. Ibid., 106.

28. Ibid., 106-107.

29. "Report of Committee on Economic Sanctions," undated, in *JFD Papers*.

30. Ibid.

31. Dulles, "Should Economic Sanctions Be Applied in International Disputes?," 107.

32. Ibid.

33. Ibid.

34. Ibid., 108.

35. Dulles, *War, Peace and Change*, 95.

36. Ibid., 96.

37. Ibid., 96-97.

38. Dulles, "Collective Security v. Isolationism," Mar. 28, 1938, *JFD Papers*.

39. Quincy Wright to JFD, Jan. 2, 1940, *JFD Papers*, 1.

40. JFD to Quincy Wright, Feb. 19, 1940, *JFD Papers*, 1.

41. Dulles, "The Aftermath of the World War," 265 (emphasis added).

42. JFD to James P. Pope, Apr. 28, 1942, *JFD Papers*, 1.

43. See, for example, JFD to Clyde Eagleton, Mar. 15, 1940, *JFD Papers*; JFD to Helen Hill Miller, Mar. 7, 1940, *JFD Papers*; JFD to Walter W. Van Kirk, Sept. 25, 1941, *JFD Papers*.

44. JFD to Richard S. Childs, Feb. 29, 1944, *JFD Papers*.

45. Dulles, "Long Range Peace Objectives," 17.

46. Ibid., 19 (brackets in original).

47. Ibid.

48. "Statement of Guiding Principles."

49. "Six Pillars of Peace," 10.

50. Ibid., 10-11.

51. See JFD to James P. Pope, 1.

52. Dulles, "The Dumbarton Oaks Proposals," Nov. 28, 1944, *JFD Papers*, 1.

53. Ibid., 2.

54. Ibid.

55. Ibid.

56. Ibid., 3.

57. Ibid.

58. Ibid.

59. Ibid., 5.

60. See Pruessen, *John Foster Dulles*.

5

The International Legal System

Another function of international organization that figured prominently in Dulles's early thought was the development of an international legal system. In order to examine this growth of Dulles's thought on this topic it will be necessary first to explore his understanding of the nature of international law. Then his views on international courts and on other methods of developing international law can be discussed.

THE NATURE OF INTERNATIONAL LAW

Since Dulles was considered by many (and indeed considered himself) to be an "international lawyer," it is not surprising that he dealt with basic jurisprudential questions of international law: Was international law effective? Was it really "law"? Initially, he seemed to respond affirmatively to these questions, but as time passed he became convinced that not only was international insufficiently developed, but what was developed did not deserve to be called law.

His early optimism was reflected in a lengthy draft on the Permanent Court of International Justice (PCIJ), written sometime in the middle to late 1920s. In this draft, Dulles advocated U. S. participation in the PCIJ. He had, however, to counter contentions that international adjudication could not be possible until "international law [was] codified." While recognizing that more codification was possible, he argued that "it may be said that there is a very substantial body of codified international law at the present time. There are hundreds of treaties and conventions between nations, all of which represent codified international law."[1] He also expressed hope for future development of customary international

law. In general, his attitude toward the current and future status of
international law was positive; one would assume from this draft that
Dulles believed that international law was effective law.

But as time went on, he began expressing skepticism about the
sufficiency and efficacy of international law. He questioned, for
instance, the precision with which a given norm of international law
could be identified. In a 1929 article, entitled "Conceptions and
Misconceptions Regarding Intervention," he explained:

> Many proceed on the assumption that international law
> exists as a very concrete thing so that one can go down to
> a library and turn to the second shelf and pull down the
> third book and find at page 297 whether a proposed course
> of action is sanctioned by international law. In fact,
> international law is far from being anything so concrete or
> readily ascertainable. We know how municipal law, the
> ordinary law of States, has been a development through
> centuries and how essentially it constitutes the ultimate
> codification of what the best practice through a period of
> time has already sanctioned. There is thus inevitably in
> international relations, a period when one must look to the
> best practice as the test of what is proper, and when one
> cannot turn to some concrete codification such as our
> present statute law.[2]

Consequently, he concluded that "it will help much in the
practicability of our discussion if we abandon the idea that
international law already exists in the sense that we can turn to a
codification or the decision of an international tribunal and there
find an explicit answer to our problem."[3] Here Dulles rejected the
notion that there was "a very substantial body of codified
international law," and instead suggested that state practice--
custom -- was the essential source of international law. This was
something, as Dulles saw it, that was not as concrete or as easy to
determine as codified law. He impled that the international system,
unlike the municipal system, was simply not very well developed; it
was still in a primitive state.

Dulles then proceeded in this article to provide a rather rough
view of customary international law. To determine the lawfulness of
intervention, he examined "the established practice of those states
who have attained the highest measure of social development."[4] He
found that "the United States alone had during the last century used
its military forces abroad over one hundred times."[5] and other well-
developed states had behaved similarly. Hence, he concluded: "I think
one must hesitate a long time before broadly condemning such
practice [intervention] on the ground that it is not sanctioned by
theoretical conceptions of what international law should be."[6] Thus,
Dulles defined customary international law as merely how civilized

states behave.   He seemed to ignore the notion that customary international law is not simply how states behave, but how they behave *authoritatively*. While it may have been true that at a certain time intervention was not necessarily a violation of international law, it was not merely so because of widespread intervention; it was because states regarded intervention as lawful, as authoritative, and largely conformed with this assumption.

As Dulles began to write on the problem of peaceful change in the 1930s, he also faced questions relating to international law. In *War, Peace and Change*, he discussed both international custom and treaties, but essentially denied them the right to be called law. International custom he dealt with in a footnote, explaining:

> There exists . . . a body of so-called "international law" which constitutes, in essence, a code of good international practice.   Nations which desire for their nationals the benefit of "antagonistic cooperation" with other peoples, tend to conform to such practices as a matter of practical expediency.   They desire and expect reciprocal action by others.   The field thus covered is primarily important to private   international   relations.   Such   so-called "international law" is not, however, so deeply rooted in the *mores* of the nations that it can withstand much strain. Nations, which, like Russia and to some extent Mexico, have abandoned capitalistic concepts and practices, tend also to abandon this so-called "international law" which would circumscribe rather than promote their national policies.[7]

Thus, while Dulles recognized the existence of customary practice, he saw it not as a set of authoritative, legally binding rules, but as "a code of good international practices" based essentially on expediency and reciprocity, and generally limited to "private international relations," that is, international business transactions.   The "rules" that did exist were not sufficiently based on the common values of states; they seemed to have little control over state behavior, with states rejecting adherence to these principles when they conflicted with self-interest.   His belief in the inefficacy of international law seemed confirmed by his repeated use of quotation remarks and the phrase "so-called" when referring to international law.

But, if Dulles ascribed little authority to customary international law, treaty law did not fare any better. It too fell into the realm of "[s]o-called international law."[8]   He explained that, while it may constitute domestic law, treaty law lacked the necessary elements to be considered international law.

Treaties serve to define the domain and status of states as between themselves, and to determine their relations. They constitute law *within a nation* to the extent that the national authority requires of its group members compliance therewith. Between the nations themselves, however, political treaties fail to partake of these qualities which alone serve to make law an instrumentality for protecting society against violence.[9]

By this definition, therefore, law must "function to solve, within a group, the problem of violence."[10] He explained that "[l]aw, from this viewpoint, is a body of rules laid down by group authority in the interest of the group members as a whole, and designed to avert the use of force by establishing conditions which acceptably balance the dynamic and static desires of the group members."[11] As noted earlier, Dulles posited three characteristics that these rules must possess: they must be made by a central authority, they must establish "a condition of flexibility," and they "must always be changeable and in fact be changed when they fail to provide the desired balance."[12] But "[s]o-called international law, which is principally embodied in treaties, largely lacks each of these three characteristics indispensable to municipal law if it is to preserve peace within the group."[13] Since there is no international authority, and since treaties are inflexible and not generally subject to change, they do not form effective law akin to municipal statutory law; they can only create "so-called" international law.

Nevertheless, Dulles asked, if treaties could perhaps be considered "sacred" by analogy to private contracts. Here too his answer was negative. Unlike the municipality, the international system has no group authority to supervise and lend its imprimatur to such agreements. He explained:

Treaties . . . cannot be expected to have "obligation" in the sense that a government imparts the legal obligation to private contracts, for there exists no international authority to accord, or withhold, such obligation. Many treaties, however, obviously have characteristics which, when present in private contracts, lead the authority to deny them legal effectiveness. The combination of these two factors tends to undermine international morality. Within an organized group, the authority takes the responsibility of overriding private contracts, so that this can occur without abandonment, by the individual, of the principle of fidelity. When, however, there exists no authority, then treaty violation, even if justified, cuts across accepted standards of honor.[14]

The lack of international sanction thus not only denies treaties the character of law, it also denies them much of the character of morality. While the British legal philosopher John Austin may have felt that "international law" could only be considered "positive international morality," due to the lack of an international authority, Dulles would not go even that far. He concluded: "In the absence of any central authority to pass judgement, one cannot consider treaties, as such, to be sacred, nor can we identify treaty observance, in the abstract, with 'law and order.'"[15]

But the sanction problem, the lack of an international authority, was not the only difficulty. International law was also ineffective, or was not even law, because it was not backed by the moral consensus of the international community. In *War, Peace and Change*, he spoke about the possibility that international practice could "become so grounded in the *mores* of the world community as to attain the status of law."[16] Many years later in 1944, he was to explain that "behind the law-making body there exists the moral consensus of the community. That is what is basic. Laws are ineffective unless they reflect that."[17] Dulles did not seem to believe that consensus had yet been established.

These views on the nature of international law that Dulles expressed in *War, Peace and Change* continued in many of his writings after he became chairman of the Commission on a Just and Durable Peace. In fact, he became more vocal in his belief that international law was not really law. In an April 1941 letter to F. Ernest Johnson of the Federal Council of Churches, Dulles criticized Attorney General Robert Jackson's approach to international law. He explained:

> My main criticism of the address is that he follows the time-honored custom of attempting to justify in terms of so-called "international law" and "justice" a course of conduct which we adopt because it is in our self-interest to do so, and which under the sovereignty system we are entirely at liberty to adopt because there is no real "international law" which is effective or designed to restrict the complete freedom of action of every nation.[18]

Dulles took this criticism even further in a September 1943 letter to Henry Luce,[19] in which he responded to an article by noted international legal scholar Philip Jessup. Dulles told Luce:

> The weakest portion of Mr. Jessup's paper, it seems to me, is that dealing with "law." *I confess to being one of those lawyers who do not regard "international law as law at all"* (p. 29) because, among other things, no nation is, or feels, bound to conform to any course of action other than its own interest and, as Mr. Jessup says,

international law "can be twisted to suit any national
interest." He suggests that we (the U.S.) are an exception
(p. 27). But that is not accurate. I can cite many treaties
we have violated . . . [Furthermore], we can -- and have-
- often passed statutes which violated treaties and the
statutes are controlling and the foreigner has no relief in
our courts.[20]

International law was not authoritative, nor did states perceive it as
such. Their behavior was dictated only by self-interest.

One reason, Dulles explained to Luce, that states did not wish
to be obligated to international law was the problem of change. He
argued:

The heart of the matter is that power to *make* law,
implies the power to *change* law. For no law -- other
than moral law -- is good forever. No nation is willing to
subject itself to such a system. It will accept -- and call
"law" -- customs and practices and treaties that it likes.
But it will not admit that anything is "law" which it does
not like. As Mr Jessup says (p. 30) we make, through our
power, our own "law." But we can hardly expect others to
accept something as "law" because it is our fiat, nor can
something we make ourselves be any objective guide for
our conduct.[21]

Presumably, what Dulles meant here was that because there was no
international authority to make and change law, states refused to be
bound by an inflexible system of treaties and customs. Indeed, they
simply would choose whatever norms they felt inclined to at a
particular time. But that method cannot provide an objective
standard. Law, Dulles seemed to suggest, must emanate from *above*
the individual members of the legal system. Consequently, he
concluded:

I think we are following a vain illusion if we assume that
the slogan "freedom under law" has sufficient substance to
be "the living principle of U.S. foreign policy," unless by
"law" we limit ourselves to "moral" law. Even as to what
that is in relation to any particular facts, many would
differ; but at least it is in principle something objective,
not subject to be made and remade just by ourselves to
serve our own convenience. "International law" achieved
its greatest influence at a time when it was deemed to
embody "moral" law and perhaps some of this viewpoint
could be recaptured.[22]

Thus Dulles seemed only to hold out the hope that perhaps a rehabilitation of "natural law" could have yielded some positive results. But he did not elaborate on this idea.

From all these statements, it would appear that he did not believe that "international law," as he knew it during this period was worth very much; indeed, it was not really law. As noted, Dulles seemed to suggest that international law might mean something if interpreted in terms of natural law. He also seemed to give some credence to the international law of the nineteenth century. In a memo of April 17, 1942, he explained that the reason the "free enterprise system functioned [well] during the nineteenth century . . [was that] there existed a system of law -- international, constitutional and municipal -- which was designed to preclude political intrusions which might upset the calculation on the basis of which private capital took long term risks."[23]   He elaborated:

> [T]here grew up a body of international law designed to prevent the quarrels of governments from upsetting international trade and investment. Private property, even belonging to enemies, was deemed to be immune from seizure in times of war. Rights of blockade were limited to the close investment of specific parts and contraband was limited to actual articles of war. Thus immunity was sought to be given to private commerce and foreign investments even against the risks of war.[24]

But these conditions that existed in the nineteenth century, Dulles concluded, no longer prevailed.[25]   He still had very little faith in the effectiveness of international law in the twentieth century.

INTERNATIONAL COURTS

Despite, and indeed perhaps because of, his beliefs about the nature of international law, Dulles consistently advocated U. S. participation in international judicial organs. He began his advocacy in 1923 when he coauthored a short legalistic memorandum, entitled "An Opinion with Respect to Acceptance by the United States of the Permanent Court of International Justice." In this piece, he and Charles P. Howland addressed "the legal problems incident to American acceptance of the Permanent Court of International Justice."[26]   They proposed that the U. S. adhere to the statute of the PCIJ with two understandings regarding the expenses of the court and the rights and privileges of the U. S., especially with respect to judges. They also dealt with the question of PCIJ jurisdiction, concluding that "[a]cceptance of the Court does not require the United States to accept its jurisdiction except in such cases as the United States may thereafter voluntarily refer to it."[27]   Additionally, they addressed the concerns about the implications of U. S. adherence to the PCIJ for the relationship between America and the League of Nations. On this point, they argued that "acceptance of the Court does not itself imply any relationship whatever to the Treaty creating the League of Nations."[28]   (According to Dulles's handwritten notation on this brief, he discussed that issue with Secretary of State Charles Evans Hughes on February 10, 1923 and then delivered a signed copy, presumably to Hughes, two days later.)

As the U. S. began to consider the acceptance of the PCIJ, Dulles continued to express his support. In 1926 he refused to be discouraged by a proposed reservation that would have limited the court's jurisdiction on advisory opinions in which the U. S. was affected.[29] Sometime between 1926 and 1928, he authored a draft setting forth his reasons for favoring U. S. participation in the PCIJ. First, he explained, the PCIJ offered the possibility of providing an alternative to war as a means of settling disputes. While there may have been much talk about efforts to outlaw war, it was "absolutely impossible to make progress in the elimination of force as an element in the settlement of international differences unless some other method of settlement is substituted, for as stated above, there will always be these differences and there must always be some way of resolving them."[30] Neither negotiation nor arbitration was sufficient. Negotiation, unless accompanied by coercion, was "nothing more than a resort to persuasion,"[31] and arbitration, unless it was imposed on one party, required the initial "spirit of cooperation"[32] just to get started. Hence, "[g]enerally speaking when international relations are seriously strained, it is impossible to negotiate an arbitration convention."[33] Consequently, "[j]udicial process remains as the one method which has been eminently successful in the solution of private differences but which has never yet been tried in any broad way in the international field."[34]

Dulles proceeded to explain how the judicial method had been successful. He cited the record of previous international courts, such as mixed tribunals and the German-American Claims Commission. While he recognized that "the matters dealt with by such courts have not been of momentous consequence from the point of view of international politics," he referred to them "chiefly because the very smooth functioning of these courts serve [sic] to illustrate what I think is a very important point, namely, that the nature of the judicial process is well devised to meet the psychological attitude of hostile or unfriendly parties."[35] According to Dulles, "[t]he judicial process . . . resembles war and is different from arbitration in that a nation can throw itself into litigation with unabated vigor and unabated confidence in the complete correctness of its position."[36] In the adversarial relationship of a court proceeding, there was no need for the disposition to compromise that was required in arbitration. He explained "that one of the reasons why the judicial process has been so successful in private controversies, is that litigation is consistent with distrust, contempt and enmity toward your adversary, whereas negotiation or arbitration is not."[37]

What is remarkable about these statements is that Dulles seemed to ignore the fact that in court proceedings the parties must have sufficient faith in the legitimacy of the institution that they can abruptly end their active adversarial relationship. When they submit an issue to the court they must be willing to accept a complete loss, which can normally be avoided in arbitration and negotiation. In essence, willingness to abide by an unfavorable court decision would seem to involve more of an "abandonment of the spirit of controversy"[38] than willingness to undergo arbitration or negotiation.

After illustrating how these claim tribunals demonstrated the suitability of judicial proceedings to disputes, Dulles then cited the success of "the greatest international court which the world has known"[39] in support of his argument. This court was, interestingly enough, the United States Supreme Court. He explained:

> At the present time we are so conscious of the unity of our nation and the Federal Government has no [so] overshadowed the State Governments, that it is difficult for us to realize the extent of the service performed by the Supreme Court as an international tribunal before which the several States have brought their differences. It requires a mental effort to recall that in the beginning our States were as divided and almost as unfriendly as are the States of Europe and that war was often imminent between them. State jealousies and rivaleries [sic] repeatedly threatened to disrupt the fragile union. Yet during these earlier days, the Supreme Court was extraordinarily successful in settling differences which inevitably arose between discordant States and such questions as boundary disputes, water rights, inter-state nuisances, relative taxing rights and innumerable [sic] others have been submitted to and decided by the Supreme Court and its decisions accepted virtually without exception.[40]

He continued to explain:

> There has been no serious dispute between the sovereign states which has not been satisfactorily settled by the Supreme Court of the United States except that of the right of a State to withdraw from the Union, and this question was never submitted to the Supreme Court. And though the Supreme Court has no way of compelling defendant States to appear before it, yet, except in only one case only, so far as I can recall, they have always appeared, and though the Supreme Court has no way of

enforcing its judgments yet almost without exception they have been accepted.[41]

From this positive experience of the Supreme Court, Dulles deduced that there was hope for "other" international tribunals.   He explained, "If the history of the Supreme Court is a safe guide, it teaches us that sovereign states will generally settle their disputes without resort to force if they are only supplied with an honorable method which does not require them to compromise or stultify themselves in their own estimation."[42]   Indeed, Dulles believed that the Supreme Court experience was a major reason "which led Secretary [of State] Hay to instruct the American delegates to the First Hague Peace Conference [1899], to bend their efforts to secure the adherence of the nations of the world to the establishment of an international court similar to the Supreme Court of the United States."[43]

But in addition to supporting the PCIJ because of the success of other international courts, Dulles also favored U. S. accession to the PCIJ because he felt that it had already proven successful in the cases it had handled.   After briefly mentioning some of the issues that the court had dealt with, he concluded:

> The variety of cases which have been submitted during the brief life of the Court, the manner in which the cases have been disposed of, the impartial attitude of the judges and the acceptance of the decisions by the litigants all point to the fact that the Court has an opportunity for usefulness which meets the highest expectations of those who have sought to establish judicial processes as a method of settling international disputes.[44]

To an extent, therefore, the PCIJ was itself a proven means of resolving international conflicts.

Through all these examples, Dulles attempted to demonstrate that the PCIJ was valuable because it could settle particular disputes. But he also supported the court because he believed that it could make a larger contribution to world peace by promoting further development of international law.   The U. S. Supreme Court had "built up a body of international law which now so defines the respective rights and duties of the several states that the possibility of a serious dispute between them is almost inconceivable."[45]   The PCIJ could perform the same task in the international arena; he explained: "There is no better way to develop international law than through such an international court as is sitting in the Hague."[46]

In addition to making a positive argument in support of the Permanent Court, Dulles also dealt with some of the more specific legal controversies surrounding U. S. participation in the court, many of which he had dealt with previously.   He reiterated, for instance, his conviction that joining the PCIJ would not establish any legal relationship to the League of Nations. Furthermore, the proposal to associate the U. S. with the court did not involve the acceptance of the Optional Clause, which related to compulsory jurisdiction. Indeed, the U. S. would only be subscribing to the PCIJ Statute generally. When a particular case arose, the U. S. *could* avail itself of the court if it so chose. He explained: "Adhesion thus means little more than extending our moral approval to the idea of an international court and paying a small fraction of the expenses of maintaining it."[47]

As time passed, Dulles abandoned much of his early optimism about the PCIJ. In a 1941 article, he explained:

> The World Court was from the beginning suspected of being politically minded. This suspicion was, in the opinion of many, confirmed by its decision of 1931 holding the proposed customs agreement between Germany and Austria to be violative of the treaty of St. Germain. The majority of one, by which this result was reached, seemed attributable to French political pressure upon the Court. Whatever the facts may have been, the result was a fatal blow to the prestige of the Court. Few remained who felt that their cause could be pleaded before the Court with assurance of an impartial, juridical verdict.[48]

But despite his belief that the PCIJ had become politicized, Dulles did not seem to have dropped his support for the concept of a world court. During the war years, when he had become involved in planning a postwar international organization, he exchanged numerous letters with Professor Manley O. Hudson of Harvard Law School on a series of issues relating to a world court. In these letters, Dulles demonstrated a great deal of support for an impartial, well-founded court.

The bulk of the Hudson correspondence took place in 1942 and 1943, and contained Dulles's responses to specific issues that Hudson had raised about the establishment of a postwar court. Some of these questions were technical in nature. For instance, the question was raised as to whether the current court, the PCIJ, should be continued. Dulles believed that this depended "on whether the Court as now constituted has achieved an international -- or supranational -- spirit which should be preserved."[49] While he believed that Hudson would know better about whether this was true, Dulles's impression was "that the Court did not achieve an objective and non-nationalistic attitude, except in affairs of minor significance."[50] Another specific question related to the relationship between the court and the new international organization. On this point, Dulles believed that "the Court should be based upon action by the States independent of any political organization."[51] He argued that there was "room for a Court irrespective of a political organization and the latter is, as events have proved, precarious.   As political organizations are formed they can stipulate for the Court as the judicial arbiter of judicable [*sic*] disputes that involve them."[52] Dulles also favored a separation of the judges from the influence of their states, and did not believe that "Judges should be representative of States" nor of "regional groups."[53] He furthermore did "not think that the great States should be entitled as a matter of right to have their nationals among the Judges," although he recognized that "if judicial eminence is a test of election it would almost automatically follow that the Judges would include substantial representation of the great States."[54]

Dulles was also asked by Hudson to respond to questions about the scope of the court's jurisdiction. For example, Dulles tended to favor regional courts "with the right of appeal to a universal court."[55] He did not favor extending jurisdiction to any court over "state crimes," explaining that he did "not think that an attempt should be made to create a judicial jurisdiction over crimes committed by States. As pointed out in the Federalist Papers to attempt to impose sanctions against States is in effect an act of war and this concept was wisely avoided in our Federal constitution."[56] He did, however, believe that under certain conditions there could be some criminal jurisdiction over individuals. If an international body were established that had "something like legislative power, then I think violation of its laws by individuals should be an offense, to try which there should be a tribunal. I would think in this event that the tribunal should be special with some right to appeal to the universal court."[57] He did not believe, on the other hand, that individuals should be able to bring claims against states.[58]

Interestingly enough, Dulles did favor granting compulsory jurisdiction to the universal court, which, as the letters progressed, he seemed to assume would be the Permanent Court. He even believed that it was possible to gain U. S. acceptance of compulsory U. S. jurisdiction. He explained:

> It seems to me not impossible to expect that the Senate would ratify a treaty conferring compulsory jurisdiction, if carefully defined, on an international court. I should think in any event that this problem must be faced frankly and I would doubt the wisdom of attempting to confer compulsory jurisdiction by some procedure other than that clearly indicated by the Constitution.[59]

But the subject matter that would fall under the compulsory jurisdiction would be limited in order not to jeopardize the possibility of obtaining initial acceptance of the compulsory jurisdiction. He elaborated: "It seems to me that compulsory jurisdiction should be confined to legal disputes. I would be disposed to confine them to disputes as to the interpretation of treaties, conventions or compacts; facts [which] if established would constitute breach thereof; the extent and nature of reparation to repair any such breach."[60]   But Dulles would have *excluded* general rules of customary international law:

> I rather question the wisdom of attempting to include disputes involving questions of international law as it seems to me this is too vague to be readily accepted as a basis for compulsory jurisdiction. To include this in effect involves inviting the court to build up a body of international "common law." Personally I would welcome this, but since it involves quasi legislative functions, I think acceptance of compulsory jurisdiction would more readily be attained with a more modest definition of the subjects of such compulsory jurisdiction.[61]

Hence, while Dulles favored the development of international "common law," he did not believe that the court should be assigned the task on a compulsory jurisdiction basis, at least initially. If it were, nations would be inclined not to accept compulsory jurisdiction and to prevent the court from getting started. It was better to gain something less than what was desired than to try for everything and gain nothing. This attitude clearly reflected Dulles's preference for a slow but sure approach to international organization, of which biographer Ronald Pruessen speaks.[62]

Dulles was also concerned about the relationship between the court's jurisdiction and the individual states. He did not "think it possible, and I am not sure it is desirable, to make provisions for a review of judgments of national courts by a permanent court."[63] (As noted earlier, if there were *regional* courts created by the universal court, however, he did believe there should be some type of appeal process.[64]) Furthermore, he did not believe that it was "practical or wise to attempt to give the court power to enforce execution of its judgments."[65]   But Dulles did not believe that the statute of the court should explicitly remove issues within domestic jurisdiction of a state from the purview of the court. He argued:

> I do not think that any provision for the compulsory jurisdiction of an international court there should be an express exception of disputes "which are within the domestic jurisdiction of any of the parties." This, it seems to me, leaves it too open to the parties themselves to contest jurisdiction in any case where they do not want it. Actually, of course, a court should feel bound not to deal with disputes which in fact relate to domestic questions just as, for instance, the courts of one state do not take

jurisdiction of controversies which relate primarily to the internal affairs of a foreign corporation.[66]

Apparently Dulles preferred that it be left up to the court to decide whether the issue did fall within the domestic jurisdiction of a state. Similarly, he also did "not think that there should be excluded disputes, the subject matter of which involves the Monroe Doctrine or the interests of third parties."[67]

Later in 1943, Dulles advocated U. S. adherence to the PCIJ as a first step toward securing international law and order. Echoing his other statements about the nature of international law, he explained that "[w]e do not, as yet, have much 'international law' because there is no international government or law making body."[68] There were treaties, but these were "not 'law' in the sense that some central body prescribes them. Rather treaties embody rules and decisions which the parties have voluntarily agreed to, or which one party has, by force, compelled another party to agree to."[69] Nevertheless, disputes relating to these treaties still arose, and "[t]hese disputes about interpretations and about facts ought to be settled by a court."[70] Similarly, there was "a certain amount of unwritten international law which reflects practices so long followed by all civilized peoples that they have achieved a certain sanctity. This body of 'law' relates primarily to the proper treatment of ambassadors, etc. Here again, there are 'rules' which an international court could apply."[71] In this draft, consequently, Dulles goes beyond his position in the Hudson correspondence and argues that the court *could* deal with issues of customary international law, but he still felt obliged to place words such as "law" and "rules" in quotation marks.

The United States, Dulles argued in this paper, should avail itself of the Permanent Court of International Justice for the resolution of disputes about these rules. In the past, "the U. S. has always refused to accept it as the judge of disputes involving treaties to which we were a party."[72] Instead, the United States had "preferred to leave disputes to be settled by force, probably thinking that we were so strong that thus we could more often get our own way."[73] But if the U. S. had changed its "mind about the desirability of a 'lawless' system, a first step we can take is to join in supporting a world court and agreeing that it may settle any disputes which involve treaties to which we are a party or which involve any other established rules of international law."[74] If the United States remained "unwilling to do that, then in fact we line up with the lawless nations, despite our protestation that we are 'peace loving' people, who desire a 'reign of law.'"[75]

Despite these strong words of support for participation in the PCIJ, Dulles did not see the court as a panacea. He explicitly recognized that many of the most important controversies could not be handled by the court because, in his opinion, there was no applicable international law.   He explained, citing the example of Panama:

> The biggest and most serious disputes cannot, however, be settled by a world court because, as yet, the nations have not any rules which a court could apply.   In 1902 Colombia and the U. S. both wanted the same thing at the same time, i.e., the site for the Panama Canal. Colombia had it and we got it because we were so much stronger that Colombia had to give it up.   Probably we ought to have been able to get it lawfully at a fair price, because we could and would build there a waterway of tremendous importance to the whole world.   People within organized groups have made rules to solve that kind of difference.   They have a rule that private property can be taken for public use, upon paying for its fair value.   But there is no "international" law to that effect.   So the Panama Canal was built by using the primitive test of superior force.[76]

Although Dulles believed that states should formulate rules on those highly political issues, "[u]ntil they do so, there will be plenty of differences that no court can solve."[77]   Nevertheless, "that is no reason for not getting started with a court to settle such disputes as are governed by an existing body of international law."[78]

OTHER MEANS OF DEVELOPING INTERNATIONAL LAW THROUGH INTERNATIONAL ORGANIZATION

As has been seen, Dulles favored the establishment of international courts not only because they would aid in settling a particular conflict but also because they would help develop international law, even though this latter function could only be undertaken gradually. He also suggested that international organization could develop international law in other ways.

In *War, Peace and Change*, Dulles supported the development of international law, but did not provide any details as to how this would be done.   As noted earlier, he advocated the formulation of a flexible regime of customary international law that would be based on the consensus of the world instead of the adoption of more treaties. He believed that if there "could develop in international affairs a viewpoint corresponding to that which is epitomized by the common law,"[79] the world would be more receptive to change.   Dulles did not go into the specifics of the way in which this attitude would be promoted.   Perhaps this would develop as part of the "ethical solution" discussed above, by which it was hoped a spirit of cooperation could be established through promotion of more international interactions.[80]   But as noted earlier, in *War, Peace and Change*, he did not propose *any specific* international institutions. Furthermore, in relation to international law, Dulles seemed in his book more concerned about developing international law not for its own sake, but in order to promote positive attitudes toward peaceful change.   Perhaps since international law was itself a means to an end, he did not examine the means to the means.

As time passed, however, Dulles gave more specific indications of how international law could be developed.   In his writings and addresses he touched on several different methods.   First, he seemed to suggest that a functional approach could develop international law. As will be seen in the next chapter, he believed that cooperation on economic and social issues could build up a spirit of cooperation among states.   It was this cooperation that would create the world consensus that was the prerequisite for a regime of customary international law.   This approach can be seen in his 1944 address on the Dumbarton Oaks Proposals, where he explained how the force problem could be handled. There were, as noted above, two methods. The first was despotism; but the second was the development of international law: "Through custom -- 'common law' -- or through a legislative body they create a system of law adequate to regulate human behavior."[81]   But that approach "was not . . . available to the authors of the Dumbarton Oaks Proposals" because there was still no "world acceptance, and therefore no effective definition, of proper and improper national conduct."[82]   Dulles then explained how such definition could be reached.

> We want world organization to bring the nations together to work for stable economic and monetary conditions; to keep the treaty structure of the world abreast of changing underlying conditions; to make autonomy the genuine goal of colonial administration and to assure to individuals everywhere spiritual and intellectual liberty.   *Out of working together on such great tasks there can come a common judgment of what is decent national conduct*, and a general agreement that, in matters of common concern, the general welfare should take precedence.[83]

Thus, to extrapolate, by cooperating on these functional issues states can reach a consensus on what is acceptable state behavior, and this consensus can form the basis for the establishment of international legal norms.

A second method that Dulles envisioned for developing international law was through the functioning of the Security Council.   Just prior to the San Francisco Conference he expressed his belief that the decisions of the Security Council, not unlike those of courts, could help establish international common law.   In a letter written for publication in the *New York Times* on March 6, 1945, he explained:

> In addition to dealing with disputes which are justiciable, the Security Council, as we have seen, will have to act in relation to disputes which at present are non-justiciable. This action would be political rather than judicial. Perhaps those acts will serve as precedents to build up a body of international "common law" so that we shall see a constant increase in "justiciable" disputes and a constant diminution of the disputes which can be settled only by political action.[84]

A third possible means to develop international law that Dulles touched on was direct legislation. In his 1944 address on the Dumbarton Oaks Proposal, he mentioned the possibility that international law could be created "through a legislative body," but he did not develop this idea much further. Perhaps the most interesting aspect of his brief reference to the legislative approach was his suggestion that the international organization could legislate for *individuals* rather than *states*. Dulles did not think it wise for the court to have jurisdiction over state crimes, but he did think it possible for the court to have jurisdiction over individuals who violate law made by the "legislative power." He thus seemed to imply that it would be wise to create international law that would apply to individuals. Although he did not go into great detail during the early period of his thought, by October of 1945 he was able to advocate "an alternative to legislation for states, namely, the adoption of laws to operate upon individuals."[85]

A final means of developing international law that appeared in Dulles's thought was codification. This method was also not very well explained in his writings. In his 1920s draft on the PCIJ, he observed in passing that it was "of course, possible, that international rights and duties can, to some extent, be clarified by codification,"[86] but did not elaborate. In *War, Peace and Change*, Dulles stated that there should be "fewer treaties"[87] because they tended to promote rigidity; he preferred the development of customary international law instead. It was perhaps in light of this skepticism about treaty law that Dulles failed to pursue the concept of codification in his early thought.

AN EVALUATION OF DULLES'S EARLY VIEWS ON INTERNATIONAL LAW AND INTERNATIONAL ORGANIZATION

From the preceding examination of Dulles's thought on international law, several general observations can be made. First, except for his early optimism, Dulles was perhaps too quick to recognize the failings of international law and too slow to acknowledge the substantial amount of international law that had developed in the early twentieth century. To an individual reading only Dulles's writings during this period, it would appear that there was no *significant* body of customary international law and that the laws which did exist dealt only with fairly narrow matters -- private transactions and diplomatic immunity. Furthermore, Dulles seemed to have ignored, with minor exceptions, the specific codification efforts undertaken at the 1899 and 1907 Hague Conferences (the latter of which he attended), and the 1929 Geneva Conference, especially with reference to the laws of war. In addition, as noted earlier, Dulles did not seem to ascribe any normative implications to the use of force provisions of the League Covenant and, although he initially praised the Kellogg-Briand Pact, by the 1940s he was once more convinced that there were essentially no international rules restraining recourse to force. Manley O. Hudson made an interesting comment in a 1944 letter discussing a report of the Committee on International Law of the New York Bar, which Dulles had helped to write. Referring to a statement in the report concerning the importance of "incorporation [presumably of international law] in multilateral treaties," Hudson commented: "If your report is to help lawyers to leadership, why don't you say what has been done along this line. Do you know my seven volumes of *International Legislation?*"[88] Perhaps Dulles did not mention what had been done because he did not believe there was anything significant.

A second observation relating to Dulles's understanding of international law is that, despite opinions to the contrary, he was neither a "legalist" nor an "anti-legalist" in his conception of the relationship of international law to foreign policy. A legalist would feel that strict adherence to international legal norms should be the foundation of foreign policy. Dulles, however, did not believe this was possible. In his 1943 letter to Luce, he explicitly criticized Professor Jessup's desire to make "freedom under law" "the living principle of U. S. foreign policy." There was no "international law" as such, and states did not want to subject themselves to those norms that did exist. Only through a slow, evolutionary process could the peoples of the world be brought together in cooperation so that eventually a world law could be formulated. But Dulles was also not an anti-legalist, if an anti-legalist is one who believes that international law should play virtually no role in determining foreign policy. His strong support for the development, however slow, of international law would seem to indicate a desire to make its promotion a goal of foreign policy. Furthermore, it seems clear that as this international law developed, it would itself serve as a guide to state behavior. In sum, Dulles did not fit into either stereotype, legalist or anti-legalist.

A final observation that can be drawn from the discussion relates to the relationship between international law and international organization. During his early period, Dulles seemed to have believed that the development of both international law and international organization was necessary in order to pursue his goal for the international system -- the establishment of a flexible world community in which states cooperated on a host of international projects and sought changes by peaceful means. Consequently, law and organization related to each other in a symbiotic way. In *War, Peace and Change*, Dulles suggested that the international common law may be the precursor of international mechanisms of peaceful change. Here, international law would serve to promote international organization. Conversely, at other points he argued that international organization efforts, such as the use of the functional method, should be used to develop international law. He did not see the sole goal of international organization as the promotion of international law. International organization should be encouraged for what it independently could contribute to international order. At bottom, just as domestic system required *both* institutions and laws, so too did a well-functioning international system.

NOTES

1. Dulles, "Draft on PCIJ [Permanent Court of International Justice]," undated (probably 1926-1928), in *JFD Papers*, 17.

2. Dulles, "Conceptions and Misconceptions Regarding Intervention," 102.

3. Ibid.

4. Ibid.

5. Ibid.

6. Ibid.

7. Dulles, *War, Peace and Change*, 38.

8. Ibid., 40.

9. Ibid., 39.

10. Ibid.

11. Ibid.

12. Ibid., 40.

13. Ibid.

14. Ibid., 45.

15. Ibid., 47.

16. Ibid., 158.

17. Dulles, "The Dumbarton Oaks Proposals," Nov. 28, 1944, *JFD Papers*, 5.

18. JFD to F. Ernest Johnson, Apr. 16, 1941, *JFD Papers*, 2.

19. JFD to Henry Luce, Sept. 29, 1943, *JFD Papers*, 1-2 (emphasis added).

20. Ibid.

21. Ibid.

22. Ibid.

23. Dulles, "Critique of Mr. Buell's Report," Apr. 17, 1942, *JFD Papers*, 3.

24. Ibid.

25. Ibid., 4.

26. Howland and Dulles, "An Opinion with Respect to Acceptance by the United States of the Permanent Court of International Justice," 1923, *JFD Papers*, 1.

27. Ibid., 3.

28. Ibid.

29. See Dulles, "Re: World Court," Sept. 7, 1926, *JFD Papers*.

30. Dulles, "Draft on PCIJ," 2-3.

31. Ibid.

32. Ibid., 3-4.

33. Ibid., 6.

34. Ibid., 7.

35. Ibid.

36. Ibid., 8.

37. Ibid., 8-9.

38. Ibid., 8.

39. Ibid., 9.

40. Ibid., 9-10.

41. Ibid., 10.

42. Ibid.

43. Ibid., 11.

44. Ibid., 14.

45. Ibid., 10.

46. Ibid., 18.

47. Ibid., 19.

48. Dulles, "The Aftermath of the World War," 269.

49. JFD to Manley O. Hudson, Dec. 29, 1942, *JFD Papers*, 1.

50. Ibid.

51. Ibid., 2.

52. Ibid.

53. Ibid.

54. Ibid.

55. JFD to Manley O. Hudson, Jan. 15, 1943, *JFD Papers*, 1.

56. Ibid.

57. Ibid.

58. Ibid.

59. JFD to Manley O. Hudson, Feb. 24, 1943, *JFD Papers*, 2.

60. Ibid., 1.

61. Ibid.

62. See Pruessen, *John Foster Dulles*, 208-209.

63. JFD to Manley O. Hudson, Mar. 23, 1943, *JFD Papers*, 1.

64. Ibid.

65. Ibid., 2.

66. JFD to Manley O. Hudson, May 19, 1943, *JFD Papers*, 1.

67. Ibid.

68. Dulles, "Draft on the PCIJ," Nov. 15, 1943, *JFD Papers*, 5.
69. Ibid.
70. Ibid.
71. Ibid., 6.
72. Ibid.
73. Ibid.
74. Ibid.
75. Ibid.
76. Ibid., 7.
77. Ibid.
78. Ibid.
79. Dulles, *War, Peace and Change*, 156.
80. Ibid., 9-26.
81. Dulles, "The Dumbarton Oaks Proposals," Nov. 28, 1944, *JFD Papers*, 2.
82. Ibid.
83. Ibid., 5 (emphasis added).
84. Dulles, "To the Editor of the *New York Times*," Mar. 6, 1945, *JFD Papers*, 2.
85. Dulles, "The General Assembly," 1, 9.
86. Dulles, "Draft on PCIJ," undated, *JFD Papers*, 16.
87. Dulles, *War, Peace and Change*, 158.
88. Manley O. Hudson to JFD, July 10, 1944, *JFD Papers*, 2.

6

Other Roles for International Organization

WORLD FEDERALISM

Yet another possible role of international organization is to promote world federalism. Under such an arrangement, states lose most or all of their sovereignty over matters of international concern and the centralized body becomes the governing authority. In the early period of his thought, Dulles used "federalism" to mean two slightly different things, initially taking a very broad interpretation of federalism and then accepting the more narrow "classical" definition, with his attitude to the concept varying according to the definition.

Dulles's first use of federalism, which appeared in an article written in 1939, was very fluid. He explained:

> The federal system recognizes that sovereignty is a bundle of powers which do not necessarily all have to be vested in the same entity or exercised with regard for the same group of people. Certain powers, for example those relating to trade, immigration, and money, operate upon a far wider circle of persons than do those relating to sanitation, education, etc. It, therefore, vests the first set of powers in a body having responsibility to a large group of people, while it leaves the second group of powers in bodies responsible only to smaller groups of persons. Our own Constitution is, of course, the best-known example of the federal system, *but the federal principle is subject to indefinite expression and many possible variations.* For instance, any number of states might agree that a matter of trade between them was a matter of common concern and, therefore, that authority over trade between these

nations should be vested in a body which derived its authority from and had responsibility toward all the peoples concerned. In this way power and responsibility tend to become coextensive, and we do away with a condition whereby certain persons are restrained and restricted by power exercised without regard for their welfare.[1]

In this statement Dulles describes a federal system in which bits of sovereignty can be given up by groups of states to deal with particular issues that extend beyond their boundaries. It is not the standard description of a *general* abandonment of sovereignty by a set number of states to an established authority. Instead, Dulles seemed to be suggesting a functional abandonment of sovereignty, with bodies organized to be coextensive with the particular problem. He corroborates this interpretation by explaining that "under the federal system, power is divided up as between different bodies having different jurisdictions. There is no single entity which has the majesty of full power."[2] As an example, he suggests that "the establishment of a common money might be vested in a body created by and responsible to the English, French, German, and American people."[3] Indeed, it is obvious that Dulles was suggesting that the organization treat functional issues, such as trade immigration, and monetary problems, rather than the issue which typically occupies world federalists -- the direct prevention of war. In consequence, the first use of "federalism" seems more appropriately interpreted as indicating a form of functionalism, which will be discussed more thoroughly later. It should be noted that in this 1939 discussion of federalism, Dulles did not specifically advocate this approach, but merely suggested it as a possibility.

His second use of the word federalism is more along the lines of the traditional definition -- a system in which sovereignty over international affairs is given up to a central authority. As noted earlier, Dulles did see the federal system, in this sense, as a possible means of balancing the dynamic and static elements of the international system. In a letter written on January 3, 1940, to Professor Eugene Staley, Dulles explained that the federal system "in effect takes powers which have a broad influence and places them in a body which is chosen by, and which owes its allegiance to, a broader group than the present national units."[4] As he explained earlier, people become the units of the system rather than the states. Dulles often used the federal experiment of the United States as an example for the international system. In *War, Peace and Change*, he explained that America's successful federalism illustrated that independent states, the colonies, could indeed give up a great deal of sovereignty and still maintain a considerable amount of independence.[5]

Nonetheless, Dulles had reservations about the prospects of realistically implementing federalism. He told Professor Staley that "[t]heoretically the Federal system is the best," but "[p]ractically I do not believe that the world is yet prepared for its extension on a sufficiently broad basis so that in this way alone the problem can be solved."[6] Furthermore, he noted in *War, Peace and Change* that "[t]he pattern of the United States cannot, of course, be applied to all the nations of the world. This is concededly not practical."[7]

These reservations about world federalism were based on Dulles's belief that a federal union would not be possible worldwide without a common political orientation and common values. And as noted earlier, he argued that "it may be that the federal system will not operate successfully unless based upon a population which is homogeneous."[8] This led him to the conclusion that a federal scheme could be implemented initially only on a less than universal basis. In a letter of July 24, 1940, however, he expressed suspicion that even the Western Hemisphere was too large for a federal arrangement.

> I have, however, some considerable doubt as to the practicability of a program so far-reaching as one that would include all of the western hemisphere in a single Federal union. This is partly because I think that security must be one of the foundations of any such union, and I doubt that we can undertake to provide this for areas so far removed as the southern part of South America. I think geographical propinquity is a factor that cannot be disregarded. I also feel that most of South America is alien, not only in language, but in political conceptions and natural and economic interests and, accordingly, an attempt to bring together so much in a single step is overly ambitious and apt to involve structural weaknesses which would make the union short-lived.[9]

A common cultural, political, and economic orientation was a prerequisite for a federal union. Perhaps an evolutionary approach to federalism would make more sense; Dulles explained that his "own preference would be to seek a more gradual extension of the Federal principle, beginning first with this continent and then perhaps extending gradually into South America, as seemed warranted by the solidity of the foundation upon which we were building."[10]

Another concern Dulles had about federalism was that it could cause states to lose some of their independence unnecessarily. In an interview broadcast on CBS on December 19, 1942, Dulles explained this fear. In response to a comment that his suggestion for "some sort of central international mechanism" would be tantamount to "a world government or a super-state," Dulles replied:

I don't believe that it calls for that and I don't think it would be desirable to try and achieve a world government in the sense that phrase is ordinarily used. We need to have an international government in the areas where people are actually inter-dependent and where what one person does affects someone else, but, there are a great many phases of our lives where what we do doesn't have any particular effect upon other people and in those areas it is much better to have a local government than it is to turn all those things over to an international government."[11]

Here Dulles's position was that international authority was necessary only in areas where states were actually interdependent. World government seems to have implied something more far-reaching, which could conceivably deprive states of their identity in areas where there were no overlapping interests. This almost seems to be a refutation of the possibility that people, rather than states, could be units of the system.

In sum, while Dulles came to advocate a central world organization, he fell short of favoring world federalism in the strict sense. Such a federation was not yet possible in a world of disparate political ideas and cultures. It also had the danger of going beyond federalism, where states maintain control over certain matters, and becoming a type of world government where states lose all independence.

REGIONALISM

In *War, Peace and Change*, Dulles dealt with international organization on the universal level only, but as time progressed he also discussed some forms of regional international organization. Although his thoughts on regionalism were tentative at first, he soon became involved in efforts to establish regional organizations and developed a firm commitment to the idea of European federation.

Before exploring Dulles's thoughts on regionalism, it should be indicated how this term is being used. Although "regionalism," in the strict sense, implies some form of organization based on geography, here the term should be taken in a broader sense. By regional organization is meant any form of international organization that binds states together on less than a universal basis. A regional organization may be primarily political, military, economic, or a combination of these functions.

As Dulles's views on regional organization began developing in the 1930s and 1940s, he vacillated between support and skepticism. In a letter to Quincy Wright, dated December 19, 1939, he endorsed the concept of regionalism. At that time he felt that "an effort should be made to achieve some form of world organization which, however, would be merely consultative and the meeting place of the chiefs of state or the ministers of foreign affairs."[12]   But, "within the framework of this central organization it might be possible to work out a series of stronger international arrangements, no one of which, however, would attempt at this stage to be world-wide in its scope, but each of which should preferably be 'open-ended' and capable of extension."[13]   These tight organizations could then be stepping stones to larger organizations."[14]   Dulles explained that those arrangements would be organized on several different bases.

> There might, for instance, be some arrangements which would be *regional*, others which would be based upon *a community of financial and commercial interests*, and others which might be based upon a *similarity of political institutions*.   The subject matter of such various agreements might be different. For instance, as illustrative of the first category, there might be an effort to develop the Federal system in Europe. As illustrative of the second category, there might be some monetary agreements as between such countries as the United States, England and France -- something like the tripartite monetary agreement formalized. As illustrative of the third type, certain countries, such as some of the "democracies", might make a tentative beginning at some form of political collaboration through a central organization, the members of which would be elected by the peoples and which might have at least a certain advisory capacity or even veto power with respect to matters of common interest.[15]

These three types of organization could conceivably have overlapping membership, with some countries belonging to only one and others belonging to several.   But these organizations, in Dulles's opinion, would probably not have enforcement mechanisms. He explained that he doubted "very much if it is feasible or desirable to endow any of these organizations with military or even economic sanctions, and much less do I believe, at this stage, in an international police force."[16]

But Dulles's views on regionalism were still quite tentative.[17] By January of 1940, he was beginning to express doubts about such organizations.   In his "Draft on Peaceful Change" (which was discussed above), he expressed fears that a federal system that developed on a less than universal basis could present problems. He explained that if the federal system can develop only where there is a homogeneous population, "the federal system may merely develop the world into groups which, while larger than any present nation, will still, as between themselves, be exclusive and resistant to change."[18]   Instead of a stepping-stone to globalism, a regional federal system could thus be nothing more than a superstate that would behave just like a conventional state but on a larger scale.

Despite this reservation, however, Dulles soon found himself involved with a number of movements specifically aimed at establishing some sort of regional organization. In March of 1940, he became a consultant to Inter-Democracy Federal Unionists, an organization headed by Clarence Streit.[19] This organization sought to establish a federal union of certain western democracies, especially the United States and Great Britain. In his capacity as consultant, Dulles drafted memoranda dealing with some of the legal aspects of establishing such a union. On November 4, 1940, for example, Dulles sent Streit a proposed joint resolution that provided for presidential authorization to enter into a federal union. This proposal empowered the president to form a union with other democracies and contained provisions that would integrate many functions of the member democracies. One provision authorized the president of the United States "to join with the other members of the Union to achieve their common defense and to perfect some common military organization as seems appropriate."[20] This military organization was to be much more than a simple alliance; it was to have supranational characteristics. The president was granted the power to "enlist and issue commissions to any person owing allegiance to any Member Democracy, it being the intent hereof that the perfection of an effective military, naval and aerial organization shall not be impeded by any distinctions flowing from differences in nationality or allegiance between the Members of the Union."[21] The draft resolution also contained provisions calling for reciprocal lifting of immigration quotas and the establishment of a Supreme Economic Council "to promote the economic welfare of the Union."[22]

While Dulles spent some time working with Streit,[23] a certain amount of skepticism on Dulles's part seems to have remained. He later questioned the practicability of some of Streit's ideas; he explained in June of 1941: "I think the educational value of what he is doing is very great, but I doubt very much that it is practical or perhaps desirable to attempt a political union as close as he [Streit] suggests."[24]

Even though the broad Atlantic union Streit had desired may have been too ambitious, *European* union seemed very practical to Dulles. In his work with the Commission on a Just and Durable Peace, he took numerous opportunities to advocate European federalism. As noted earlier, one of his criticisms of the Atlantic Charter was that it contained provisions that could be interpreted as restricting the possibility of European union. In his discussion following the critique of the Atlantic Charter, Dulles explained:

> We should seek the political reorganization of continental Europe as a federated commonwealth of some type. As stated above, there must be a large measure of local self-government along ethnic lines. This can be

assured through federal principles which in this respect are very flexible. But the reestablishment of some twenty-five wholly independent sovereign states in Europe would be political folly.[25]

He advocated this union not purely for the interest of Europe, but for those of the United States as well. He argued:

> Twice within the last twenty-five years the United States has become deeply involved in the wars originating between the independent, unconnected sovereignties of Europe. It has been demonstrated that the world has so shrunk that European wars can no longer, as during the last century, be confined to Europe. Therefore, it is not merely of self-interest to Europe, but of vital concern to us, that there be not restored in Europe the conditions which inherently give rise to such wars. From a purely selfish standpoint any American program for peace must included a federated continental Europe. From the standpoint of the peoples concerned, their economic interdependence calls for political mechanisms to assure that their resources and markets be coordinated for maximum peaceful utility.[26]

It is interesting to see here, once again, Dulles's belief that war results from a system that is factually interdependent but composed of legally independent, unconnected, sovereign states.

Dulles's concerns about Europe were also, as would be expected, reflected in his work with the Commission on a Just and Durable Peace. When the "Six Pillars of Peace" was published in March of 1943, the idea of regional collaboration, particularly European collaboration, was not excluded. In the Comment to Pillar One, which provides for an overall political organization, it was explained that this would not preclude regional arrangements:

> The degree of collaboration can properly be related to the degree of interdependence and thus any universal scheme may contain within its framework provision for regional collaboration. To continue there the uncoordinated independence of some twenty-five sovereign states will assure for the future that, as in the past, war will be a frequently recurrent event.[27]

Although neither the commission nor Dulles developed the specifics of how other regional arrangements should be set up, in principle they endorsed such organizations.

FUNCTIONALISM

Throughout Dulles's early discussion of the roles of international organization there is, as has been alluded to previously, a strong emphasis on the functional approach to peace. Before examining how Dulles demonstrated this functionalist tendency, however, it is first necessary to define the concept of functionalism.

The Definition of Functionalism[28]

Functionalism is an approach to world peace, most eloquently developed by David Mitrany,[29] that seeks to establish international organizations to deal with economic and social issues. By linking peoples together on these issues it is hoped that a spirit of cooperation will develop that will slowly "spill over" into the political realm, making interstate conflict less likely. The initial step begins by founding a series of organizations, each aimed at a particular economic or social problem. There is no set size (that is, continental, regional, or global) for the organizations; they are, instead, to be coextensive with the particular problem they seek to address. If it is a problem affecting several states, such as river navigation, then it will comprise those states (in this case those that are riparians). If the problem involves all states, as in the case of an infectious disease, the organization would encompass all states. For these organizations there is no set *political* goal; it is rather hoped that as states cooperate on these issues a web of interdependence will be established and national boundaries will become less and less significant.

This theory of functionalism is based on several important assumptions. First, it is assumed that the essential source of international conflict is economic and social problems. Problems such as poverty, hunger, disease, lack of adequate transportation and communications, the abuse of human rights, and so on, are seen as the precipitators of political problems. Second, it is assumed that since these problems transcend particular state boundaries, states, acting independently, are inadequate to deal with these troubles; a government that is not coterminous with the problem is insufficient. Third, functionalism assumes that these economic and social problems can temporarily be separated from political problems, but that eventual cooperation on the former will result in cooperation on the latter. Fourth, it is believed that it will eventually be possible for individuals to shift their loyalty from the nation-state to the new transnational groups. As economic and social issues are regulated, it is anticipated that humans will begin to lose excessive devotion to the inadequate state.

Functionalism and Dulles

While Dulles's views do not entirely mirror the works of the proponents of functionalism, they do, nevertheless, contain many tenets of the functional approach to international peace. First, despite his discussions of other causes of war, Dulles seems to have believed that social and economic difficulties were indeed a major cause of war. Second, as repeatedly noted throughout the previous discussion, he believed that in an interdependent world, the sovereign state was ill-suited to deal with many of these problems. Third, he believed that cooperation in economic and social areas could build up an international consensus, a world community which, as noted earlier, was the *conditio sine qua non* for certain higher types of political cooperation. In this discussion only the first and third elements will be examined, since Dulles's belief in the inadequacy of the state has already been examined.

The Causes of War. As noted above, in *War, Peace and Change*, Dulles explained that a major cause of war was the tension that existed between the dynamic and static forces in the world. In this early period of his thought, however, he also acknowledged other causes of war. As early as April of 1921, he made an interesting response to Simeon E. Baldwin on the question of convening a Third Hague Conference to discuss rules on declarations of war and the consequences of war on treaties. He said that he doubted the wisdom of further discussion of such issues, but added:

> I would have hoped that our Committee could have directed attention to rules of international law applicable to peace conditions, and the formulation and observance of which would tend to eliminate the causes of war. Such subjects as international communications, international waterways, the status of less advanced and mandatory countries with reference to the "open door" -- these seem to me to offer a fertile field for discussion and one which is perhaps more constructive and more in line with present needs than such a subject as the manner in which a declaration of war should be formulated.[30]

Dulles here suggests that by dealing with economic and social issues such as communications, waterways, and underdevelopment, conditions may be created that would eliminate the cause of war.

During his work with the Commission on a Just and Durable Peace nearly twenty years later, he also referred to economic and social problems as causes of war. In a speech of May 28, 1941, Dulles explained that depression and unemployment were major factors leading to war. As populations become depressed, it became much easier for ruthless leaders to gain power by taking advantage

of the poor economic conditions.[31]   Indeed, underemployment was a
clear cause of arms production: "Our economic world came to a state
such that in Germany and England -- and we may now add the
United States -- a solution of the problem of unemployment has been
found only in armament production."[32] Furthermore, Dulles's general
thesis,   that   economically   arrogant,   sovereign   states   produce
deleterious economic effects on their dependent neighbors, confirms
the idea of economic causality of war; indeed, as noted previously,
these economic problems that gave rise to war were a major impetus
to his advocacy of European union.

Dulles also seemed to have believed that the abuse of human
rights could lead to war.   The last "Pillar" of the "Six Pillars of
Peace" provided that "[t]he peace must establish in principle, and
seek to achieve in practice, the right of individuals everywhere to
religious and intellectual liberty."[33]   The comment on this principle
explained it as follows:

> Wars are not only due to economic causes. They have
> their origin also in false ideologies and in ignorance.
> Peace,   furthermore,   cannot   be   preserved   merely   by
> documentary acts that create political bodies and define
> their   powers   and   duties.   Such   bodies   can   function
> effectively only as they can count upon a public opinion to
> understand and support them.
> It is, therefore, indispensable that there exist the
> opportunity to bring the people of all the world to a fuller
> knowledge   of   the   facts   and   a   greater   acceptance   of
> common   moral   standards.   Spiritual   and   intellectual
> regimentation that prevents this is a basic underlying cause
> of war.   As such it is not a matter of purely domestic
> concern, and government and parties must recognize this if
> the world is to achieve a durable peace.[34]

If, in other words, the people are denied religious and intellectual
freedom, they will be susceptible to deception and it will be more
difficult to establish common moral standards.   Hence, they can be
more easily mobilized for war by those who deceive them.

The following year, in 1944, the commission released another
statement (which Dulles endorsed) that recognized that economic and
social factors led to war. In the statement the commission succinctly
expressed its belief that because these factors are causes of war, an
international organization must address them: "[W]e do insist that
international organizations should be designed, not to maintain a
faulty world status, but to seek inventively to eradicate the political
and   economic   maladjustments,   the   spiritual   and   intellectual
deficiencies, the inadequacies of international law, which basically
cause war."[35]

Functionalism as a Means of Diluting Sovereignty. Dulles began examining the possibilities of functionalism in the late 1930s in a rudimentary way by suggesting that economic cooperation among people could promote a spirit that would lessen conflict.   In the "Road to Peace," he stated that international rigidity could be broken down through "encouraging economic fluidity."[36] He explained that "[n]ational boundaries lose much of their significance if there exists national policies which permit a diffusion of economic advantages. Export   and   imports,   emigration   and   immigration,   and   the international flow of capital, even though these must necessarily be regulated, can bring about a large measure of international flux without shock to national boundaries."[37] Similarly, in *War, Peace and Change*, Dulles's discussion of using the "ethical principle" to help prevent international conflict suggested functionalist tenets.   In addition to calling for a lessening of tariff and trade restrictions, he suggested a more open border policy.   He argued that "[m]easures could undoubtedly be taken to facilitate the movement of people across boundary lines."[38] In such measures "our primary objective is to change the popular impression which one people has of the boundaries of another.   The present picture is too frequently that of bleak and forbidding barriers erected in total disregard of their external consequences."[39]   Unfortunately, he continued, most states take the attitude: "I am sovereign; I do as I choose, without accounting to anyone and I choose to keep out foreigners, their goods and their chattels.   Boundary barriers thus created inevitably arouse resentment abroad and a desire for leadership able and willing to push back or break open such boundaries,"[40] and hence, war. But, cooperation in economic and immigration issues could ameliorate this problem.

> It is possible, on the other hand, to treat these matters as a common problem of economic balance and to seek to impart an understanding of the domestic considerations which require protective action. There is, indeed, already a growing disposition to treat international trade as a matter of bilateral negotiation rather than of international fiat. This new technique can serve to alter greatly the old conception of boundaries. It may, indeed, prove feasible in certain cases to go further and to secure desired protection by the voluntary act of foreign nations restricting their exports or emigration.[41]

Thus, through cooperation and a common treatment of these problems, including the recognition of domestic difficulties, it would be possible to diminish the significance of boundaries.

   This germ of functionalism became full grown during Dulles's work with the Commission. In fact, early in his work, he was convinced that a postwar organization should be *primarily* concerned with financial and economic issues.   In 1942, he described three functions for an international organization, all of which related to economics:[42]

> 1) I would have the Executive Organ create a Monetary or Banking Corporation . . . empowered to provide monetary media through which needed exchange of goods between nations could be facilitated . . . .
> 2) I would have the Executive Organ authorized to charter commercial companies, as seemed to it desirable, to engage in the business of effecting international movements of goods from one country to another . . . .
> 3) I would have the Executive Organ authorized to negotiate compacts with the several nations whereby their tariffs and trade quotas would be fixed.[43]

Explaining this proposal Dulles said: "By these three initial steps we will have begun that dilution of sovereignty which all enlightened thinkers agree to be indispensable. . . .   We will have avoided the mistake of assuming, at the beginning, tasks so vast, so difficult and so unexplored that failure is likely."[44]   Rather than elaborate on a grandiose plan for world organization, Dulles felt that if these economic tasks were undertaken, it would be the beginning of the end of sovereignty.   His preference for a functional approach was also revealed in his criticism of Clarence Streit; he remarked that "I would favor economic and financial union, letting the political union work out of them if and when this became a natural development."[45]

By 1944, elements of the functionalist approach had become major parts of Dulles's thought.   As concrete proposals for the United Nations were being made, Dulles felt the best hope for world peace lay not in security provisions, but in those that provided for cooperation in a number of functional areas.   He explained on November 28, 1944:

> We want world organization to bring nations together to work for stable economic and monetary conditions; to keep the treaty structure of the world abreast of changing underlying conditions; to make autonomy the genuine goal of colonial administration and to assure individuals everywhere spiritual and intellectual liberty.   Out of working together on such great tasks there can come a common judgment of what is decent national conduct, and a general agreement that, in matters of common concern, the general welfare should take precedent.   That will, on the one hand, greatly reduce the occasions for the use of

force, on the other hand it will make it possible to arrange
so that force can be quickly and decisively used, when it
needs to be used at all.[46]

Here was the essential functionalist thesis: cooperation on economic
and social matters will breed a spirit of common interest that will
spill over into the political realm, giving rise to an attitude that
makes the use of force less likely, but allows states to join together
when collective security is necessary. As Dulles said in a December
1944 letter to Ernest Hopkins: "I just do not think the force
provisions [of the Dumbarton Oaks Proposal] will work, or can be
made to work, unless the other activities of the world organization,
particularly in the field of economics and human rights, develop a
feeling of fellowship and a feeling that there is positive value in
international organization so that it is worth while fighting to
preserve it."[47]

DECOLONIZATION

During the early period of Dulles's thought, he also became
concerned about the role that international organization could play in
dealing with the colonial question. He endorsed the Mandate system
that the League of Nations established to deal with colonies and after
World War II continued to support international colonial regulation.

In *War, Peace and Change*, Dulles favorably discussed the League
Mandate system for its possible role in facilitating open trade and
cross-border interaction.[48] After having explained how in industrial
countries the extent of economic cooperation as a means of
mitigating the sovereignty problem is somewhat limited, he takes a
more positive view with respect to colonies.

When we move on to those nations which are less highly
developed, and particularly when we consider colonial
areas, a much more ambitious program may be found
practical. In such areas monopoly of opportunity is not
maintained by or for the benefit of the local population.
The boundary barriers do not protect a highly developed
form of society which might suffer severe dislocation were
the protection abruptly withdrawn. In the colonial areas
the sovereignty system is operated by the colonizing or
mandatory power to the end that its nationals may have a
preferential right of exploitation. There would seem to be
no insuperable obstacle to opening up vast areas of the
world through the application of the "mandate" system as
proposed by President Wilson, namely, that the territory is
to be administered in trust, first for the well being and

advancement of the local populations, and then for the
benefit and equal opportunity of the whole world.[49]

This comment is revealing in several respects. First, in this passage
Dulles's major concern seems to be that because colonies have poorly
developed industrial bases, and because they are being run by another
country, they have less need of protective trade barriers.
Consequently, they can be opened up to promote international
commerce, the flourishing of which will help prevent conflict.
Implicit in this argument is the belief that competition over colonies
was a major cause of World War I.[50] With free trade, however, the
monopoly would effectively be broken. Second, however, Dulles did
believe that the interests of the inhabitants should take precedent
over the interests of the imperial power (even though in this passage
his main concern was that colonies be opened up for commerce).
This was still, in his mind, merely making colonialism more tolerable
and *not* abolishing colonies altogether, or even granting some form of
self-rule.[51]

As time passed, Dulles continued to advocate the use of a
mandate system, stressing more and more the importance of such
international regulation for the interests of the colonies. In his 1941
pamphlet, "Long Range Peace Objectives," he explained:

All non-self-governing colonies, with the possible exception
of those where self-government is already advanced, should
be placed an international mandate. This was the original
concept of President Wilson, perverted by the Treaty of
Versailles. The purpose of the mandate should be, first, to
assure the moral, social and material development of the
native inhabitants and their ultimate self-government, and
in the meantime to assure that other peoples shall have
access to their resources and trade on equal terms.

Such mandating, if carried out in a genuine
international spirit, would prevent colonial areas being used
as pawns to advance national policies of imperialism,
strategy or prestige.[52]

Once again Dulles's approach was very similar to that taken in *War,
Peace and Change*, even in his desire to assure "access to their
resources and trade on equal terms." Unlike his argument in *War,
Peace and Change*, this argument made it clear that the ultimate aim
of the new mandate system was self-government. It is interesting to
note, however, that some colonies that already have a good deal of
self-government would not necessarily be placed under international
control.

In keeping with Dulles's views on colonies, the official
statements of the Commission on a Just and Durable Peace also
advocated international supervision of colonial territories. Principle

Seven of the "Guiding Principles" of 1942 proclaimed that

> the government which derives its just powers from the consent of the governed is the truest expression of the rights and dignity of man.   This requires that we seek autonomy for all subject and colonial peoples.   Until that shall be realized, the task of colonial government is no longer one of exclusive national concern.   It must be recognized as a common responsibility of mankind, to be carried out in the interests of colonial peoples by the most appropriate form of organization.   This would, in many cases, make colonial government a task of international collaboration for the benefit of the colonial peoples who would, themselves, have a voice in their government.   As the agencies for the promotion of world-wide political and economic security become effective, the moral, social and material welfare of colonial populations can be more fully realized.[53]

This principle varied slightly from Dulles's general line.   In the commission's statement, colonies were held to be an international concern, but there was not as strong an advocacy of the international regulation of colonies.   Dulles had begun by stating that all colonies would be subject to international control "with the *possible* exception of those whose self-government is already advanced" (emphasis added).   In this principle, the commission seemed to be approaching the issue from the other side, explaining that "in many cases" an international regime would be utilized.

When the commission issued the "Six Pillars of Peace," it included a stronger statement on colonialism.   Pillar Four stated that "[t]he peace must proclaim the goal of autonomy for subject peoples, and it must establish international organization to assure and to supervise the realization of that end."[54]

The comment to that pillar explained that there was "ferment among many peoples who are now subject to alien rule.   That will make durable peace unattainable unless such peoples are satisfied that they can achieve self-rule without passive or active resistance to the now constituted authorities."[55]   But for particular colonies, total self-rule may not be immediately possible: "We realize that autonomy, in certain cases, is not now desired, and in other cases is presently impractical."[56]   Individual states, however, should not be the sole arbiter of this matter since "judgments to this tend to be warped, and certainly are suspect, when made by the governing power itself."[57]   Consequently, "[t]here must be international agencies, which embrace persons free from the self-interest which comes from identification with a particular governing power, and which are charged with the duty to see that pledges of ultimate autonomy are honored, and that, in the meanwhile, there is no exploitation for alien ends."[58] Thus, all colonies would be subject to some form of international supervision.

Interestingly enough, both Dulles and the commission were less clear regarding the precise nature of supervision. Dulles seemed to suggest that it would vary depending upon the nature of the colonial power. In a 1942 interview, he spoke rather positively about British colonial rule. He explained that he believed "that it is genuinely their [British] policy at the present time to try to bring along these people to autonomy and ultimate independence."[59] Consequently, he said, "I would not necessarily take the colonies away from the administration by Great Britain."[60] (The implication is that *some* colonies would indeed be taken from an imperial power.) Nevertheless, there should still be "an over-all international body which would have the opportunity to supervise and scrutinize and make sure that the countries which were actually administrators are making good on their promise and were not really using their control for purposes purely on exploitation in holding these people back."[61]

ARMS CONTROL AND DISARMAMENT

Another function that international organization is often envisaged as performing is to control or limit armaments.[62] During the early period of Dulles's thought, he recognized the importance of arms control, but did not regard it as the most important function of international organization. In this period, three general ideas ran through his writings. First, he believed that the presence of large armies and navies could indeed be a source of war. As early as 1930, he explained: "It has always been recognized that the maintenance of powerful armies and navies was itself one of the most fertile causes of war."[63] This was because massive armament "promotes international fear and jealousy,"[64] and "establishes within each nation a large and influential body trained for war and for whom rapid advancement and large reputation can come only with the opportunity to practice their profession."[65] Moreover, "constant awareness of great military and naval establishments renders impossible the creation of a public state of mind which harmonizes with the idea of renunciation of war as an instrument of national policy."[66]

In subsequent works, Dulles continued to express his belief that massive armament could lead to war. In *War, Peace and Change*, he explicitly rejected the notion that general *armament* could help the cause of world peace by serving as a deterrent. While recognizing that making war more destructive could have a deterrent effect, he argued that it was "unsafe to place our hope of peace upon the terrifying influences of vast armaments," since "[t]he consequences of being wrong are too appalling."[67] A major problem was that "the achievement of such armament in itself requires the highly emotional state which is capable of precipitating a totalitarian war."[68] In order to gain public support, something "akin to war psychology"[69] must be created. But the generation of such psychology, which cultivates a "sense of peril from abroad,"[70] is only a small step away from actual armed conflict.

A second notion present in Dulles's early thought is that arms reduction will only be a result of peace; conditions that give rise to the need for armament must be ameliorated before disarmament can take place. In a 1930 article, Dulles explained that no major arms reduction had occurred because there existed a "state of mind" generating the belief that vast forces were necessary for the protection of certain vital needs. He explained that "[t]here is no people who would willingly support an armament designed only for offensive purposes."[71] Instead, big "navies are maintained primarily because of the belief that they are required for the defense of vital national interests, and of these the most vital, in the case of nations unable to feed themselves, is the ability at all times to maintain access to overseas sources of food."[72] And "[o]f but slightly less importance in the case of nations whose internal economy is largely based on overseas exports, is the necessity of maintaining at all times a substantial market for their surplus goods."[73] Consequently, in this article Dulles argued that granting immunity to food ships in times of war would help alleviate the need for such armaments since states would not have to maintain navies to assure access to food.[74]

In *War, Peace and Change* (where, incidentally, Dulles rejected the argument that states' interests were purely defensive) he went even further. While "[v]ast military establishment may even . . . become a precipitating cause of war," "it would be a cause only in a secondary sense."[75] He explained that "[i]f limitation of armament comes, it will be a result rather than a cause of peace."[76] He continued: "So long as the force system prevails, then armament has utility. So long as it has utility, so long will armament survive and the greater the utility, the greater will be the armament (subject to the limitations of finance)."[77] Before there can be any meaningful reduction of armaments, there must be an alternative to force as a mechanism of change: "[T]he existence of the force system is the cause of armament and we cannot expect armament to be placed permanently in a non-competitive basis unless we first demote force from its role of supreme arbiter of change."[78] Consequently, Dulles did not discuss disarmament in his pamphlet of September 18, 1941, "Long Range Peace Objectives," because it was, along with several other issues, "at the present time highly disputable and I do not consider . . . [i]t essential to inaugurating an era of peace."[79] Other issues, such as the means of peaceful change, were of primary importance.

A final element in Dulles's discussions of arms limitation is the desire that any arms agreement that is reached not be one-sided. He did not want to see a repetition of the aftermath of Versailles. In *War, Peace and Change*, he repudiated the French theory of "arming, to a high degree, the satisfied nations which are interested in preserving the *status quo* and disarming the dissatisfied nations who would be disposed to seek change."[80]　Although the Treaty had provided for general disarmament, "such representations were deliberately kept vague, so that the French thesis could be carried out without violation of any specific mandatory treaty clause."[81] Dulles rejected this one-sided arrangement, arguing in part that it is very difficult to determine who is and who is not a "satisfied power." Furthermore, in keeping with Dulles's general belief in the inevitability of change, such an approach would presumably be anathema in any case.

The desire to prevent a one-sided arms reduction was also echoed in publications of the Commission on a Just and Durable Peace. The "Statement of Guiding Principles" of December 11, 1942, favored "international control of armaments."[82]　However, such control was to be mutual: "For one or more nations to be forcibly deprived of their arms while other nations retain the right of maintaining or expanding their military establishments can only produce an uneasy peace for a limited period."[83]　Consequently, "[a]ny initial arrangement which falls short of this must be looked upon as temporary and provisional."[84]　Similarly, the "Six Pillars of Peace," called for "procedures for controlling military establishments *everywhere*."[85]

NOTES

1. Dulles, "The Church's Contribution Toward a Warless World," reprinted in H. P. Van Dusen, ed., *J. F. Dulles, The Spiritual Legacy of John Foster Dulles*, 144-145 (emphasis added).

2. Ibid., 146.

3. Ibid.

4. JFD to Eugene Staley, Jan 3, 1940, *JFD Papers*, 2-3.

5. Dulles, *War, Peace and Change*, 124-127.

6. JFD to Eugene Staley, Jan. 3, 1940, *JFD Papers*, 2-3.

7. Dulles, *War, Peace and Change*, 127.

8. Dulles, "Peaceful Change," Draft of Jan. 23, 1940, *JFD Papers*, 9.

9. JFD to Alec Besso, July 24, 1940, *JFD Papers*, 1-2.

10. Ibid., 2.

11. Dulles, "The People's Platform" (transcript), Dec. 19, 1942, in *JFD Papers*, 7-8.

12. JFD to Quincy Wright, Dec. 19, 1939, *JFD Papers*, 1.

13. Ibid.

14. See Claude, *Swords Into Plowshares*, 106-107, for the discussion of regionalism as a "stepping stone."

15. JFD to Quincy Wright, Dec. 19, 1939, *JFD Papers*, 1-2.

16. Ibid., 2.

17. Ibid., 1.

18. Dulles, "Peaceful Change," 9.

19. See Clarence Streit to JFD, Mar. 21, 1940, *JFD Papers*.

20. Dulles, "Memorandum," undated, *JFD Papers*, 1.

21. Ibid.

22. Ibid., 1, 2.

23. Pruessen, *John Foster Dulles*, 186-187.

24. JFD to Hugh Wilson, quoted in Pruessen, *John Foster Dulles*, 209.

25. Dulles, "Long Range Peace Objectives," 12.

26. Ibid., 12-13.

27. Dulles, "Six Pillars of Peace," 8.

28. This definition draws heavily on the work of Inis L. Claude, Jr. See especially Claude, *Swords Into Plowshares*, 378-407.

29. See Mitrany, *A Working Peace System*.

30. JFD to Simeon E. Baldwin, Apr. 26, 1921, *JFD Papers*, 2-3.

31. Dulles, "The Church's Role in Developing the Bases of A Just and Durable Peace."

32. Ibid., 13.

33. "Six Pillars of Peace," 11.

34. Ibid.

35. Commission on a Just and Durable Peace, "A New Year's Statement to Public Leaders and Our People," Jan. 1944, *JFD Papers*, 2.

36. Dulles, "The Road to Peace," 499.

37. Ibid.

38. Dulles, *War, Peace and Change*, 129.

39. Ibid., 129-130.

40. Ibid., 130.

41. Ibid.

42. I draw heavily here from Pruessen, *John Foster Dulles*, 207-209.

43. Dulles, "Toward World Order," May 5, 1942, quoted in Pruessen, *John Foster Dulles*, 208.

44. Quoted in Pruessen, *John Foster Dulles*, 209.

45. JFD to Hugh Wilson, June 13, 1941, quoted in Pruessen, *John Foster Dulles*, 209.

46. Dulles, "The Dumbarton Oaks Proposals," Nov. 28, 1944, *JFD Papers*, 5.

47. JFD to Ernest Hopkins, Dec. 14, 1944, *JFD Papers*.

48. I draw on R. Pruessen's discussion here as well. See Pruessen, *John Foster Dulles*, 165-168, 173-176.

49. Dulles, *War, Peace and Change*, 131.

50. See Pruessen, *John Foster Dulles*, 175-177.

51. I am indebted to Inis L. Claude, Jr., for this understanding. See Claude, *Swords Into Plowshares*, 353-376.

52. Dulles, "Long Range Peace Objectives," 13-14.

53. Federal Council of Churches, "Statement of Guiding Principles," 4-5.

54. "Six Pillars of Peace," 9.

55. Ibid.

56. Ibid., 9-10.

57. Ibid., 10.

58. Ibid.

59. Dulles, "The People's Platform," 10.

60. Ibid.

61. Ibid.

62. See Claude, *Swords Into Plowshares*, 286-311.

63. Dulles, "Immunity of Food Ships in Time of War," 1930, *JFD Papers*, 4.

64. Ibid.

65. Ibid.

66. Ibid., 4-5.

67. Dulles, *War, Peace and Change*, 90.

68. Ibid.

69. Ibid.

70. Ibid.

71. Dulles, "Immunity of Food Ships in Time of War," 5.

72. Ibid.

73. Ibid.

74. Ibid.

75. Dulles, *War, Peace and Change*, 94.

76. Ibid., 93.

77. Ibid.

78. Ibid., 94.

79. Dulles, "Long Range Peace Objectives," 17.

80. Dulles, *War, Peace and Change*, 91.

81. Ibid.

82. Federal Council of Churches, "Statement of Guiding Principles," 5.

83. Ibid.

84. Ibid.

85. "Six Pillars of Peace," 7 (emphasis added).

PART TWO

THE U.N. YEARS
(1945-1952)

PART TWO

THE LEAN YEARS
1895–1915

7

The Founding of the United Nations

DULLES AND THE WRITING OF THE CHARTER

As World War II was coming to an end, Dulles found his role in international affairs changing. Having been a private citizen involved in advocating the establishment of a new international order, he was now to become an official participant in the founding and functioning of an international organization. In April of 1945, largely due to the pressure exerted by his friend, Senator Arthur Vandenberg,[1] Dulles was appointed to an advisory role with the U.S. Delegation to the United Nations Conference on International Organization -- the so-called San Francisco Conference. In this capacity he was involved in almost all major discussions of the Delegation, as well as meetings with other delegations. In some instances, he was responsible for presenting the U.S. position to the Conference.

It would be tedious to chronicle all of Dulles's activities surrounding the founding of the United Nations. Instead, several major areas in which Dulles played a role will be examined.

Domestic Jurisdiction

One of the most controversial questions associated with international organization is how to divide jurisdiction between the international agency and the component units of the system: How much domestic jurisdiction are the states to have, and how is this to be safeguarded? This question was the subject of extensive debate at San Francisco. Dulles's views on domestic jurisdiction underwent interesting developments during the course of his work with the U.S.

delegation. Initially, he questioned the need for a comprehensive provision on domestic jurisdiction; later, however, he came to accept the necessity of such a provision and, in fact, became instrumental in presenting this position to the conference.[2]

Not long after Dulles joined the Delegation, he expressed misgivings about the provision on domestic jurisdiction in the Dumbarton Oaks Proposals. This provision was contained in Chapter VIII, *Section A* (*Pacific Settlement of Disputes*); it provided that "[t]he provisions of paragraph 1 to 6 of Section A [relating to the power of the Security Council to investigate disputes, to call upon states to use peaceful means to settle disputes, and to decide whether a dispute is likely to endanger international peace and security] should not apply to situations or disputes arising out of matters which by international law are solely within the domestic jurisdiction of the state concerned."[3]

On April 16, at a U.S. Delegation meeting, Dulles explained that

> he had objected to this paragraph at the time of his discussions with Secretary of State Hull in the fall of 1944. It was, he thought, a contradiction in terms to say that a matter which threatened the peace of the world was solely a matter of "domestic jurisdiction." How could this be? We had to have limitations as to Section B dealing with action concerning threats to the peace or acts of aggression, but the whole effect of Chapter VIII would be destroyed with such a limitation in it. The Security Council should have authority to consider any matter which threatened the peace of the world.[4]

Dulles objected to a blanket statement that would have prevented the Security Council from even *discussing* a potentially threatening issue, but he did recognize the need for a limitation with respect to the Security Council's *acting* against a threat to the peace. Senators Vandenberg and Connally, however, doubted that the charter would get through the Senate without such a provision on domestic jurisdiction. Dulles believed "that the trouble with international law was that it had reserved the right of any state to do as it pleased, although the Dumbarton Oaks Proposals represented an attempt to break this principle. He wondered whether something might not be gotten through the Senate."[5] He explained the "it was just a matter of talk in the Security Council in any case."[6] Senator Connally, however, believed "that 'talk' would imply responsibility and action."[7]

In the end, Vandenberg and Connally carried the argument. On April 18, the delegation agreed to a slightly different provision that still kept the essential principle of domestic jurisdiction intact. It provided that "[t]he provisions of paragraph 1 to 6 of Section A should not apply to situations or disputes arising out of matters which are within the domestic jurisdiction of the state concerned."[8] The word "solely" had been removed, as had the reference to the use of the principles of international law for determining domestic jurisdiction. There was no opposition from Dulles at the time. Apparently, he had become convinced of the need for this provision.

As discussions with other delegations took place, Dulles became one of the main supporters of the U.S. position. He was assigned to a subcommittee on domestic jurisdiction and, at a May 3 meeting of the "Big Four," he presented the report of the subcommittee. At that time he argued "that the exemption for domestic jurisdiction should cover the whole Charter, as the matters to which it applies are not limited to VIII, A,"[9] and proposed that the provision be written in a separate chapter of the charter. On June 14, after the four sponsoring governments had agreed on a provision, it was Dulles who presented the position of the sponsors to Committee I of Commission I. He

> emphasized that the four-power amendment dealt with domestic jurisdiction as a basic principle, and not, as had been the case in the original Dumbarton Oaks Proposals and in Article 15 of the Covenant of the League of Nations, as a technical and legalistic formula designed to deal with the settlement of disputes by the Security Council.[10]

This different approach was necessitated

> by the change in the character of the Organization, as planned in the discussion at San Francisco. The scope of the Organization was now broadened to include functions which would enable the Organization to eradicate the underlying causes of war as well as to the crises leading to war. Under the Social and Economic Council the Organization would deal with economic and Social problems. This broadening of the scope of the Organization constituted a great advance, but it also engendered special problems.[11]

He explained these problems:

> For instance, the question had been raised as to what would be the basic relation of the Organization to member states: Would the Organization deal with the governments of the member states, or would the Organization penetrate directly into the domestic life and social economy of the member states. As provided in the amendment of the sponsoring governments, Mr. Dulles pointed out that this

principle [domestic jurisdiction] would require the
Organization to deal with the governments.[12]

Dulles continued to elaborate, giving a specific example: "Under the
Economic and Social Council the Organization had a mandate to
raise the standards of living and foster employment, etc., but no one
in the 10-member Council would go behind the governments in order
to impose its desires. The amendment recognized the distinct value
of the individual social life of each state."[13]
   Thus, Dulles rejected (at least in his official capacity) the
notion that the organization should have transnational powers that
would be applied directly to individuals. He also rejected the concept
contained in previous versions of the provision that the test of
international law should be applied to determine domestic jurisdiction,
pointing "out that international law was subject to constant change
and therefore escaped definitions."[14] He explained that "[i]n this era
the whole internal life of a country was affected by foreign
conditions."[15] Consequently, Dulles "did not consider that it would
be practicable to provide that the World Court determine the
limitations of domestic jurisdiction or that it should be called upon to
give advisory opinions since some countries would probably not accept
the compulsory jurisdiction clause."[16] Dulles concluded his remarks
to the committee by explaining that this provision was not, however,
the last word on this issue; it was merely what was possible at the
time. He explained that

> this principle was subject to evolution. The United States
> had had long experience in dealing with a parallel problem,
> i.e., the relationship between the forty-eight states and the
> Federal Government. Today, the Federal Government of
> the United States exercised an authority undreamed of
> when the Constitution was formed, and the people of the
> United States were grateful for the simple conceptions
> contained in their Constitution. In like manner, Mr. Dulles
> foresaw that if the Charter contained simple and broad
> principles future generations would be thankful to the men
> at San Francisco who had drafted it.[17]

This turnabout on the issue of domestic jurisdiction represents
an interesting twist in Dulles's thought and actions. In light of his
work with the Commission on a Just and Durable Peace, Dulles might
have been expected to continue to advocate strongly a narrower
definition of domestic jurisdiction. Ronald Pruessen explains:

> Throughout the late 1930s and his work with the
> Commission on a Just and Durable Peace, he had been
> critical of the way so many governments failed to
> appreciate the broad international implications of actions

that seemed essentially domestic in nature. Currency regulations, trade policies, or immigration restrictions, he had often argued, could have as great an impact on people across the globe as on those within the nation establishing them. In the economic field especially, this had been a major preoccupation for him. He had often urged the need to begin diluting formal sovereignty in this respect, to allow some kind of internationalization of once exclusively domestic jurisdiction.[18]

Why then did Dulles quickly agree to a comprehensive provision on domestic jurisdiction and then defend this provision before other delegations at San Francisco? It may be that he realized that the establishment of a *workable* international organization was preferable to an unsuccessful attempt to establish the *perfect* international organization. In the course of the debates, he may have come to realize that what was possible at San Francisco was far short of his ultimate goals, but it was a beginning; consequently, he stressed the *provisional* nature of the organization and its potential for eventual change. As Pruessen explains, Dulles "surely would have sensed the link between some of the early statements made in his delegation and his own arguments about the need for a realistic, elemental beginning for the new organization. . . . Here was one of those situations in which what might have been desirable in an abstract sense would have given way to what was practical."[19]

Another possible explanation, which Pruessen also advances, was that Dulles may have begun to see that there were cases when international organization could be detrimental to American foreign policy goals. Pruessen argues that Dulles "himself had shown no special desire to avoid meddling with American independence and freedom of movement in the past, concentrating instead on the way in which cooperation with others could bring economic and political benefits," but "[w]hat might have begun to emerge in the work on 'domestic jurisdiction' questions was an awareness that the fundamental goal of national interest was more important than the methods which he had usually advocated for serving it."[20]

The Security Council, Enforcement Action, and the Veto

Dulles's views on the authority of the Security Council are also surprising in light of some of his earlier statements. In general, he was not much worried about the council's right to initiate collective military action, but rather about other powers that it could exercise. During an April 26 debate of the delegation, he expressed his fear that the provision of the Dumbarton Oaks Proposal dealing with the authority of the Council was too broad, or at least could be so interpreted. This provision provided that, once peaceful settlement had failed, the council "should take any measure necessary for the maintenance of international peace and security in accordance with the purposes and principles of the Organization."[21]   Leo Pasvolsky explained that a possible interpretation of this section was that "[t]he Security Council . . . would have unlimited powers to avert a threat to international peace and security and could even impose the terms of settlement."[22]   Dulles responded "that it was a sweeping power, and Mr. Pasvolsky replied that if there was a threat to the peace the Security Council had to have very wide powers of action."[23]   To this, Dulles replied "that under this power the Security Council could give the Sudetenland to Germany or could give Alaska to Russia in order to keep the peace."[24]   Congressman Sol Bloom and Commander Harold Stassen assured Dulles that for such Security Council action there would still need to be agreement among the five permanent members, but this did not satisfy him.   He explained, "[B]ecause of the veto power the United States would not be subjected to the imposition of terms of settlement, but that it would be terrific to put small powers to such a threat."[25]   Even the United States could suffer if its executive branch representative so chose: "if we should have as President or as delegate to the Security Council someone who believed that the immigration or tariff policies of the United States should be changed, then by not exercising the veto he could enable the international organization to force the United States to change them."[26]   Enforcement action *per se* was acceptable, but a broad interpretation of the power of the Security Council, urged Dulles, would be inappropriate.   He "thought it right to say to the member states, 'If you want to go to war, the Organization will impose diplomatic and economic sanctions or call out contingents of armed forces to bomb your cities,'"[27] but to impose another type of settlement was beyond the power of the council.

In light of the concerns of Dulles and some of the other members of the delegation, efforts were made to draft alternative language.   The following day, he and two other U. S. delegates proposed that the provision be revised to indicate, among other things, that the Security Council "'may invoke the measures provided for by Paragraphs 2 and 3 of this section.'"[28]   This would make it clear that the Security Council's power would indeed be limited to diplomatic, economic, and military sanctions as set forth in paragraphs 2 and 3.   With some minor changes and renumberings, this proposal was adopted by the U.S. Delegation.

The actions of Dulles on this provision are most interesting since they seem to conflict with principles developed in his earlier period.   As noted previously, Dulles's major concern was for international organization to ensure peaceful change.   He had spoken about the need for boundaries to lose their significance and even for territorial adjustments to be made when necessary.   But in the debates over the power of the Security Council, he seemed to be most afraid that the council would institute adjustments to territory or order a country to revise its immigration policy. It almost seems a complete reversal. Previously Dulles had expressed doubt about the collective enforcement powers of the new organization and had praised the peaceful change aspect; now he accepted enforcement powers but rejected others. Unlike his position on domestic jurisdiction, his position on this matter did not change in response to delegate opposition; he had argued his stand on narrower Security Council power from the beginning of the delegation meetings. Why he took this position is debatable. One can only speculate that in this case he also felt that the international community was not yet ready for an international organization with the power to effect change within a country. As he pointed out later, he did not want the council to be "the arbiter of the world."[29]

Despite these concerns, however, Dulles did want the Security Council to have power within its proper area. As noted above, he did not object to granting the council the authority to order enforcement actions. He also did not want to delay the entry into force of the powers of the council. When a French amendment would have required the consent of additional states before the Security Council could assume authority over aggression by "enemy states," Dulles explained "that the object of this [the U.S.] Delegation with respect to this paragraph was to insure that the authority of the Security Council should be established at the earliest possible moment."[30] He "was of the opinion that to make necessary the consent of more states as the present [French] draft did, would be to make the establishment of the authority of the Security Council more difficult."[31]

In addition to those questions relating to the Security Council, Dulles also had to concern himself with the veto issue. In general, he did not seem particularly pleased with the concept of the veto, but rather seemed to accept it because an agreement had already been made at Yalta that could not be changed. When a draft of the Four-Power interpretation of the veto was presented to the U.S. Delegation, he was quite critical. This paper attempted to justify the veto on the basis that "'it would be absurd for some dispute -- not only affecting the peace and security of the world in general, but also of direct interest to one of the five members having primary responsibility for the maintenance of peace and security -- to be dealt with without regard to, or even over the objective of, that member.'"[32] But if this really were the case, asked Dulles, why did the veto *not* apply to parties to a dispute for issues relating to Section A of this chapter, which dealt with the right of the Security Council to *investigate* a dispute? He believed that the draft "was a bad paper because it was an attempt to justify logically something that was logically indefensible."[33] He suggested "that any statement made should emphasize the chronological sequence whereby unanimity had been required under the League of Nations and progress had been made in the Charter of the proposed organization although perfection had not yet been reached."[34] At another point, Dulles commented on a subsequent draft interpretation:

> The statement under consideration, he declared, had been precipitated by a request for interpretation. It did not ask for a justification of the substance of the Yalta proposal. This statement implied substantial agreement on the *meaning* of the Yalta formula. Apparently, however, there was disagreement on how the formula could be defended. MR. DULLES wondered why an attempt should be made to present a joint defense. He was of the opinion that it was no matter for a joint defense, especially since some of the members of the Delegation [e.g. Dulles] did not believe in the Yalta formula. He suggested that the statement under consideration be confined to a presentation of the meaning of the Yalta formula as it was now understood by the four powers. He thought that the defense of the formula could be made elsewhere, perhaps on the floor of the Conference. It would be difficult, he thought, to get agreement on the merits of the formula.[35]

In subsequent discussions of the meaning of the veto, Dulles did want to ensure that the veto would not be applied to the discussion of issues by the Security Council. When the Soviets stated on June 1 that their interpretation was that the permanent members could use the veto to prevent an issue from being debated, he and the rest of the U.S. Delegation, strongly fought this move.[36] In a memorandum, Dulles recognized the motivation for such a proposal, explaining that "[t]he Soviet political system does not encourage or even admit of free discussion of the kind we rely upon to clarify different viewpoints and bring out ways of solution."[37] But, as Ronald Pruessen explains, Dulles felt that the Soviet "approach could not be allowed to set the overall tone of the new organization."[38] He furthermore believed that acquiescence in this Soviet proposal could "seriously impair the future influence of the U.S. in world affairs."[39] One aspect of this was that acceptance "would be deemed by it [the USSR] to be a sign of weakness. It might make it extremely difficult for the U.S. again to prevail in any international negotiations with the U.S.S.R. and it would tempt the U.S.S.R. to keep on crowding the U.S. until dangerous friction developed."[40]

Beyond those questions of interpretation, Dulles also held on to hopes that the veto could someday be altered.[41] On June 14, he explained that "[i]t was important . . . to make clear that the 'dead hand' of one of the major powers need not necessarily be continued in perpetuity."[42] He continued to point out that "[t]he world . . . is a living thing and cannot possibly be held by a 'dead hand' in spite of the language of the Charter."[43] He argued "that the present

Conference was dropping Japan and Italy from the ranks of the Organization despite the fact that these two nations had held permanent seats on the Council of the League of Nations" and "thought that some way should be found to point to this fact and to point out that the Conference was not necessarily accepting the idea that the five major powers would retain the permanent veto power."[44]   This was vintage Dulles, a thinker concerned about not freezing the status quo.

Peaceful Change

As noted, Dulles's concern for peaceful change was visible on his comments on the veto issue, even if some of his comments about the Security Council authority seemed to argue to the contrary. This interest in peaceful change was also evident in some of the other areas he addressed at San Francisco. Early in the proceedings, when Senator Vandenberg introduced an amendment explicitly mentioning treaties or other international agreements as creating situations in which the assembly should be empowered to recommend alternatives, Dulles was naturally very supportive.[45]   As observed previously, he had constantly attempted to have treaties mentioned explicitly in the Dumbarton Oaks Proposals. He also wanted to liberalize the amendment procedures for the charter and convey the idea that the charter was not to be interpreted as though it had been written in stone. During the early sessions, he commented that he "thought it would be very useful to be able to say that the Charter was not the last word, that it was just a start and so that people could have hope that at some future date change might be made."[46]   Later he explained that he "was in favor of classifying as a procedural matter, covered by the provisions of paragraph 2 of Section C, Chapter VI [and hence a matter not subject to the veto] the concurrence of the Security Council in the call for a general conference [to review the charter]."[47]   He even advocated the inclusion of a provision in the charter that would indicate that the Charter was not to be interpreted as a static document: "Mr. Dulles said he thought it a question of policy whether there should be a paragraph explicitly recognizing the need for subsequent revision. He himself thought it might be desirable to recognize that the Charter is inadequate as it stands and that it would be a good idea to improve it later."[48]

In his desire to portray the charter as a fluid and changeable instrument, Dulles seemed not to waver. As late as June 14, in the passage previously quoted in connection with the veto, Dulles still advocated a flexible charter. He felt that a three-fourths vote of all members should be sufficient to adopt an amendment to the charter, and did not favor allowing the use of the veto by the permanent members on this issue. This was a minority view within the U.S. Delegation, and he "remarked that he was not in agreement with the

Secretary [of State] and declared that he wanted his position clarified for the sake of the record although he knew there was no possibility of changing the position of the Delegation."[49]   He explained that he "thought that the inflexibility of the amendment procedure would be the focal point for attack."[50]

These statements clearly reflect the essence of Dulles's early thought, and may also help explain his willingness to accept certain limitations on the new international organization.   If he firmly believed that the charter was only a "start," that could and should be altered as circumstances changed, it is not surprising that he would condone certain provisions that seemed to be at odds with his early thought.

Economic and Social Issues

The functional approach to peace, as has been noted, held out a great deal of promise for Dulles.   During his work with the Commission on a Just and Durable Peace, he advocated organized cooperation on a whole host of economic and social issues as a means to international peace.   When Dulles became an active participant in the founding of the new international organization, however, his position became a bit different from what would have been expected.   While he did not reject the importance of the economic and social functions of the organization, he did express fears about the U.N.'s going too far in that direction.   In an early discussion about the possible expansion of the authority of the Economic and Social Council, Dulles explained "that the Protestant church groups with which he was affiliated have a tremendous interest in this whole economic and social field, but that they have all felt that the present proposals regarding economic and social cooperation set forth in the Dumbarton Oaks documents were fully adequate."[51] In other words, these activities should not be expanded.

Much of Dulles's concern reflected a fear that the increasing activity in the economic and social field could infringe upon the domestic jurisdiction of states.   On May 16, in response to a draft that enumerated the rights and duties of the Economic and Social Council, he commented that he "opposed it on the ground that it would give the Organization direct power to legislate on matters of domestic concern."[52]   Later, Dulles was troubled by a proposal to mention "full employment" as a goal of the organization in the charter.   He felt that in the context of the section, employment could be interpreted as a problem that transcended domestic affairs. He "pointed out that the opening paragraph of the Section under consideration presupposed that the conditions were necessary for the maintenance of peaceful relations. If this was so, was it not possible that full employment could become a matter of international concern and therefore no longer subject to the domestic 'jurisdiction clause'?"[53]   If poor employment conditions were posited as a conceivable cause of conflict, could not the Security Council intervene by claiming that a threat to the peace existed?   Indeed, when an attempt was made to list "raw materials" as a potential concern of the organization, he opposed such a move, arguing "that the Organization was becoming top-heavy with economic functions; this became obvious when the Charter was viewed as a whole."[54]

Interestingly enough, while Dulles was expressing these concerns to the delegation, publicly he was not wavering from a commitment to economic and social cooperation as a means to peace. In a speech delivered on May 17, he explained that the delegation had "been very happy to see written into the Charter the conception of equality of peoples without regard to race, language, religion, or sex."[55]   He contended that "a more prominent place has been given the objective of achieving individual human rights and liberties in accordance with the basic thought that those liberties belong to all people without discrimination.   The place of these human rights has been tremendously enlarged by the amendments that have been already agreed to at San Francisco."[56]   He also praised the new institutions established to deal with economic and social issues.

> We also feel that the activities of the Assembly through the Economic and Social Council and through its Commissions, such as the Commission on Human Rights, are going to go far to make this World Organization one which will be sustained by the nations -- not because it has behind it military force, which is a rather precarious and undesirable form of support, but because it is doing so much good for all the peoples of the world -- so much good, in fact, that no people will tolerate any government which seeks to destroy the organization.[57]

These changes in the charter, Dulles argued, "should help build a world in which there will be much less human discontent and human unrest."[58]   If they occurred, "it obviously would eliminate the forces which breed the military dictators and the gangsters who have been disrupting the peace of the past decade."[59]   Thus, he concluded, the delegates at San Francisco were concerned "not only with machines for maintaining peace," but also with "establishing procedures for eradicating the major causes of war."[60]

This speech seems to be perfectly consistent with the functional approach Dulles had accepted in his early thought.   There were no reservations about encroachments upon domestic jurisdiction or concern about the scope of these new functions.   Instead of being troubled by the possible expansion of economic and social activities, he seemed pleased that they had been expanded.   Does the apparent difference between this speech and Dulles's comments during the meetings of the U.S. Delegation indicate a hypocritical private-public dichotomy? It may indicate Dulles's desire to portray the charter publicly in the best possible light in an effort to ensure Senate ratification and public support for the fledgling organization. His concern in private, on the other hand, may reflect the belief that the organization was not yet ready for some of the far-reaching activities in the economic and social field.

Regional Arrangements

A major controversy at San Francisco revolved around the relationship between the new global organization and potential regional arrangements. The Dumbarton Oaks Proposals had contained a provision allowing collective action against the enemy states of World War II to be exempted from the requirement of Security Council authorization. In light of this provision, the Latin American countries wanted a similar provision to preserve the military prerogatives of the Inter-American System, which they believed should be free from Security Council constraints. This effort produced heated debates in which Dulles found himself involved.[61]

In general, there were two phases of Dulles's views on regional arrangements. Early in the debates, he advocated a strong role for regional organizations with a great deal of independence from the Security Council. He believed that if rules could be established that prescribed acceptable and unacceptable state behavior, enforcement actions by regional organizations could be exempted from the veto. He argued

> that the use of force should rest on law, it would work automatically, and that perhaps it would function better regionally than it would universally. He thought, therefore, that the Security Council should facilitate the development of regional arrangements. If it were always necessary to submit procedure under regional arrangements to the Security Council, the Great Powers would be able to exercise a veto and the International Organization might prove an obstacle to peace in that case.[62]

Dulles was afraid that some permanent member, with no real interest in the case, might intervene to prevent action in a given region. According to the record, "[b]oth MR. DULLES and COMMANDER [Harold] STASSEN interposed that this would permit France and China, for example, to veto American regional action in the Western Hemisphere."[63]

Leo Pasvolsky and other members of the U.S. Delegation opposed broad authority for regional arrangements, fearing this could gravely weaken the global organization. Pasvolsky explained that "he did not want the Inter-American System destroyed, . . . but to weaken the authority of the Security Council in regional matters would be tantamount to throwing all Europe into the hands of the Soviet Union, and would break the world up into regional units."[64] Dulles reiterated his contention that "if the legal basis for collective security were established by regional arrangements and were approved by the Security Council, then it would work automatically."[65] But Pasvolsky responded "that this position presupposed a world under which the same law applied everywhere; that because there were lacunae in the law, political decisions entered the field."[66] Rather than responding to the merits of this argument, Dulles replied "that the position adopted by Mr. Pasvolsky would have prevented the formation of the American Union."[67]

As time passed, however, Dulles began to recognize that failing to make regional action subject to the veto could be a two-edged sword. On May 4, he commented on the dilemma, explaining

> that there had developed in this hemisphere genuine regional arrangements. If the veto power was allowed to operate. we might not be able to take advantage of this system, and meanwhile we might find we had given in to a Russian proposal which would permit the Russians to use force in Europe and undermine the whole system of collective security. The two main difficulties . . . were that (1) It was not clear whether bilateral agreements were included among regional agencies and arrangements under Chapter VIII, Section C [the Dumbarton Oaks provision permitting regional arrangements]; and (2) the loose language of Chapter VIII, Section C, paragraph 3 and Chapter XII, paragraph 2 [the exemption from Security Council authorization for actions against enemy states], might permit the negotiation of agreements in such a way that one would get in fact an interlocking regional system resulting in the complete absence of control of that system by the Security Council.[68]

In effect, Dulles returned to one of his old fears that too much emphasis on regionalism could bar effective functioning of the global organization.

On the same day, an amendment was proposed to further clarify the right of states to establish alliances or bilateral pacts against the enemy states.[69] This amendment further stimulated even more the desires of Latin American countries and their supporters to have a similar exemption.[70] Hence, Arthur Vandenberg proposed that the Charter explicitly exempt from Security Council control "measures which may be taken . . . under the act of Chapultepec . . . until such time as the Organization [the United Nations] may, by consent of the Governing Board of the Pan American Union, be charged with this function. . . ."[71] This proposal sharply divided the United States

Delegation.   The opponents asked, if the U. S. obtained a specific exemption for its sphere of influence, what would stop the USSR from seeking the same?

Dulles essentially sided with the opposition on this issue. Although he had toyed with the idea that the Soviets might tolerate a single exemption from the Western Hemisphere,[72] he concluded that the best way to approach the issue was *not* to exempt specifically the Inter-American System.   Dulles prepared a memorandum on the issue in which he now seemed to argue that a special exemption for the Inter-American System was unnecessary since the inherent right of self-defense would allow a Western hemispheric organization to take necessary action.   As Arthur Vandenberg explained, "Dulles argued that there is nothing in Dumbarton Oaks which prohibits 'self-defense' and that under the Chapultepec agreement 'self-defense' in the Western Hemisphere is a partnership affair and that the Monroe Doctrine is still part of it."[73]   Dulles explained that

> at no point would the member states give up their right to use force in all circumstances . . . they pledged to refrain from the use of force in a manner inconsistent with the purposes of the organization.   Since the prevention of aggression was a purpose of the organization, action to prevent aggression in the absence of action by the Security Council would be consistent with the purposes of the organization. . . . If a European country vetoed action to prevent aggression in the Western Hemisphere, we would be entirely free to use force.[74]

Dulles also approached the issue from a slightly different angle: perhaps it was merely a waste of time to worry about the Chapultepec agreement; the Inter-American organization would probably never be established.   He argued

> that there is no correlation between the existing treaty system in this hemisphere and the Dumbarton Oaks Proposals.   The Act of Chapultepec simply recommends the ratification of the treaty in the future.   Before there would be a conflict, there would have to be a conference held to consider the draft of a treaty.   He questioned whether this could ever happen.   Moreover . . . the treaty would have to be ratified by twenty-one republics, which he thought was altogether unlikely.   Only after these two hurdles were surmounted would there perhaps be a conflict between the Dumbarton Oaks Proposals and the treaty system.   He thought there were 99 chances out of 100 that the issue of such a conflict would never have to be faced.[75]

Here Dulles was arguing in the alternative (a reflection, no doubt, of his legal training) that the delegation was probably concerning itself with a problem that would never occur. (Of course, history proved Dulles's prediction quite inaccurate when the Charter of the Organization of American States entered into force a few years later.)

As the debates on regional organization continued, Dulles adhered to both of these arguments. First, since the right of self-defense was inherent, there was no need to make a special provision for the Americas; and second, even though "it was hard to reconcile on paper the establishment of two police groups, the regional and the world," there "was no real clash because it was highly unlikely that a local police group would be established in the Western Hemisphere."[76]

The U.S. Delegation haggled over the issue and eventually the majority decided, contrary to Dulles's wishes, to make some mention in the U.N. Charter of the Inter-American System. But Dulles continued to work on the matter. As Ronald Pruessen explained, "[a]ccepting the unavoidable, Dulles became deeply involved with the inter-delegation bickering that was designed to produce an appropriate Charter clause. He spent hours in subcommittee meetings, using his highly respected legal ingenuity to devise acceptable language."[77] The proposal that emerged specifically mentioned the "inherent right of self-defense" and cited the Act of Chapultepec as an example of an arrangement established for that purpose. It provided, in part, that "[i]f the Security Council fails to prevent aggression by any state against any member state, such member state possesses the inherent right to take measures of self-defense. The right to take measures of self-defense against armed attack shall apply to arrangements, like those embodied in the Act of Chapultepec, under which all members of a group of states agree to consider an attack against any one of them as an attack against all of them."[78]   While this amendment did not conform to Dulles's initial preference not to mention the act, he could nevertheless accept it. He responded to arguments that the act not be mentioned by explaining

> that there were two reasons for doing so: First, the Latin American states would like it, and secondly, reference to the Act of Chapultepec puts a limitation on the arrangements. Specific reference to it would tend to prevent arrangements purporting to be like it, but not having the same solid basis. Reference to the Act, therefore, has a limiting force. It prevents throwing the door open to less sound and historical arrangements.[79]

After some minor changes in this new draft, it was adopted by the U.S. Delegation and presented to the other sponsors.[80]

In the meetings with the other four powers, Dulles emerged as a spokesman for the U.S. position. He and his colleagues encountered problems, however, with their proposal. As Russell and Muther explain, "[t]he new wording . . . proved still unsatisfactory to both the British and the Soviet delegates, who objected that it would lead to a series of regional organizations acting independently of the world institution."[81] Even though Dulles "emphasized that the United States did not want to encourage regionalism,"[82] "the session was adjourned to give the British and American foreign ministers a chance to seek a meeting of the minds."[83] At this meeting Dulles pled for an understanding of the U.S. proposal in terms of American foreign policy goals. He explained

> that it was not only a question of the Security Council having the opportunity to act, but it was the question of the United States carrying forward within the new world organization its traditional policy of the Monroe Doctrine as expanded and further defined in modern times; that the United States now regards an attack on any one of the American Republics as an attack upon the United States, and in that event the United States wished to exercise collectively its right to self-defense.[84]

In the face of stiff opposition from the British, however, a compromise draft was prepared that reserved "the inherent right of self-defense, either individual or collective, in the event that the Security Council has failed to maintain international peace and security and an armed attack against a member state has occurred."[85] On behalf of the U. S., Dulles once again proposed that the Act of Chapultepec be mentioned, but the British remained adamant in their opposition and the U. S. finally acquiesced. To convince the Latin American countries of the continuing commitment of the United States to Western hemispheric solidarity, some changes were made in other areas of the charter, and the U. S. promised that the president would make a statement pledging to negotiate a treaty "to give preeminence to the undertakings of the Act of Chapultepec."[86] Explained Dulles, "this statement . . . was the price we had to pay for omitting reference to the Act of Chapultepec in the document."[87]

The regional problem surfaced only once more in late May when France submitted a proposal to give still more leeway to defense pacts made to check the rise of "enemy states." As Russell and Muther explain, these regional defense arrangements were initially to be exempted from Security Council control "only until the organization assumed responsibility for security in relation to the enemy countries, 'by consent of the Governments concerned.'"[88] But in late May, the French proposed "to spell out that 'Governments committed by treaties of mutual assistance' would 'by common consent' have to grant the Security Council responsibility for preventing further aggression; and only thereafter would they have to seek Council permission before taking action under the treaty."[89]

As noted above, Dulles opposed this effort to expand the consent necessary for the Security Council to assume authority. He explained that "in his opinion the new wording will admit all the United Nations to the decision as to whether the Security Council could assume jurisdiction over the prevention of aggression by enemy states."[90] Under the previous wording "it had been his interpretation that authority over the control of enemy states would be granted to the Security Council on the 'request' of any two parties to a regional arrangement."[91] He questioned "why Australia should have the right to prevent the United Kingdom and Russia from turning over their authority under a regional arrangement to the Security Council."[92] Eventually, other changes were made to meet some of France's concerns, but the words "the governments concerned" were left in the draft.[93]

Several observations can be made about Dulles's role in the regional arrangements issue. First, although he initially desired to give more independence to regional organizations, he came to realize that strong regional arrangements could quickly degenerate into spheres of influence operating outside of the control of the global organization. (Indeed, his initial preference for strong regional organizations may have been a reflection of his Republican affiliation. The Democrats, notably Cordell Hull, had tended to oppose giving regional arrangements a very independent role, fearing that such organizations could prevent the success of the universal organization and encourage a Western hemispheric isolationism. The Republicans, on the other hand, seemed to prefer strong regional organizations, hoping to build a well-functioning Inter-American system.) Second, as Ronald Pruessen has argued, "Dulles's approach to the regional organization issue says much about his belief in the inevitably rudimentary nature of a new international organization."[94] Pruessen explains: "His emphasis on the 'inherent right of self-defense' and the ability of the United States to *assume* its freedom of movement for protection of its interests coincided completely with his earlier statements. Though hypothetically desirable, he had argued in 1944 and early 1945, there was no way nations were going to be rushed into surrendering the perquisites of sovereignty."[95] Third, Dulles's activities in this area indicate his flexibility in dealing with political affairs. While he would express his views on an issue, he was generally willing to accept what the practical considerations of the situation dictated, and could change course reasonably easily. In this respect, his behavior at San Francisco was very like that of a lawyer. He would state his position, but would work just as strongly with whatever his "client" finally decided. This characteristic, which was seen in the discussion of domestic jurisdiction as well, could seem hypocritical: how could someone so forcefully advocate one position and then, when overruled, not only acquiesce in that position but actually become its leading proponent? To a trained lawyer, however, this ability to bend with the client would not be perceived as hypocrisy.[96]

The International Court of Justice

Most of Dulles's work on the International Court of Justice came after the completion of the charter, and will be examined later. He did, however, make a number of comments about the court while a member of the U.S. Delegation.   These comments generally confirmed Pruessen's view that Dulles believed that the new organization could only be a "rudimentary" agency. From the outset, Dulles expressed support in theory for compulsory jurisdiction for the court, but realized that such jurisdiction was not yet possible. On April 30, he "observed that everybody would like to have the compulsory jurisdiction clause, but that we would have to move toward it through the process of evolution. He thought that the United States' acceptance of the Court Statute with the Optional Clause would be as great a step at present as would be practical."[97] The "optional clause" allowed states the "option" of accepting compulsory jurisdiction if they so chose. They could still remain parties to the court's statute, however, whether or not they accepted the clause.

Other Issues

In addition to these major issues, Dulles was also involved in a number of other concerns at San Francisco, including "the Principles" of the organization, the trusteeship question, and the development of international law.

Dulles was very skeptical about spelling out the specific "Principles" of the United Nations in the founding document. According to the minutes of a U.S. Delegation meeting, he "questioned what this chapter [Chapter II: Principles] was intended to accomplish and said that he did not understand what the principles were. In part they were long-range purposes and in part, specific undertakings by the member governments."[98]   Consequently, he "thought that they were extremely dangerous in their present form, and he did not see what role they were supposed to play."[99]   He explained that "[i]n particular . . . the looseness of the commitments bothered him; e.g., all members undertake to give every assistance or they undertake not to give assistance. What, he asked, does this mean?   He thought it was important to clear up the confusion involved in this chapter."[100]

Dulles further commented "that he did not know what was meant by the term 'principle' and that he thought the rather generalized and vague commitments in that chapter might jeopardize getting the charter through the Senate."[101]   As an example, "he referred . . . to the obligation to settle disputes by peaceful means,"[102] which was one of the specific principles in Chapter II.   He subsequently commented that "the obligation contained in this paragraph was a dangerous one and raised the question as to what would happen if a member refused to accept a method of pacific settlement."[103]

Dulles's concern here seems to reflect his lawyer's preference to avoid making law of vague pledges.   Interestingly enough, the principles contained in the "chapter" eventually became the principles of article 2 of the charter, which forms the normative basis of the United Nations system.

As noted previously, the colonial question also had concerned Dulles.   At San Francisco, he had a few things to say about the proposed trusteeship system.   On one occasion, he made it clear that while he favored "self-government," he did not necessarily favor "independence."   He explained that

> he tended to agree with Mr. Stassen that the concept of independence might not assist in the establishment of future peace.   Just as in the last war when there was criticism of those who set up many independent states in Europe, we would be subject to the same type of criticism.   It would be progress if we could speak of self-government integrated within an overall framework.   Mr. DULLES added that the church groups with which he was associated were satisfied in all their statements with self-government or autonomy as objectives of the trusteeship system and had never insisted on independence.[104]

These views are generally consistent with his developed early thought; he wanted self-determination but believed that total independence could cause more harm than good.

Another issue that Dulles discussed during the founding of the U.N. was the question of developing international law.   In April, when the U.S. Delegation was considering the "Purposes" section of the charter, he expressed reservations about a proposed amendment to the Dumbarton Oaks proposals that would have added the words "and with due regard for the principles of justice and equity and in accordance with the rule of law"[105] to the section.   He believed "that the reference [to the rule of law] was altogether ambiguous and that it would be a mistake to put in the reference in its present form."[106]   He explained "that the reference to the rule of law had been cut out in the first paragraph since there was no adequate body of law at the present time,"[107] but, he added, "since we all want to develop a body of international law, he could see the great value of putting in a reference to the *promotion* or *development* of international law as a basis for peace.   This law . . . could be developed by decisions of the court and the codification of international law."[108] These views were very much in keeping with Dulles's early thought; at present, international law was not very well developed, and thus could not yet be a viable guide to state conduct. Dulles felt it should, nevertheless, be prompted through court precedents and codification efforts.

DULLES'S EVALUATION OF SAN FRANCISCO

In the weeks and months that followed the San Francisco Conference, Dulles became an outspoken advocate of United States ratification of the charter. During this period, several major themes ran through his thought. First, in several addresses, he expressed the belief that the charter made great progress toward implementing the "Six Pillars of Peace" developed by the Commission on a Just and Durable Peace. In a speech delivered on July 10, 1945, entitled, "The Charter - An Important Step Toward Durable Peace," he explained:

We now have the Charter of a World Organization. It is not a perfect document. It does, however, go far to realize the first phase of making peace just and durable, as proposed by our "Six Pillars of Peace." That statement was issued over two years ago, before any of the governments had formulated a position on the matter of world organization. We can take satisfaction in having charted the course along which nations have moved.[109]

Thus, Dulles believed that because the charter reflected the "Six Pillars of Peace," the commission could take credit for having shown the way to international organization. He went on to indicate how each pillar was included in the charter. Pillar One provided for a "'political framework for a continuing collaboration of the United Nations and, in due course, of neutral and enemy nations.'" This, explained Dulles, "[w]e now have."[110] Pillar Two "dealt with economic and financial problems," which under the charter was "made a task of an Economic and Social Council."[111] Furthermore, the charter "recognized that conditions of stability [presumably economic] and well being are necessary for peaceful and friendly relations among nations," and "[a]ll members are pledged to action to achieve that end."[112] The third pillar, which dealt with peaceful change, was also addressed at San Francisco since, under the charter, "[t]he General Assembly may recommend measures for the peaceful adjustment of any situation, regardless of origin, which it deems likely to impair the general welfare or friendly relations among nations."[113] Pillar Four dealt with the plight of "subject peoples."[114] On this issue, "the member nations declare that the administration of non-self-governing peoples is a sacred trust to be administered with a view to developing self-government and free political institutions," and "[t]here is established an international trusteeship system."[115]   Pillar Five, which "called for 'procedures for controlling military establishments everywhere,'" was also dealt with in the Charter: "The General Assembly is to consider the principles governing disarmament and the regulation of armament, and make recommendations about this.   The Security Council, in turn, is bound to formulate plans for the regulating of armament and possible disarmament."[116]   Finally, Pillar Six, which "called for a peace which would establish the right of individuals everywhere to religious and intellectual liberty,"[117] was also largely incorporated into the charter. Dulles explained that "[a] basic purpose [of the charter] is respect for human rights and for fundamental freedoms of all without distinction as to race, language, religion or sex," and there was "to be a special Commission to achieve these goals."[118]   Dulles also echoed his belief that the charter embodied principles from the "Six Pillars" in testimony before the Senate Foreign Relations Committee on the question of charter ratification.[119]

A second element present during Dulles's discussion of the charter at this time was his recognition from the outset that the charter was only a *beginning* move toward peace, and not its ultimate realization.   In his Senate testimony, he explained:

I recognize that this Charter does not do what many people would like -- to guarantee at a single step perpetual peace.   We would all like to see that.   But the world does not move at a single step from a condition of virtual anarchy to a condition of well-rounded political order.   Those steps are made falteringly.   There are missteps; there have been missteps. . . .   It may be that permanent peace will be achieved only by trial and error; but it will never be achieved at all if we are afraid even to try.[120]

Because the charter was only a first step, it contained many inadequacies that Dulles was not afraid to acknowledge.   In an article that appeared in the October 1945 issue of *Foreign Affairs*, he explained:

The political inadequacy of the United Nations Organization is obvious.   Any political order which eliminates major violence over a long period of time must depend largely on laws defining, concretely and acceptably, what conduct is admissible and what is not. They need to be changed frequently as to adapt the basic judgments they express to constantly changing conditions and so as to assure an acceptable balance among members of the society who incline to pull in different directions.

The achievement of such a body of laws calls for a
lawmaking process.   And to enforce them there is
required, in addition to the pressure of public opinion, a
judicial system and a police force which will act
automatically as the law directs.[121]

But the problem was that the charter did not establish laws or set
up law-making and law-enforcing bodies. Dulles explained that "[t]he
Charter itself did not establish rules of conduct which the
organization is committed to enforce.   It does set forth certain
general principles; but these are expressed as self-denying ordinances,
not as law which the Organization enforces. The Security Council is
under no injunction to move against violations."[122] Dulles rejected
the notion that the charter was, in fact, a law-creating instrument.
Apparently, he did not accept the understanding that provisions, such
as the article 2(4) prohibition on the unilateral use of force, would
become binding norms of international conduct once the charter
entered into force. Strangely enough, he seemed to adhere to the
belief that because aggression was not defined in the charter, it was
not prohibited. He explained that "[s]ome consideration was given to
a possible prohibition of 'aggression.' But, as Mr. Eden observed at
San Francisco, aggression is a concept without any precise agreed
content."[123] He continued to explain that "[s]ome expansions and
contractions of zones of national influence are reprehensible and
some may be desirable."[124] Thus, he added, "[i]t is not easy to find
words which would define and prohibit such exploits as the initial
acts of Hitler and Hirohito and yet permit the expansion of the
U.S.S.R. from the low ebb to which Russia fell under the Tsars and
authorize Great Britain to 'erase the sore spots in Europe' as now
proposed by Professor Laski."[125] (This is a remarkable statement,
seemingly indicating that Dulles believed that the charter allowed
certain "expansion," i.e., the use of force for certain "justified"
territorial aggrandizement. This interpretation of the charter has
been nearly universally rejected.)

According to Dulles, the delegates at San Francisco "abstained
from seeking to legislate perpetual peace by a single Article
sanctifying for all time things as they are,"[126] but "after that
deceptively easy way had been rejected, the problem of legislation
was seen as immensely difficult."[127] He explained that the states "at
San Francisco had not yet reached the position where they
constituted a true community with common judgments about
conduct."[128]   Furthermore, "many of them did not want the
establishment of any law which would be superior to their own
particular will and conscience. Wisely, then the Conference did not
attempt to write laws for the Organization to enforce."[129]

But, not only did the charter not make law, it "also failed to
establish a body to make laws hereafter."[130] Although "[t]he
Security Council . . . might conceivably build up a body of

international common law through its reasoned action in dealing with international disputes, . . . it is not likely that an adequate body of law could develop in this way in time to meet the necessity which will face the world,"[131] due to the voting process in the council. The General Assembly also suffered from problems in the voting procedures: "In the Assembly, where each state has one vote regardless of size, a small minority of the people could impose its will on the great majority."[132] Thus, it too could not be deemed to be a legislative body. Finally, in light of these problems and the veto, the San Francisco Conference "could not establish any effective enforcement procedure."[133]

Dulles summarized these inadequacies as to law, law making, and enforcement in an August 1945 letter to Lieutenant Elmo G. Montag, who had written him about the education of an international police force. Dulles explained:

> we have not found any way of making international laws. That was one of the great troubles we ran into at San Francisco and the reason why the proposed military contingents cannot go into action in any case, however flagrant, unless the Security Council first, after consideration, so decides. The making of that decision is a quasi-legislative act which calls for unanimous consent of at least all of the five major powers. Therefore, the situation is as it would be if there were a policeman on the street but he had no law telling him whom to arrest. If a situation arose such that he thought someone should be arrested, he would first have to go to the town council and have a meeting called and await the outcome of a political discussion where the voting and rules were such that authority to act would be very doubtful.[134]

Dulles concluded that while "[i]t is interesting and important to think in terms of a police force," "it is more important in terms of how to get laws which a police force can enforce."[135] But "[t]o achieve an effective law-making process requires a good deal more sense of community and sense of fellowship and common moral judgment than exists at the present time."[136]

Despite these inadequacies, however, Dulles believed that the charter was a worthwhile instrument; it achieved the most that was possible at the time. He explained in his *Foreign Affairs* article that "[t]he present Charter represents a conscientious and successful effort to create the best world organization which the realities permit. Of course, anyone who is free to disregard realities and to act only in the realm of theory can write a 'better' Charter. A reasonably intelligent school boy could do that."[137] Nevertheless, "[t]he merit of the present Charter lies in the fact that its words correspond with the realities. What in the abstract are defects become in reality

merits. The Charter was deliberately made to mirror the hopes and
fears, the trusts and distrusts, the strength and infirmities of the
human environment in which it must live and work."[138]   In sum,
Dulles recognized the limitations of the charter but believed that
these were necessary, given the existing political climate. He did
continue, however, to emphasize, as he had done at San Francisco,
that the charter was not the final word: "Under present conditions it
[the charter] could not advantageously be made materially different.
But some day it ought to be different.   The delegates at San
Francisco were almost unanimous about that."[139]

The third theme seen in Dulles's evaluation of the San
Francisco Conference was a belief that the greatest potential for the
promotion of peace lay in the economic and social activities provided
for in the charter. In a speech delivered on June 29, 1945, to the
Foreign Policy Association in Philadelphia, he explained how the
Dumbarton Oaks emphasis on the Security Council had been rejected
at San Francisco. He argued that "[t]he first days of the Conference
showed how difficult it would be for the Five to provide . . .
unanimity,"[140] as differences arose among the major powers.
Consequently,

> the Big Five themselves demonstrated to the Conference
> that the future peace of the world ought not to be rested
> wholly upon their ability quickly to agree on future
> measures to repress aggression.   All hoped that the
> Security Council would turn out to be an effective body.
> But no one could be sure. So we all agreed to do what
> some of us had long wanted -- we agreed to develop the
> possibility of the Organization's taking remedial action to
> diminish the causes of war.[141]

He further elaborated on these efforts to strike at the causes of
war.

> We wrote a preamble affirming our faith in fundamental
> human rights -- in the dignity and worth of the human
> person -- in the equal rights of men and women, and of
> nations large and small. We dedicated the Organization to
> promote social progress and better standards of life in
> larger freedoms [sic]; to practice tolerance; to heal
> economic and social sores. We bound the Organization to
> seek justice, to develop international law, and to promote
> respect for human rights and for fundamental freedoms for
> all without distinction as to race, sex, language or
> religion.[142]

He then went on to praise the charter provisions on peaceful
change, the Economic and Social Council, and the trusteeship system.

For Dulles it was important that allied unity be maintained through cooperative efforts on these functional issues. In his *Foreign Affairs* article, he discussed how the General Assembly could promote this. He explained:

> Fellowship based on a war coalition usually disintegrates after the enemy's defeat. The way to prevent this from happening to the United Nations is to continue them in combat against the material and spiritual enemies of human welfare. To organize that combat is the primary responsibility of the General Assembly, and to do it successfully calls for a high order of statesmanship.[143]

He elaborated that to maintain this unity it was important "that the Assembly choose projects which are likely to succeed."[144]

While not rejecting extremely technical projects, Dulles did feel that "the compilation of scientific data on meterological and hydrographic matters does little to promote the fellowship of people."[145] He believed that "[t]hough such tasks should of course continue to be undertaken, they are no substitute for activities which will develop the enthusiastic loyalty and support of the peoples of many lands and afford a powerful outlet for their dynamic impulses."[146] He then explained a number of specific tasks. For instance, the organization should "encourage the development and codification of international law,"[147] but not just as between states. He explained that there was "an alternative to legislation for states, namely, the adoption of laws to operate upon individuals."[148] In light of the Nuremberg Trials, "[t]he time is . . . propitious to begin to frame international law which will not be merely applicable retroactively but will operate in the future to deter individuals anywhere from wilfully or maliciously plotting or inciting international disorder."[149] Furthermore, "once individual duties are made a subject of international law, it becomes logical also to define the international aspects of individual rights."[150] If such actions were taken, "[a] cause of war might be curbed,"[151] since "[b]y promoting that development the General Assembly could begin to give practical content to the affirmation by the peoples of the United Nations of their 'faith in fundamental human rights, in the dignity and worth of the human person.'"[152]

Dulles also felt that the assembly should seek "the solution of international problems of an economic character."[153] He explained that "[t]he conditions of trade and finance ought to be such that nations can acquire, on a fair exchange basis, the food, raw materials and other products which do not lie within their own resources and which they need for the maintenance of tolerable standards of living."[154] Dulles believed that "[a] success here would do much to eliminate some of the underlying causes of war."[155] Similarly, he advocated General Assembly work "to promote international cooperation in the field of health."[156]   All these cooperative activities would, he hoped, promote an international spirit of fellowship conducive to peace.

It is interesting to note the continuity of Dulles's post-San Francisco position on these functional issues with his early thought. Even though at the conference he apparently had reservations about broadening the scope of certain economic and social activities, in the speeches that followed he held these activities out as the cornerstone of the charter.

The final theme present in Dulles's thought after San Francisco was the belief that the charter was worthy of support because it was consonant with United States foreign policy goals.   Much of his testimony before the Senate Foreign Relations Committee dealt with this issue.   He began by explaining that the charter provided an alternative to an individual approach to the enemy states.   The United States could thus avoid a repeat of the Versailles experience. He argued that "the reason why Germany recovered ber [sic] military might was not because the Treaty of Versailles was a soft treaty; it was because the Treaty of Versailles was not enforced.   The reason why it was not enforced was that the victors fell out among themselves."[157]   Since "we do not want to do that again," "the only practical alternative is to adopt the San Francisco Charter."[158]   But, Dulles explained, the charter should not be accepted "merely because [it] is the lesser of two evils," but because "the document before you charts a path which we can pursue joyfully and without fear."[159]

After this introduction, Dulles did not immediately demonstrate how the charter had many positive aspects that coincide with U. S. goals, but rather illustrated how the charter *did not have negative effects* on U. S. policy.   He explained that under the charter the United States would "remain the masters of our own destiny," arguing that "[t]he Charter does not subordinate to any supergovernment. There is no right on the part of the United Nations Organization to intervene in our domestic affairs.   There can be no use of force without our consent.   If the joint venture fails, we can withdraw."[160] He continued to explain that the United States would not have to worry about an independent U.S. Representative to the Security Council acting contrary to American goals; it was the United States, not the individual, who was a member of the council.[161]

Following this discussion of the "negative" benefits of the charter, Dulles developed some positive reasons for joining the organization.   He cited the ways in which the economic and social activities would be helpful in promoting unity and illustrated how the charter reflected the "Six Pillars of Peace."

Dulles then proceeded to refute the opponents of the charter who contended that the document put the United States in a precarious position.   He rejected the accusation that the charter was simply a military alliance, insisting that "there is not a word which commits the United States in advance to use its armed forces."[162]

He also rejected the idea that the charter represented an effort by the large nations to dominate the small, noting that the small nations were not afraid that the big states would dominate them, but rather feared that the Security Council would *not act* due to the veto.[163] He responded to the allegation "that this Charter will perpetuate colonial imperialism."[164]   In his view, it was clear that the charter did not totally eliminate colonialism, but "the greatest step in advance that has ever been made in modern times is the fact that by this Charter every colonial power, without exception, subscribed to the proposition that the administration of colonial people is a sacred trust to be administered with a view to their ultimate self-government and the establishment of their free institutions."[165] Dulles also rejected the notion "we cannot go into this Charter because of the huge public debt of the United States and the large sums that we have expended in aid to others by way of lend-lease."[166]   He explained that there was "not a single word or line in this Charter which by affirmative implication commits the United States to any financial aid whatever, any more than it commits the other nations to financial aid to the United States."[167]

Not surprisingly, most of the questions to Dulles by Committee members revolved around fears that the charter would overcommit the United States.   Under questioning from senators, Dulles insisted that if the United States adopted the charter, the country would not abrogate its constitutional process.   He explained that the specific arrangements for establishing military contingents would have to be negotiated with the United Nations and ratified by the Senate at some future date.   At that time the Senate could provide whatever it pleased.   While Dulles was reluctant to comment on the probable size of these forces, he eventually admitted that he did not believe they would need to be very large, since they were not designed to be used against a great power or the enemy states.[168]

Dulles was also asked about the question of withdrawal from the organization; once again, he stated "that there was a right of withdrawal, the reason being that the agreement was not of a type which in any sense merged the member states into a new government or under which they gave up any of their independence."[169]   But although there was a *legal* right, he explained that "morally, in my opinion, a nation ought not withdraw without reasons which are at least good to it."[170]

Senators additionally questioned Dulles about the relationship between the charter and the Monroe Doctrine.   On that point, he explained that the Monroe Doctrine was "a doctrine of national self-defense"[171] and that "there is nothing whatever in the Charter which impairs a nation's right of self-defense,"[172] nor the right of collective self-defense as expanded through the Mexican Conference and the Act of Chapultepec.[173]   Senator Warren R. Austin asked Dulles to confirm the "fact that the San Francisco Conference does not change the autonomous conditions of the regional arrangement with respect to the western hemisphere created by the Act of Chapultepec . . . until the Security Council takes the steps that are necessary for security."[174] Dulles explained:

> It changed it in this respect only, Senator Austin. Without the Security Council and the new world organization we could have had in this hemisphere a regional organization which was wholly autonomous and which could act on its own initiative to maintain peace in this hemisphere without reference or regard whatsoever to any world organization. As it results from the Charter at San Francisco, the world security organization is given the first opportunity to maintain peace everywhere, using presumably regional organizations which it is invited to do but not absolutely compelled to do.
>
> If, however, the Security Council fails to maintain peace and despite the existence of the Security Council there is an armed outbreak, then the regional organization moves in without regard to the Security Council.[175]

Thus, the Western Hemisphere organization was always able to act in collective self-defense if the Security Council could not act. It is interesting to note that despite article 52, paragraph 2 of the charter, which obligates members to attempt to settle disputes through regional arrangements before referring them to the council, Dulles assumed that the Security Council was "given the first opportunity to maintain peace everywhere."[176]

NOTES

1. See Pruessen, *John Foster Dulles*, 236-237.

2. In this discussion, I draw heavily from Pruessen's work. See his *John Foster Dulles*, 239-252.

3. "Dumbarton Oaks Proposals for the Establishment of a General International Organization," reprinted in Russell and Muther, *A History of the United Nations Charter*, 1024.

4. "Minutes of the Tenth Meeting of the U.S. Delegation," April 16, 1945, *1 Foreign Relations of the United States*, 1945, 308 (footnote omitted).

5. Ibid, 309.

6. Ibid.

7. Ibid.

8. "12th Mtg., U.S. Delegation," Apr. 18, 1945, *1 Foreign Relations of the United States*, 1945, 332-333.

9. "3rd Four-Power Consultative Mtg," May 3, 1945, *1 Foreign Relations of the United States*, 1945, 582.

10. "Summary Report of the 17th Mtg. of Committee I/1," Jan. 14, 1945, Doc. 1019, I/1/42, 6 U.N.C.I.O. Docs. 507 (1945).

11. Ibid.

12. Ibid, 508.

13. Ibid.

14. Ibid.

15. Ibid.

16. Ibid.

17. Ibid.

18. Pruessen, *John Foster Dulles*, 248-249.

19. Ibid, 250.

20. Ibid. (footnote omitted).

21. "Dumbarton Oaks Proposals," in Russell and Muther, 1024.

22. "18th Mtg. U.S. Delegation," Apr. 26, 1945, *1 Foreign Relations of the United States*, 1945, 418.

23. Ibid.

24. Ibid.

25. Ibid, 418-419.

26. Ibid, 419.

27. Ibid, 420.

28. "21st Mtg., U.S. Delegation," Apr. 27, 1945, *1 Foreign Relations of the United States*, 1945, 475.

29. "28th Mtg., U.S. Delegation," May 3, 1945, *1 Foreign Relations of the United States*, 1945, 577.

30. "59th Mtg., U.S. Delegation," May 31, 1945, *1 Foreign Relations of the United States*, 1945, 1003.

31. Ibid.

32. "53rd Mtg., U.S. Delegation," May 25, 1945, *1 Foreign Relations of the United States*, 1945, 875.

33. Ibid, 876.

34. Ibid.

35. "55th Mtg., U.S. Delegation," May 26, 1945, *1 Foreign Relations of the United States*, 1945, 916 (emphasis added).

36. Pruessen, *John Foster Dulles*, 247.

37. Dulles, "Memorandum," June 8, 1945, quoted in Pruessen, *John Foster Dulles*, 248.

38. Pruessen, *John Foster Dulles*, 248.

39. Dulles, "Memorandum," June 8, 1945, quoted in Pruessen, 248.

40. Ibid.

41. R. Pruessen also makes this point. Pruessen, *John Foster Dulles*, at 247.

42. "71st Mtg., U.S. Delegation," June 14, 1945, *1 Foreign Relations of the United States*, 1945, 1298.

43. Ibid, 1299.

44. Ibid.

45. "10th Mtg., U.S. Delegation," Apr. 16, 1945, *1 Foreign Relations of the United States*, 1945, 297-301.

46. "12th Mtg., U.S. Delegation," Apr. 18, 1945, *1 Foreign Relations of the United States*, 1945, 335.

47. "18th Mtg., U.S. Delegation," Apr. 26, 1945, *1 Foreign Relations of the United States*, 1945, 439.

48. Ibid, 441.

49. "71st. Mtg., U.S. Delegation," June 14, 1945, *1 Foreign Relations of the United States*, 1945, 1298.

50. Ibid.

51. "8th Mtg., U.S. Delegation," Apr. 11, 1945, *1 Foreign Relations of the United States*, 1945, 265.

52. "42nd Mtg., U.S. Delegation," May 16, 1956, *1 Foreign Relations of the United States*, 1945, 765.

53. "51st Mtg., U.S. Delegation," May 23, 1945, *1 Foreign Relations of the United States*, 1945, 854.

54. "60th Mtg., U.S. Delegation," Jun. 1, 1945, *1 Foreign Relations of the United States*, 1945, 1027.

55. "Draft of Talk of Mr. John Foster Dulles" (Based on stenographic transcript of Mr. Dulles's remarks of 5/17/45), in *JFD Papers*, 2.

56. Ibid.

57. Ibid.

58. Ibid, 3.

59. Ibid.

60. Ibid.

61. The analysis draws heavily upon Pruessen, *John Foster Dulles*, 243-246.

62. "10th Mtg., U.S. Delegation," Apr. 16, 1945, *1 Foreign Relations of the United States*, 1945, 303.

63. Ibid, 302.

64. Ibid, 303.

65. Ibid, 304.

66. Ibid.

67. Ibid.

68. "29th Mtg., U.S. Delegation," May 4, 1945, *1 Foreign Relations of the United States*, 1945, 596.

69. Russell and Muther, *A History of the United Nations Charter*, 692.

70. Ibid, 693.

71. Quoted in ibid, 694.

72. *1 Foreign Relations of the United States*, 1945, 644.

73. Vandenberg, *The Private Papers of Senator Vandenberg*, 189.

74. Quoted in Pruessen, *John Foster Dulles*, 244.

75. "35th Mtg., U.S. Delegation," May 10, 1945, *12 Foreign Relations of the United States*, 1945, 657.

76. "36th Mtg., U.S. Delegation," May 11, 1945, *12 Foreign Relations of the United States*, 1945, 665.

77. Pruessen, *John Foster Dulles*, 245.

78. "37th Mtg., U.S. Delegation," May 12, 1945, *1 Foreign Relations of the United States*, 1945, 676.

79. Ibid.

80. Ibid, 686.

81. Russell and Muther, *A History of the United Nations Charter*, 699.

82. 3rd Five Power Informal Consultative Meeting on Proposed Amendments (Part I), May 12, 1945, *1 Foreign Relations of the United States,* 1945, 697.

83. Russell and Muther, *A History of the United Nations Charter*, 699.

84. "Memorandum by Mr. Robert W. Hartley of the United States Delegation of a Conversation held at San Francisco," May 12, 1945, *1 Foreign Relations of the United States*, 1945, 700.

85. Robert W. Hartley, "Minutes of Informal Drafting Session," *1 Foreign Relations of the United States*, 1945, 705.

86. "39th Mtg., U.S. Delegation," May 13, 1945, *1 Foreign Relations of the United States*, 1945, 720.

87. Ibid.

88. Russell and Muther, *A History of the United Nations Charter*, 707.

89. Ibid.

90. "59th Mtg., U.S. Delegation," May 31, 1945, *1 Foreign Relations of the United States*, 1945, 1004.

91. Ibid, 1005.

92. Ibid.

93. Russell and Muther, *A History of the United Nations Charter*, 707-710.

94. Pruessen, *John Foster Dulles*, 246.

95. Ibid.

96. I draw heavily on R. Pruessen's analysis on this point. See ibid, 239-252.

97. "23rd Mtg, U.S. Delegation," April 30, 1945, *1 Foreign Relations of the United States*, 1945, 492.

98. "5th Mtg., U.S. Delegation," Apr. 19, 1945, *1 Foreign Relations of the United States*, 1945, 224.

99. Ibid.

100. Ibid.

101. Ibid.

102. Ibid.

103. "6th Mtg., U.S. Delegation," *1 Foreign Relations of the United States*, 1945, 229.

104. "45th Mtg., U.S. Delegation," May 18, 1945, *1 Foreign Relations of the United States*, 1945, 795.

105. "5th Mtg., U.S. Delegation," Apr. 19, 1945, *1 Foreign Relations of the United States*, 1945, 220.
106. Ibid.
107. Ibid, 222.
108. Ibid. (emphasis added).
109. Dulles, "The Charter - An Important Step Toward Durable Peace," July 10, 1945, *JFD Papers*, at 1.
110. Ibid.
111. Ibid.
112. Ibid.
113. Ibid.
114. Ibid.
115. Ibid, 1-2.
116. Ibid, 2.
117. Ibid.
118. Ibid.
119. U. S. Senate, "The Charter of the United Nations: Hearings Before the Senate Committee on Foreign Relations," 79th Cong., 1st Sess. (1945) (statement of John Foster Dulles), 640, 642.
120. Ibid, 644.
121. Dulles, "The General Assembly," 2-3.
122. Ibid, 3.
123. Ibid.
124. Ibid. (emphasis added).
125. Ibid.
126. Ibid.
127. Ibid.
128. Ibid.
129. Ibid, 3-4.
130. Ibid, 4.
131. Ibid.
132. Ibid.
133. Ibid.
134. JFD to Lt. Elmo G. Montag, Aug. 2, 1945, *JFD Papers*.
135. Ibid.
136. Ibid.
137. Dulles, "The General Assembly," 5.
138. Ibid.
139. Ibid. at 6.
140. Dulles, Address at the Foreign Policy Association Luncheon, Jun. 29, 1945, *JFD Papers*, 2.
141. Ibid, 2-3.
142. Ibid, 3.
143. Dulles, "The General Assembly," 2.
144. Ibid, 7-8.
145. Ibid, 8.
146. Ibid.
147. Ibid, 9.

148. Ibid.
149. Ibid.
150. Ibid.
151. Ibid, 10.
152. Ibid, 9.
153. Ibid, 10.
154. Ibid.
155. Ibid.
156. Ibid.
157. U. S. Senate, "Hearings on the Charter of the United Nations," 640.
158. Ibid.
159. Ibid, 641.
160. Ibid.
161. Ibid.
162. Ibid, 642.
163. Ibid, 642-43.
164. Ibid, 643.
165. Ibid.
166. Ibid, 644.
167. Ibid.
168. Ibid, 645-646, 651-655.
169. Ibid, 647.
170. Ibid.
171. Ibid, 649.
172. Ibid, 650.
173. Ibid.
174. Ibid.
175. Ibid.
176. Ibid.   For an interesting discussion of this issue, see Inis L. Claude, Jr., "The OAS, the UN and the United States," reprinted in J. Nye, ed., *International Regionalism* (Boston: Little, Brown, 1968) 3, 11-13.

8

The First Sessions
of the United Nations

In light of Dulles's involvement in the founding of the United Nations, it is no surprise that he became a member of the U.S. delegation to the first session of the General Assembly. From 1946 until 1950 he had the opportunity to work as an official participant in the international organization he had worked so hard to establish. During this time he was able to deal with a number of issues that related directly to his early thought on the roles of international organization. This chapter will examine the most important issues with which Dulles was involved during his membership in the U.S. delegation.

THE TRUSTEESHIP ISSUE

When the first session of the United Nations General Assembly began in early 1946, Dulles was chosen to be the U.S. representative on the Fourth Committee, which was to deal with the establishment of the Trusteeship Council and other issues relating to colonies and non-self-governing territories. Rather than giving a detailed description of all of Dulles's activities with the Fourth Committee, this discussion will explore several major aspects of his work on the trusteeship and colonial issues.

Forming the Trusteeship Council and the Problem with the USSR

Under Chapter XII of the U.N. Charter, an international trusteeship system was to be established to regulate colonial territories falling into three categories: 1) those administered under the

League Mandate system; 2) those of the enemy states of World War II; and 3) those voluntarily subjected to the system.[1] A Trusteeship Council was to be set up to establish the specific policies governing the administration of these trusts, but since the council would consist of an equal number of trustee and non-trustee states, it could not be established until specific trusteeship agreements were reached and at least three trustee states were identified.[2]   According to article 79 of the charter, these agreements were to be concluded "by the states directly concerned"[3] and then approved by the General Assembly or by the Security Council in the case of strategic trusts. One of the most controversial issues associated with the trusteeship agreements was determining the "states directly concerned." The Soviet Union believed that it "was a state directly concerned in any trust territory," since "the Soviet Union considered itself as concerned in any major economic, political, or geographic question anywhere in the world."[4] The United States, however, took a more narrow view. Dulles, as the U.S. representative on the Fourth Committee, became the chief negotiator with the Soviets on this issue.

During the course of the first and second sessions of the General Assembly, Dulles met with numerous Soviet representatives to attempt to resolve the problem. But as draft trusteeship agreements were being worked out with former mandated powers, no compromise had been reached with the Soviets. According to Alger Hiss, by November 1, 1946, Dulles had begun to feel that the Soviets were trying to prevent the establishment of the Trusteeship Council. Explained Hiss, Dulles felt

> that the Russians are planning a campaign of obstruction to the proposed agreements. They have indicated that they will emphasize the need for provisions looking toward early independence which would be inacceptable [sic] to the mandatory powers. If the Russians have a veto right they would then be able to prevent the establishment of the trusteeship system. Mr. Dulles said that he was inclined to feel that although the establishment of the trusteeship system is important, that establishment is really of less substantive importance than is the propaganda issue which the Russians are raising about what states are really the defenders of the dependent peoples. He said that once the trusteeship agreements were approved there will be relatively little of substance which the Trusteeship Council will itself accomplish and, as in the case of the mandate system, the administering powers will be responsible in fact for what goes on in their territories. . . . He indicated that he was anxious that we not get in a position of appearing to rush through the Assembly against Russian opposition agreements which are satisfactory to colonial

powers.   He said he thought the Russians would try to
class us with the colonial powers.[5]

It was Dulles's fear that unless an agreement was made with the
Soviets, the biggest problem would be the propaganda loss suffered by
the United States. The Soviet Union would appear to be the great
defender of the subject people, while the United States would seem
to be one of the exploitative colonials.

In light of these considerations, Dulles continued his efforts to
resolve the question of "the states directly concerned" with the
Soviets. On November 7, he introduced a proposal in the Fourth
Committee that would have provided for consideration of draft
trusteeship agreements by a subcommittee that would receive input
from all states and consult with the mandatory powers. The subcommittee would then bring the agreements to the full committee
prior to reference to the General Assembly. Theoretically, this would
allow for all states to present their views on the agreements, without
necessitating a final definition of "states directly concerned." Dulles
explained that "[s]uch procedure would give all nations interested
equal opportunity to present their views," and "without prejudice to
any rights they might possess in accepting the decision of a two-
thirds majority of the General Assembly, they would forego formal
classification as States directly concerned as well as formal signature
of the preliminary agreement."[6] The Soviets, however, did not seem
willing to accept this proposal to by-pass a formal designation of
"states directly concerned."[7]

As   the   subcommittee   continued   to   consider   the   draft
Trusteeship Agreements, Dulles met with the Soviet delegates to try
to resolve the issue. The Soviets seemed to soften their position,
explaining on November 30 that they would be willing not to be
considered a state directly concerned in regard to *African* mandatory
territories, but only under a general agreement that they would be a
state directly concerned "as regards other areas, notably the Pacific
Islands."[8] They seemed most concerned about U. S. fortifications on
Pacific territories, believing that such fortification violated the
charter. Dulles disagreed with their legal interpretation and
attempted to argue in terms of "vital interests." Just as the United
States would not forgo its fortifications or submit such activities to
the Security Council for approval, so the USSR would not be willing
to do the same with respect to the Kuriles. He contended that "the
United States would not agree to a double standard under which the
Soviet Union did not subject to Security Council control areas in its
possession which it deemed vital; whereas the United States, as to
comparable areas in its possession, would be subject to control and
inspection by the Soviet Union."[9] (Despite this disagreement,
however, Dulles concluded his memorandum by explaining that "[w]hile
the discussion was extremely frank, the atmosphere throughout was
friendly and cordial[,] and it was agreed that we would each think

the matter over to see whether there was any possible basis for agreement which would permit of going ahead harmoniously on the trusteeship matter."[10])

As the session progressed, although the Soviets seemed willing at times to compromise, the United States was unable to reach agreement with them. In November and December of 1946, Dulles made repeated efforts to persuade the Soviets to take a more informal approach to the definition of "states directly concerned," but did not succeed. On December 9, he informed the subcommittee of the Fourth Committee that since he had been unable to reach an agreement, the United States would revert to its original position to adopt draft trusteeship agreements without passing on the question of who the "states directly concerned" were. The subcommittee adopted his proposal, as did the full committee on December 11. After a debate in the General Assembly on December 13, eight trusteeship agreements were adopted.[11]   The Soviet Union, however, began boycotting the meetings of the Trusteeship Council.

In a very rough draft of a speech to be delivered on January 16, 1947, Dulles reviewed his role in establishing the trusteeship system. He pointed out that the U.S. Delegation had to work "in the face of a disposition on the part of certain states, notably the Soviet bloc of states."[12] He explained that

> there were a great many difficulties in the way because while they [Soviets and their allies] professed their desire to see the Trusteeship Council set up it seemed actually they would have preferred to be in a position of being able to point out to dependent peoples that due to the reactionary attitude of the colonial powers it had been impossible to set up a trusteeship system and therefore there was no alternative but for the dependent peoples to take the matter of dependency in their own hands and through revolutionary ways seek self dependence and self governance.[13]

This would be the propaganda victory of which Dulles had spoken.

Dulles went on to explain that it was true "that the United States delegation seemed to be lined up pretty much with the colonial powers."[14] But this was due to two factors. First, he argued, much of the U. S. haggling with the colonial powers had taken place in private; had these negotiations been public, "they would have been spectacular and everybody would have realized the concern the United States had in the welfare of the people and in drafting a bill of rights."[15] Second, although the draft speech is incomplete at this point, Dulles seemed to suggest that the United States appeared to be associating with the colonialists because it realized that if the agreements had been any more anti-colonial, they would not have been accepted by the colonial powers.

The Former Japanese Colonies

One of the major colonial issues directly affecting the United States was the disposition of the former Japanese mandates that the United States had come to occupy during the war. During late 1945 and early 1946, the United States was uncertain about how it would handle these territories; disagreements arose among the State, Navy, and War Departments. On October 9, 1946, fearful of the impression that American inaction would leave with other states, Dulles sent a memorandum to the secretary of state. In this memorandum, he discussed a conversation with Secretary of the Navy James Forrestal. Dulles explained:

> I stated that in my opinion from an over-all standpoint the United States needed to demonstrate to the rest of the world its capacity to act decisively in relation to international affairs. There were, I said, a number of countries who were doubtful as to whether we had that capacity and whether it was safe for them to associate themselves with us. I said that the indecision shown with reference to the Japanese Mandated Islands would, if prolonged, weaken our position in the world; that the differences of opinion between the State Department, War Department, and Navy Department were well known and could not be continued without giving the world the impression that in such matters our Government was unable to make up its mind and come to a decision.[16]

He thus felt that if the United States were to maintain the appearance of a world power, it must demonstrate its capacity to make decisions.

Although Dulles believed that "*some* decision was of first importance, irrespective of what that decision was," he personally favored "strategic trusteeship rather than annexation."[17] He explained that there had been "a long history beginning with the Atlantic Charter which had given other nations reason to believe that we would not annex outright and if we did so it might set an example for others to do likewise with a result that the entire trusteeship system might collapse."[18] He rejected Navy protestations that the United States could not secure the necessary military rights under such an arrangement, believing that such rights were attainable under a trusteeship agreement.

Eventually, the United States decided to pursue a strategic trusteeship in this area. On November 7, 1946, Dulles read a statement by President Truman expressing the United States' willingness to put the former Japanese mandates under U.S. trusteeship.[19] Whether or not Dulles was, in fact, the moving force behind this policy decision, he later claimed a great deal of responsibility for it. In a 1949 draft on his "distinctive contributions to U.S. foreign policy, as manifested through the United Nations General Assembly," he explained that "[t]here was vacillation and indecision in Washington, which was extremely embarrassing from the standpoint of our foreign policy. I brought this to a head by conferences with the President, Forrestal, and the State Department so that the decision was made to place the islands under strategic trusteeship."[20] He explained that while "the Soviet Union could have exercised a veto power, . . . I was largely instrumental in preventing that."[21]

The Relationship Between the Trusteeship Council and Provisions for Non-Self-Governing Territories

As noted earlier, Chapter XII of the U.N. Charter, which established the trusteeship system, deals only with certain types of territories -- former mandates, colonies of enemy states, and those voluntarily submitted under the system. Only those colonies would be regulated by the Trusteeship Council. Under Chapter XI of the charter, however, *all* colonial powers pledged to administer consciously their territories in an effort to provide respect for human rights, self-governance, and economic and social development. They also committed themselves to submit regular reports to the secretary-general on development in these areas.[22]

Initially, Dulles seemed to have been most concerned about the territories under Chapter XI. While the General Assembly was considering a resolution dealing with "the conversion of the old League of Nations mandates into trusteeships under the United Nations,"[23] Dulles

wondered whether the General Assembly in its resolution should not call on other states, not just to mandating powers, since there were other types of territories eligible for trusteeship in addition to the mandated territories. He was particularly concerned . . . with the necessity of appealing to dependent people throughout the world and of reassuring them at this meeting of the General Assembly that the United Nations was taking steps to promote their welfare. The Trusteeship Council was the only organ of the United Nations which could not be created at this time. He had reluctantly come to this conclusion on the basis of the technical difficulty of creating the Trusteeship Council and he, therefore, thought it all the more important to make plain to public opinion throughout the world that the question of trusteeship and the broad question of dependent territories was not being completely neglected at the first meeting of the General Assembly.[24]

Hence, in light of the initial problems in establishing the Trusteeship Council, Dulles wanted the assembly to issue a broad appeal to all colonial powers in an effort to demonstrate that the U.N. could take some action. His skepticism about the trusteeship system led him to see more hope in the Chapter XI provisions of the charter. As noted above, by November of 1946, he believed that the council would be largely powerless. Instead, he regarded "Chapter 11, which relates to dependent territories generally and of course covers a far greater area of the world's surface and a far greater population group than does the trusteeship system, as more important than the trusteeship system itself."[25]

In 1947, the U.S. delegation opposed a resolution of India that "propos[ed] that the Members which administer territories referred to under Article 77(c) of the Charter should place under trusteeship such of those territories as are not to be given immediate self-government."[26] Dulles led the opposition to this resolution both in the Fourth Committee[27] and at the plenary session. In the plenary session, he reaffirmed his delegation's commitment to decolonization and belief in the trusteeship system, but he felt it necessary to oppose the Indian Resolution for several reasons. First, he believed that a move to call upon all administering states to place their colonies under the Trusteeship Council would be "a vote of non-confidence in the operation of Chapter XI of the Charter."[28] In fact, he argued, the Chapter XI provisions of the charter had been successful. He explained that "[i]t is pursuant to the provisions of this Chapter, since it came into force, that approximately five hundred million non-self-governing people have attained, or are at the present time, we believe, on the verge of attaining, independence."[29] Dulles recognized that this movement to independence was not suddenly caused by the inclusion of Chapter XI in the charter, explaining that "[i]t is very rare indeed that a declaration like Chapter XI . . . or any declaration of independence, accomplishes great deeds merely by words."[30] Normally, "[t]he function of words is primarily to crystallize a great sentiment which already prevails, and, by its crystallization and implementation, to make it more effective."[31] This, according to Dulles, was what Chapter XI did; it crystallized existing decolonization sentiment and then facilitated the means for its realization.[32] It would thus be wrong to express a lack of confidence in this system.

A second reason that Dulles opposed the Indian resolution was that the U.S. delegation believed it was "quite preposterous really for this General Assembly to adopt a resolution saying that the Trusteeship System is, as originally proposed and adopted, the surest and quickest means of enabling the people of dependent territories to secure self-government or independence."[33] While the United States believed that the trusteeship system was "a good method of securing independence,"[34] it could not call it the "surest and quickest"; the system had yet to be tested. Additionally, Dulles explained, a U.S. vote in favor of the resolution would imply that Alaska and Hawaii would have to "pass through trusteeship," a process that would be opposed by the inhabitants. If a provision were to be established, Dulles concluded, there should be two resolutions: one calling on states to act under Chapter XI; the other dealing with the second category (enemy states' colonies) of the trusteeship system.

The Italian Colonies

One of the last important colonial issues with which Dulles was involved was the plight of the former Italian colonies. According to the Italian Peace Treaty, the General Assembly was left to determine the disposition of these territories,[35] giving the assembly what Dulles called "an authority without precedent in the history of the United Nations."[36]   In 1948 and 1949, he served as the major United States spokesman on these territories, and, although he was not participating in the fall of 1949 when the issues were resolved, he later explained that "the basic work had been done when I was in charge of the matter."[37]   The solution the United States and its allies proposed provided "that Libya be granted independence in ten years, but that in the interim its three principal constituent parts be administered by Great Britain, France, and Italy; that a portion of Eritrea be absorbed by Ethiopia and the remainder by the Anglo-Egyptian Sudan; and that Somaliland be placed under Italian trusteeship."[38]

Although Dulles supported this proposal, according to Ronald Pruessen, "[h]e did fret somewhat about the blatant continuation of a quasi-imperialistic European presence in Northern Africa, particularly an Italian presence so soon after World War II."[39]   Pruessen explains what Dulles told the French Foreign Minister:

The Italian colonies must be looked on as part of the general problem of Europe and Africa.   Tensions between the East and West and the iron curtain have largely interrupted East-West developments and require us to think in terms of North-South, i.e., Western Europe and Africa.   There are in Africa vast resources which can be developed to the natural advantage of Africa and West Europe and more than make good the loss of access to the natural resources of eastern Europe and the loss of Asiatic colonies.   This North-South development, however, requires friendly collaboration between the native peoples and the peoples of Europe. . . . If the Italian colonies were dealt with in a manner which excited a Moslem Holy War or a race war of black against white, then the foundation for North-South development would disappear.[40]

Here, Dulles's main concern for promoting good relations with Africa was to maintain access to the resources of the colonies.[41] But in light of his other statements on the subject, it seems impossible to suggest that access to resources was his only desire or that he was not genuinely concerned about the interests of subject peoples.

In general, several conclusions can be drawn from Dulles's work on the trusteeship and colonial issues. First, he continued to be a strong supporter of self-government for colonies, reaffirming essentially the position he had taken with the Commission on a Just and Durable Peace. Second, however, he realized that the United States as an "anti-colonial" power had to tread very delicately in order not to alienate its allies, hence, much of the hard negotiations on colonial matters had to go on in private, rather than in the committee or assembly room. Third, in his work on colonial issues, Dulles began to be confronted with Soviet intransigence and their use of the United Nations for propaganda purposes. As noted earlier, he believed they wished to appear to be the "true" spokesman for the subject people at the expense of the West. This Soviet behavior he was to encounter in other areas of the United Nations, and it, no doubt, had a great influence on the development of his later thought on the USSR.

THE INTERIM COMMITTEE

As the first session of the General Assembly progressed, Soviet-United States disagreement also became apparent on issues relating to peace and security. Unable to accept the U.S. position on matters such as Korea and Austria, the Soviet Union frequently made use of the veto to block Security Council action. In an effort to respond to this "problem" and the problem of extremely short work sessions of the General Assembly, the United States, with Dulles as its spokesman, proposed the creation of a new body, an Interim Committee. As Dulles later explained, "[i]n view of the paralyzing effect of the veto on the Security Council and the fact that the Assembly was normally in session only about two and a half months of the year, it seemed important to have available a body representing all of the members of the United Nations, which could exert an influence at least of a deterrent character throughout the year, free of veto."[42] The Interim Committee, Dulles hoped, could also serve to reinvigorate "[p]ublic opinion in [the United States], which is crying for some revitalization of the United Nations."[43]

In a rough draft of a speech dated October 9, 1947, Dulles enumerated four functions for the Interim Committee. First, the committee would have "preparatory functions."[44] It would "consider matters in relation to the maintenance of international peace and security and friendly relations among nations which may be listed with the Secretary General for inclusion on the agenda at the next regular session."[45]   If necessary, it "would consider the subject, investigate the facts, and make its views available to the next session of the Assembly."[46] The committee could even request that a special session of the General Assembly be called if it believed that the issue was "urgent."[47]   Second, the Interim Committee would have "'follow-through' functions."[48]   He explained that "if this present session of the General Assembly makes recommendations in relation to international peace and security and friendly relations which call for continuing attention, the General Assembly might in particular cases assign that responsibility to the Interim Committee."[49]   Third, the committee would be able "to get underway the work necessary to enable the General Assembly to make recommendations regarding the general principles of cooperation in the maintenance of international peace, as contemplated by Article 11(1) of the Charter, and initiate studies for the purpose of promoting international cooperation in the political field."[50]   Fourth, since the Interim Committee was only to be established on a trial basis, it would have the task of determining whether such a committee should be permanently established.[51]

Soon after the United States proposal was presented to the First Committee, a subcommittee was established to discuss the matter.   On November 6, 1947, the full committee approved a resolution to set up the Interim Committee and, despite strong Soviet Bloc opposition, the General Assembly adopted the resolution on November 13.[52]

The most interesting aspect of Dulles's involvement with the Interim Committee is what it revealed about his approach to the Soviet Union and the role he felt the Soviets played in the U.N. These views can be seen both in his discussions within the U.S. delegation, in meetings with other delegates and in his debates in the First Committee and Plenary Sessions.

It was clear that a major reason for the Interim Committee was to deal with the problem of a Security Council blocked by the Soviet veto. But in a meeting with the British Delegation, Dulles did not see the Interim Committee as a simple way to get around the Soviet-blocked council or as a competitor for the Security Council. He explained that "while there might be some degree of competition between the two bodies he thought it might not extend beyond the stage of healthy competition."[53]   He felt that "on the contrary the Security Council would be strengthened as we could at least hope that the existence of this Assembly body might result in more efficient operations of the Security Council (the Soviet attitude in the Security Council might be more reasonable)."[54]

But while Dulles denied that the United States was trying to "use the United Nations as an instrument of American foreign policy against the Soviet Union,"[55] he seemed to have become increasingly convinced that the Soviets posed a special threat that had to be countered. In a conversation with Dr. Aranha of the Brazilian

Delegation, ostensibly on the Interim Committee, Dulles explained broader concerns about the USSR:

> The problem as I expressed it to Dr. Aranha is simply the matter of how far the Soviet Union can spread its system of despotism and the police state throughout Europe and perhaps the rest of the world. . . . I stated that we had no desire to force freedom upon countries who do not themselves desire it, and that we are perfectly able to take care of ourselves, if the rest of the world prefers to get along without us. We are not like the Russians who are endeavoring to impose a police state upon others. We are only acting through the Charter in the thought that the Members of the United Nations are desirous of living a life of their own. The notion that we are using the United Nations as an instrument of our national policy is totally wrong and misleading.[56]

It was clear, however, that Dulles had become much more overtly critical of the Soviets.

Despite these feelings, Dulles did not want to go too far in anti-Soviet actions. During the preliminary discussions of the Interim Committee, the United States was considering a proposal to investigate the problems of the veto when Dulles cautioned "that it is most important not to give the Soviets any decent excuse to withdraw from the United Nations."[57] In light of some opposition, both Soviet and ally, he expressed fears that if the Interim Committee were to "function for the purpose of crystallizing world public opinion through discussions like the General Assembly itself,"[58] problems would arise. He explained that there would be political objections "out of fear for the discussions in the Committee will accentuate the U.S.-U.S.S.R. conflict and perpetuate the wrangling and the name calling."[59] Consequently, Dulles "suggested a test which the Interim Committee might follow in selecting matters for its agenda: The Committee should consider only major matters with which the General Assembly could not adequately deal without prior preparation through study and investigation, such as the Korean and Palestinian question."[60] He also expressed general concern about other tasks that the committee had originally been seen as performing.[61]

When Dulles actually presented this issue to the First Committee and the Plenary Session of the General Assembly, he had to respond directly to Soviet bloc criticisms. With two formidable opponents, Andrei Vyshinsky and Andrei Gromyko, Dulles dealt with both the legal and policy arguments raised by opponents to the Interim Committee.[62] The key policy objection, as Dulles saw it, was the fear that the Interim Committee would subvert the concept of great power unanimity by throwing issues relating to peace and security into the hands of a General Assembly committee in which the U.S. enjoyed an "automatic majority." He explained that "[t]he USSR delegation suggests that one or two nations, by a mixture of coercion and inducement, always control a majority of votes in the General Assembly, and that therefore the voting results are, as they say, mechanical and do not reflect honest and independent judgment."[63] This was, however, an inaccurate assessment. Although there seemed to be mechanical voting "in at least one bloc [i.e., the Soviet],"[64] "[i]n general, . . . the record of the General Assembly, during the sessions it has so far held, shows little sign of mechanical voting."[65] In fact, Dulles argued, the proposal for creation of the Interim Committee demonstrated how there was no automatic action. It too went through many changes before emerging from subcommittee.[66] Furthermore, the Soviets themselves had indicated that there could be no mechanical majority; Dulles explained, "[i]n the very speech in which the theory of mechanical majorities was expounded, it was also said that the United States apparently did not dare to submit the Marshall Plan for consideration of the Organization of the United Nations."[67] But "[i]f the United States did not dare to submit a plan to the General Assembly because it feared that body's moral judgment, what greater testimony could there be to the independent moral judgment and authority of this General Assembly."[68] Conceivably, the prerogatives of the assembly could be abused in the future but, said Dulles, "I believe we can trust the General Assembly itself to be vigilant in protecting its own dignity and to avoid a cheapening of its verdicts."[69]

In sum, several observations can be made about Dulles's activities with the Interim Committee proposal. First, his actions here, like those relating to the Trusteeship Council, demonstrated that he was becoming troubled by apparent Soviet intransigence in the United Nations.[70] His comments to Dr. Aranha illustrated his harsh feelings about the USSR. Second, despite his concern, he did not want the Soviets to withdraw from the organization. He even seemed to express hopes that the Soviets, who vowed not to participate in the Interim Committee, might eventually join the Committee.[71] Third, Dulles seemed to be somewhat oblivious to the true advantage the United States enjoyed at the United Nations in the late 1940s. Certainly, there was haggling over specifics, but nevertheless, the United States did practically have an "automatic majority."

HUMAN RIGHTS

During his work with the Commission on a Just and Durable Peace, Dulles had been a strong advocate of the promotion of human rights by the new international organization. After the United Nations came into being, he initially advocated the formulation of a universal bill of rights. In a summary of a statement he delivered in 1946, he explained that he felt the Human Rights Commission should "develop a uniform bill of rights which will come into operation as rapidly as possible in all parts of the world."[72]

As problems with the Soviet Union became apparent, Dulles seemed to have suggested that human rights might even be an appropriate "strategic rallying point."[73] In what appears to have been a Dulles memorandum of 1947, he explained that "[t]he present crucial international issue is the issue of the free society against the police state."[74] Accordingly, "[t]he United States should take the lead in placing that issue emphatically in the foreground and basing it on moral principle. In this way world public opinion might be mobilized more effectively than could result from a mere confrontation of American and Soviet power."[75] Specifically, the free world could be united against Soviet oppression through the common activity of drafting an international bill of human rights. Dulles explained,

> The process of making the concept of human rights and fundamental freedoms explicit in an International Bill provides a common task which can unite the free forces of the world, in whatever land they may be. It can be made a dramatic focus of man's world wide struggle for freedom, and can stand as a symbol of hope for dependent peoples as well as for men and women whose rights are denied by totalitarian governments. That process can spell out the moral principle on which the free societies can take their common stand.[76]

From this memorandum, it appears that Dulles wanted to use the human rights document as a weapon for the United States and its allies against the Soviets. The unification on moral issues, such as human rights, took on a purpose akin to collective security. He explained that "[t]he U.S.S.R. seems clearly bent upon extending the police state system and is employing any methods, short of war, to accomplish its ends."[77] The problem was that "Russia might miscalculate how far she can go" and therein "lies a primary danger of war."[78] But, "[t]he chance of that miscalculation can be minimized if a sufficiently powerful segment of the world makes convincing its unyielding commitment to the principle of a free society."[79] Although Dulles would "not accept as a foregone conclusion that such an emphasis on moral principle will further divide the world into two major spheres," even if he were mistaken, "this division will come at a point which will commend itself to men of good will everywhere."[80] He explained that "we can reasonably hope that Russia will respect a strong moral front, established in good faith and not merely as an expedient, and may as a result increase her cooperation."[81] Essentially, what Dulles was saying was that if through aggressive American leadership[82] the democracies could stand firm in their dedication to human rights by drafting a human rights document, the

Soviets could become convinced of Western solidarity and learn not to underestimate Western commitment to protect the free world. They would thus be deterred from aggression by moral force.

In these comments, however, Dulles was implicitly acknowledging that this international bill of rights could not be a truly *universal* document. It was being drafted not to express the common expectations of all nations on human rights, a prerequisite to law that Dulles recognized, but rather as an expression of the Western conception of human rights, a conception that could unite the West *against* the East. As time passed, Dulles explicitly acknowledged the impossibility of a universal *legal* document on human rights. In a letter to Eleanor Roosevelt, dated June 10, 1948, he explained that:

> I believe that it is illusory to expect any universal covenant which will really be both adequate and effective. There are such fundamental philosophic and religious differences between the Member States with respect to the nature of man that any covenant that could be universally adopted would be meagre or illusory and probably it would depend on a use of words which had a double meaning.[83]

Dulles still believed that the General Assembly should move forward to adopt a nonbinding declaration, but seemed convinced that covenants on human rights would only be successful among smaller groups of states. He explained:

> I think that the Assembly might as well grapple with the reality of the problem and recognize that just as less than universal pacts may be necessary under Article 51 to develop national security on a less than universal basis, so under Article 56, in order to develop observance of human rights and respect for human freedoms, it may be useful to supplement what can be done universally by what, at the present time, can only be done on a less than universal basis.[84]

Here Dulles was not concerned about using human rights documents as an instrument against the Soviets, but rather about establishing whatever level of international human rights law was possible, given the conditions of the time.

As the Universal Declaration on Human Rights developed, it began to resemble the union of numerous "sets" of human rights definitions rather than their intersection.[85] Dulles, in keeping with his earlier feelings, was concerned that the various "rights" mentioned in document would be interpreted as "legal rights." For instance, one provision stated that "'everyone has the right of access to public employment.'"[86] In the United States, he argued, communists did not have access to public employment. This was no major problem, however, since the declaration did not establish a *legal* obligation. But it needed to be explained "that the Declaration is a general statement of principle and aspiration and not a legal document, standing in relation to a future covenant of human rights, in the same way that the American Declaration of Independence was related to the Bill of Rights."[87]

Nevertheless, though he wished to emphasize the nonbinding nature of the declaration, Dulles still supported its formulation. He fought against efforts to delay the adoption of the declaration,[88] and once it was adopted, he publicly praised the instrument. In a speech delivered over the NBC radio network on December 22, 1948, Dulles hailed the declaration as "concrete action" of "first importance."[89] He compared its potential impact with the influence of the French Declaration on the Rights of Man, which "caught the imagination of peoples throughout much of the world [with its] repercussions . . . [that] shook many dictators off their thrones."[90] The Declaration further represented a dynamic aspect of international organization that could functionally promote peace. Echoing previous statements, he explained that "[p]eace, if it is to last, must be used as an opportunity for peacefully changing conditions so as to give human beings fuller and more equal opportunity."[91] He continued to explain that "[t]he United Nations Assembly has established a universal human goal toward which the nations and the peoples can strive together in fellowship. If they respond, the United Nations will have set in motion forces that, by working for human liberty and justice, work also for peace."[92]

Two conclusions can be drawn from Dulles's views on human rights. First, he remained committed to U.N. action in human rights, believing that cooperation on human rights could eventually promote peace. Second, however, Dulles began to realize that his initial expectations about human rights, however modest, were still too high. He had begun to believe that the United Nations was not yet able to reach agreement on a universally acceptable human rights covenant, consequently only less than universal legal instruments could be possible at the time. Indeed, this realization seemed to parallel Dulles's view about other aspects of the United Nations. As he saw the Security Council blocked by the Soviet veto in a way he had not anticipated, he had begun to doubt that collective security, even in a limited sense, was possible.

THE DEVELOPMENT OF INTERNATIONAL LAW

Another area of concern for Dulles during this period of his life was the development of international law. In general, his views on this subject remained consistent with those held during the early phase of his thought. First, he continued to believe that the international legal system was inadequate. As noted earlier, he attributed almost no legal significance to the Charter provisions on the use of force. While at the United Nations, he initially adhered to this view. In a speech of November 17, 1947, for instance, he explained that one reason the veto was necessary was the fact that there was no real law to guide the Security Council. He contended that "[t]oday international law is not sufficiently adequate or sufficiently precise to provide a clear answer to many problems that may confront the Security Council."[93] Specifically, Chapter VII should be subject to the veto because, among other reasons, the council's "power of action is so vast, [and] so unrelated to any defined law."[94]   Once again, he seemed to reject the notion that Article 2(4) established at least some "international law" on the use of force. Nonetheless, his views were to change somewhat.

Second, and as a corollary of his belief in the inadequacy of international law, Dulles continued to believe that international law should be developed. He emphasized, once again, that this could be done with Security Council precedents and General Assembly actions, both through informal customs and through the development of international legal instruments. He also echoed his belief that international law should be developed so that it could apply to individuals as well as states. In a summary of a 1946 statement, he argued that "we should seek, as far as possible, that the international law developed should be applicable to individuals."[95]   Three years later, he explained his belief that one of the major problems of the Versailles settlement was that it applied to states and not individuals. He argued that

> It can, I think, be said that the revival of Germany's military power and their ability to wage World War II came about wholly because the authors of the Treaty of Versailles ignored the reasoning of the Federalist Papers, namely, that laws which operate only upon states in their corporate capacity have no effective sanction except war, and war is a sanction which is not often invoked by those who seek, through law, to prevent war.[96]

Consequently, he explained that earlier, during a 1947 discussion of German disarmament, he had "urged that, in light of past experience, any future prohibitions should operate not merely on the German state, but on German individuals, and that the magnitude of the penalty should be reasonably related to the magnitude of the offense."[97]

Dulles realized that enacting this type of international law would not be easy. When the United Nations was considering a draft resolution on the codification of international law that would have called for an International Criminal Code, he worried about how these principles could be applied to individuals. In the case of the United States, argued Dulles, even if an international criminal code were created it could be easily overridden by subsequent statute: "[h]e pointed out . . . that in the United States a legislative act which is more recent than an international act supersedes the international act."[98]   He went on to explain "that the individual was in a dilemma whether he owed allegiance to the international criminal code or to the national law. He recalled that he had advocated an international law that operated on individuals as well as on states. However, there was still a need to find out how to make the international law superior to national law, especially since the Constitution provided that the laws of Congress were the supreme law of the land."[99]

Over the course of the first years of the United Nations, Dulles did recognize that several positive steps were being taken to promote the development of international law.   On November 17, 1947, he explained that the General Assembly "was trying to make good the present inadequacy and indefiniteness of international law."[100]   In 1946, "the Assembly set up a Committee to study how best to carry out that [Charter] mandate and this present [1947] Assembly presumably will get under way the actual work of developing and codifying international law."[101]   He further emphasized that "the Assembly charged the new Interim Committee to study how to develop 'the general principles of cooperation in the maintenance of international peace and security' (Article 11(1)) and how to promote 'international cooperation in the political field' (Article 13(1)(a))."[102]   He also acknowledged that "efforts are being made to develop agreed rules of conduct and standards in certain special fields.   This is one of the tasks of the Atomic Energy Commission and additional rules may come out of the work of the Commission on Conventional Armaments."[103]

Despite these advances, Dulles remained troubled about the progress toward the development of international law.   He was also "greatly disappointed" when the American Bar Association chose to oppose the adoption of the Convention on the Prevention and Punishment of the Crime of Genocide.   In a statement released September 9, 1949, he felt it was "hard to see how a beginning can ever be made in developing international law if the nations are not willing to ban effectively the crime of genocide -- the killing of masses of human beings merely because of their race or religion."[104]   He hoped the United States would not follow the lead of the ABA; "[i]t is not often that the United Nations General Assembly, representing virtually all of the nations and people of the world can come to a unanimous agreement, and it would be lamentable if the United States, which has always been at the forefront in developing international law, should now take the lead in repudiating this first great Convention on human rights."[105]

Of course, Dulles did not have utopian hopes for establishing a regime of international law.   In an article in which he responded to those who wanted "'world government'" "to enact so-called world laws,"[106] Dulles stated that there was "no illusion greater than that results can be reached merely by setting up a body to pass laws and giving it a police force."[107]   Reiterating his earlier views, he explained that "[u]nless laws reflect the opinion of the community to which they apply, so that they are voluntarily accepted by the great majority, they are either disregarded or become enforceable only by what in fact is war, whereby one part of the community attempts forcibly to impose its views on another part."[108]   His concerns here were not so much with the problems that United Nations development of international law presented, but rather with the problems of developing international law through a "world federation."[109]   He did, however, recognize the problems that competing philosophical frameworks created for the United Nations. With both human rights, and, as will be seen, collective security, Dulles had come to believe that true universalism was not yet possible, as there was not yet an underlying common moral community to support a fully developed legal system.

COMMUNIST AGGRESSION

As noted previously, during the first sessions of the United Nations, Dulles was exposed to Soviet intransigence on numerous issues and this, no doubt, influenced his views on the Soviet Union. Simultaneously, however, he began to see Soviet and Soviet bloc aggression in various parts of the world.   Much of this aggression was not the traditional variety, where troops of one state overtly attacked another, but rather indirect aggression, where a state threatens another subversively by supporting indigenous rebels. This section will examine two cases of Soviet-backed aggression with which Dulles was involved: Greece and Korea.

Greece

In 1946, Greece became increasingly convinced that Yugoslavia, Albania, and Bulgaria were supporting Greek communists in their effort to overthrow the Greek government.   At that time, the Greek government took the matter to the Security Council, and a majority "concluded that there existed a threat to the peace under Chapter VII of the Charter and had proposed that Greece's northern neighbors should be required to desist from their illegal operations."[110]   But "action along those lines had . . . been prevented by the use of the veto by the Union of Soviet Socialist Republic."[111]   Consequently, in 1947, the problem was taken to the General Assembly and a Special Committee was established to investigate these allegations of unlawful use of force against Greece. In addition, the "Assembly . . . also called upon Greece and its northern neighbors to co-operate in removing the threat to the peace."[112]   By March of 1947, Greece had asked the United States for unilateral assistance.   On March 12, President Truman pledged to aid Greece (and Turkey), explaining that the United States could "not allow changes in the status quo in violation of the Charter of the United Nations by such methods as coercion, or by such subterfuges as political infiltration."[113]

In the fall of 1948, the Special Committee presented its report to the First Committee. According to Dulles, the Special Committee concluded that "the co-operation which had been called for by the General Assembly, did not exist and that the efforts to assist the communist attempt to overthrow the Government were being continued by Greece's northern neighbours, which had persistently refused to co-operate in the United Nations' effort to remove the threats to Greek territorial integrity."[114] While the First Committee was considering measures to recommend to the General Assembly, Dulles made a speech strongly condemning Soviet sponsored activities generally. He explained that "[w]herever one looks, whether it be to Europe, Africa, Asia or the Americas, there is apparent the same pattern of effort, namely the incitement, from without, of coercion, fear and violence within to achieve international political objectives."[115] He continued to explain that "[t]here is nothing surprising about this uniformity, for it reflects what communists throughout the world have been consistently taught and what they are being taught today."[116] Specifically, "[t]he Soviet, they are told, will not be safe until the non-communists nations have been so reduced in strength and numbers that communist influence is dominant throughout the world, and that, in such efforts, the Soviet Communist Party is the 'vanguard,' the 'shock-brigade of the world proletariat.' Is is furthermore taught that this result cannot be achieved by peaceful reform but only by methods of revolution."[117] While states have the right to the particular type of government they want, "the Charter does not countenance using *violence* to achieve international ends."[118] He explained that "Article 2(4) binds all the Members broadly to 'refrain in their international relations from the threat or use of force.'"[119] Only peaceful change was permitted, and hence "[t]here is . . . a basic contradiction between the Charter theory of *peaceful* change, by evolution, and the communist doctrine of *violent* change, by revolution."[120] Thus, Dulles explained, "[s]o long as Soviet communism does preach and practice revolution as a means to destroy the social order elsewhere and to achieve world-wide political ambitions, many are bound to wonder whether the communist governments signed the United Nations Charter with integrity of purpose."[121]

Despite the fact that the Security Council was blocked by the Soviet veto, Dulles believed that hope still lay in the General Assembly. He explained that "[t]he Assembly can expose the facts and by so doing can build up a moral judgment so widespread and so weighty that no nation will ignore it. Marshal Stalin said of the League of Nations that 'despite its weakness the League might nevertheless serve as a place where aggressors can be exposed.'"[122] Continued Dulles, "[h]e put his finger on a great power--the power of exposure. It does not work with precision or with immediacy, but it is, in the long run, a power to which all are sensitive for history has proved that those who flout it pay, some day, a heavy penalty."[123] Even though, argued Dulles, the General Assembly resolution calling "upon Albania, Bulgaria, and Yugoslavia 'to do nothing which could furnish aid and assistance' to the Greek guerrillas," was not obeyed, the General Assembly had not failed.[124]   He explained that the assembly had not,

> to be sure, achieved immediate obedience to its will. But the General Assembly was never given authority to command obedience. It depends primarily on the power of public opinion and to build that up takes time, patience and persistence. Already, however, the General Assembly has had an influence. It has had an influence in promoting aid to Greece. It has had an influence even along the northern frontier. The representative of my Government who served on the Special Committee believes, and I understand others believe, that if it had not been for the presence of the Special Committee in Greece, the military aid given by the northern neighbors of Greece would have reached far greater proportions than, in fact, had been the case. There can, I think, be no doubt that the northern neighbors of Greece have, in fact, been restrained by the presence of the Committee and its power of exposure at this "town meeting of the world."[125]

Hence, the moral authority of the General Assembly had at least helped prevent the conflict from expanding. In short, concluded Dulles, the situation in Greece was bad, but it was "not *fatally* bad, for Greece survives."[126] And "Greece not only survives but, thanks to its own efforts and those of the United Nations and of other friendly states, Greece is steadily making progress in the rehabilitation of the country and in making good the terrific losses which Greece suffered when she resisted Nazi aggression and became its victim."[127] He thus favored a resolution calling for the continued work of the Special Committee and opposing aid to the Greek rebels. This course, he felt, "assures a continuing exposure which will make it certain that, if there is continued violation of the Charter, world opinion will grow steadily more condemnatory, more resolute and more potent to restrain aggression."[128] (Dulles echoed this view in a subsequent speech before a Plenary Session of the General Assembly on November 27, 1948.)[129]

Dulles's comments on Greece reveal several interesting things. First, they reflect his faith in the ability of the General Assembly to promote change by influencing public opinion. Dulles had always been skeptical about the possibility of the success of the Security Council, and had tended to emphasize the potential of the assembly instead. Second, his statements on Greece tended to contradict some of his previous comments about the inadequacy of the international law regarding the use of force. In this connection, he had indicated that there was little in the way of authoritative norms that could guide the Security Council in making decisions under Chapter VII of the Charter. Nevertheless, he now seemed to be rather clear about the legal obligation involved in Article 2(4). It is possible that this inclusion of Article 2(4) was due to an instruction he had received, but, on the other hand, it is also possible that he was beginning to understand the normative significance of the prohibition on the unilateral use of force, or, at least, to recognize its political utility. Third, Dulles's comments about Greece once again reveal a growing concern over Soviet expansionism and the role that communist ideology played in Soviet foreign policy.

Korea and the "Uniting for Peace" Resolution

Following the surrender of Japan, the Korean peninsula had been occupied by Soviet troops to the north of the 38th parallel and United States troops to the south. Since 1947, the United States had been urging the United Nations to develop a program for Korean independence. At this time, Dulles became the chief spokesman for the United States on this issue. He later explained the activities that he helped coordinate in the early stages of the Korean problem:

Our military people wanted to get our army out of Korea, which was felt to involve an over-extended position. We wanted, however, contemporaneously to get the Soviet troops out of North Korea and actually to set up an independent state under U.N. sponsorship which the Soviet Union could not destroy without open attack upon a creation of the United Nations. So we worked out a program for simultaneous withdrawal of troops, the holding of supervised elections, and ultimate recognition of the Government by the U.N.[130]

Unfortunately, this proposal was not well received by the USSR. Explained Dulles,

The Soviet Union refused to allow the Commission to operate in North Korea, but we went ahead in South Korea, which represents two-thirds of the people, and the result has been that the occupying forces have, in fact, been withdrawn from all Korea and a Government set up in South Korea in pursuance of U.N.-supervised elections, which has a fair chance of survival with some temporary economic aid from the U.S., and assuming that there is not open attack upon it with Soviet aid.[131]

Dulles wrote these words in December of 1949; within six months, an "open attack" had indeed occurred.

On June 15th, 1950, North Korean troops, with Soviet support, crossed the 38th parallel. The issue was taken to the Security Council immediately. The Soviets at the time were boycotting the proceedings of the Council in protest of the seating of the Nationalist Chinese representative on the Council. In consequence, on June 27, the council was able to adopt a resolution recommending that "the Members of the United Nations furnish such assistance to the Republic of Korea [South Korea] as may be necessary to repel the armed attack and to restore international peace and security."[132] Pursuant to this resolution, a United Nations force, under the coordination of the United States, was established and sent to Korea. Soon, however, the Soviets returned to the Security Council and further action on the issue was blocked by their veto.

In light of the inability of the Security Council to initiate any further action in Korea, the United States Delegation began formulating a resolution to grant the General Assembly the right to *recommend* collective action. As various proposals were being drawn up, Dulles was given the task of consulting with other delegations in an effort to develop an acceptable draft to present to the First Committee.

In these consultations, Dulles had to deal with numerous legal and political concerns about what became known as the "Uniting for Peace" Resolution. On the legal side, Dulles had to assure delegates that the proposed resolution did not violate the charter. For instance, French representative Jean Chauvel was troubled "as to whether the General Assembly could constitutionally recommend to the Members of the United Nations the designation of armed forces available for collective use, and could thereafter recommend collective use if the Security Council failed to act to meet aggression."[133] His concern seemed to be based on provisions in the charter providing that any questions relating to peace and security "on which action is necessary shall be referred to the Security Council by the General Assembly either before or after discussion."[134] In response to this concern, Dulles explained that "this provision of Article 11(2) does not in any way impair the broad authority of the General Assembly to discuss and make recommendations."[135] He argued that "[t]he only limitation is, we think, contained in Article 12(1), which says that 'While the Security Council is exercising in respect of any dispute or situation the functions assigned to it in the present Charter, the General Assembly shall not make any recommendation with regard to that dispute or situation unless the Security Council so requests.'"[136] Maintaining military units available for the use of the assembly was not, argued Dulles, a question requiring Security Council action. Furthermore, the General Assembly would not be violating Article 12(1) by dealing with a matter before the Security Council since "the Security Council would have had its opportunity and would have failed to act."[137]   In addition, the assembly would not be taking "action," a function reserved for the Security Council, since any resolution that it adopted in a particular case would be only a *recommendation.* Concluded Dulles,

> It would, I suppose, hardly be contended that the provisions of the Charter prevent the Members from acting collectively against aggression except with the approval of the Security Council, where the veto exists. If that were so, the Charter would not be a bulwark, but a trap tying the hands of the law-abiding nations which would serve the purpose of any Great Power aggressor. Surely if the Members want to, they can create military units available for collective defense and if they want to, they can put those units into action. Article 51 makes this entirely clear. We feel that the Charter enables them to use the General Assembly as the place for working out this voluntary system to carry forward the fundamental objectives of the Charter. This would be based on recommendation only. To get this result, the Members do not have to go outside the framework of the United Nations. The Charter is, happily, a flexible instrument and responsive to growing needs.[138]

For Dulles, the charter was not an impediment to voluntary General Assembly measures directed against an aggressor.

Dulles also had to deal with political objections to the "Uniting for Peace" Resolution. One representative of the Indian delegation told Dulles that India was worried about "the possibility that it [the "Uniting for Peace" Resolution] would be regarded by the Russians as an effort toward alliance against them and might cause them to leave the United Nations."[139] Echoing previous statements, Dulles "made it clear . . . that it was not the purpose or intent of the United States to drive the Russians out of the United Nations."[140] He explained "that in his opinion although it was impossible to predict Russian action, the taking of this step by the Assembly would not force the Russians out nor be used as a pretext by them to leave the United Nations unless they had decided for other reasons to do so."[141]

By October 3, several states had consented to cosponsor the "Uniting for Peace" Resolution,[142] and Dulles was given the task of shepherding it through the First Committee and the Plenary Sessions. Several interesting themes, very similar to those present in his discussions of the Greek issue, ran through his comments on the resolution. First, he demonstrated a very strong desire for the establishment of some type of effective collective security system. In a speech before the First Committee, he recognized that the initial Security Council action in Korea was possible only by happenstance. He explained:

It was doubtful, firstly, whether the Security Council would have acted if at the decisive moment, for extraneous reasons, one of the permanent members had not been absent; secondly, whether, if the General Assembly had not sent a commission to Korea three years ago, the Council would have had the information needed to justify prompt and decisive action; thirdly, whether United Nations forces could have saved the Republic of Korea if the United States had not stationed troops in Japan five years ago to enforce compliance with the terms of armistice; lastly, whether the aggressor would have failed in Korea except for what amounted to, from his standpoint, extraordinarily bad fortune.[143]

In short, the modified system of collective security that existed at the time was not reliable, and consequently, "[i]f potential aggressors were to be deprived of all hope of success, a reliable system would have to be created instead of matters being left to chance."[144]

The new system, Dulles seemed to suggest, would not be perfect, but would provide more of an assurance that aggression would be met by collective action. On October 13, he explained that "[t]he action which is contemplated is indeed momentous. It may determine, perhaps decisively and finally for our generation, whether or not the nations of the world really want an effective, as against a paper, system of collective resistance to aggression."[145] He continued: "[t]he goal is security based on collective strength and subject to law. The proposals before the Committee, while not perfect nevertheless do seem to the sponsors to be the closest thing we can realistically get at the present time to achieve the result of collective strength under law."[146]

A second theme present in many of Dulles's statements on this issue was a fear that without some form of collective security, the world would degenerate into the old alliance system. On October 13, he asked the First Committee: "What are the alternatives before us? If at this time of admitted peril the United Nations in this General Assembly hesitates to recommend ways whereby its Members can unite their strength to maintain international peace and security, what will happen?"[147] Answering his own question, he continued: "We all know what will happen. There will inevitably be increased dependence on military alliances, the strength of which will not be subject to law or to any such representative universal body as this United Nations."[148] If this were to occur, there could "be no comparable assurance that aggregations of power outside this Organization will be as responsive to the overall welfare of the peoples of the world as can be assured by this Organization."[149]

A third element in Dulles's discussion of this issue was a strong critique of the Soviet Union. Some of his earlier statements contained little in the way of criticism of the USSR, but the Soviet opposition to the resolution may have caused him to become more overtly critical of them. By November 1, 1950, Dulles was uncompromising in his comments about the Soviets. He explained that the dispute was not simply a national political conflict, contending that "[t]he United States has no national ambitions which clash at any point with the welfare of the Russian people, and between our nations there are no territorial disputes and no commercial disputes."[150] There was the problem of the unpaid lend-lease money, "but no one anywhere thinks that the United States will go to war to collect its debt."[151] The problem transcended these issues; simply put, "[t]he issue on which we part is the issue of whether freedom and diversity in the world shall be systematically stamped out and replaced by enforced conformity with the pattern of Soviet totalitarianism."[152] If a state chose to adopt a communist government, that was its decision. Unfortunately, "[n]o people yet have come under the yoke represented by the USSR brand of imperialist communism except by violent coercion."[153] In consequence, "[t]he United States will not be a party to that programme and thus, so long as it remains the programme of the Soviet Union, the possibilities of negotiation are limited."[154] (Dulles added, "I say 'limited,' which is not to say that the possibilities are non-existent."[155]) In light of these Soviet challenges to the independence of states, Dulles believed it was necessary "to create enough collective strength to protect the freedom of the people who want to be free."[156] Not surprisingly, Dulles's comments about the Soviet Union provoked a lively response from his Soviet counterparts.[157]

In sum, as Dulles had begun to deal with Soviet activities in Greece, Korea, and other areas, he became increasingly convinced of the need to expose Soviet actions and to take appropriate action. The action he had in mind was the formulation of a type of collective security system operating under the auspices of the General Assembly. This, he hoped, would show the commitment of the vast majority of the member states to stand up for freedom and independence, and to deter potential aggressors.

DULLES'S EVALUATION OF THE UNITED NATIONS

During the five years that Dulles worked at the United Nations as a member of the U.S. delegation, he had numerous occasions to provide an overall assessment of the functioning of the new world organization. In various speeches, articles, and letters, he drew several major conclusions about the United Nations. First, he believed that despite a pervasive disillusionment about the organization, the United Nations as a whole had been very successful. The disillusionment reflected greatly exaggerated expectations that had developed about the organization. People had expected, he argued, that the United Nations would bring about a world peace shortly after its establishment. When the Security Council soon became blocked by the veto and states were unable to set up the military contingents provided for under Article 43, people became convinced that the organization had failed.[158] In fact, he contended,

> the United States Delegation [at San Francisco] saw that it was unlikely that the United Nations could be a means for "enforcing peace" by using the military and economic might of the great powers to impose policy upon which they agreed. We saw that the only kind of power that could be counted on at this stage of world development was moral power and the power of world opinion.[159]

From this standpoint, the United Nations had indeed been successful. The General Assembly had been able to function reasonably well as a center for "exchanging and harmonizing attitudes."[160] As a "Town Meeting of the World," the United Nations brought together representatives from over fifty states to discuss common problems. This debate promoted international fellowship,[161] and helped formulate world public opinion. This public opinion, argued Dulles, "has tremendous influence upon the conduct of men and nations." He explained:

> Public opinion does not work with the precision and speed that may be desired and that may be desirable. Nevertheless, it is a powerful force. I have served at every regular session of the General Assembly, as well as at the San Francisco Conference of the United Nations and I have been increasingly impressed by the extent to which national policies are influenced by ability, or inability, to make a presentation which will win the support of public opinion. Every delegation at the United Nations tries to make a case which will win public support, and at times changes its position if it seems that the original position cannot win public support.[162]

As this unification of public opinion was taking place, a body of common moral beliefs was also developing. This common moral attitude, Dulles hoped, would lead to the development of a basis upon which an international legal structure could be built.[163]

Although the USSR was not as easily persuaded by public opinion, the General Assembly debate served two purposes in relationship to the Soviets. It allowed other delegations to "get an understanding of why Soviet leadership acts as it does";[164] that is, to understand the ideological motivation behind actions. In addition, the United Nations exposed Soviet hypocrisy. Dulles explained that

> as the Delegates at the United Nations have come together at their "town meeting" and have told each other of their

experiences, a single pattern has been exposed and it has been seen that the Government which has attempted by propaganda to get the reputation of being a "peace lover" was, in fact, the government that was teaching its followers throughout the world the use of violence and making plans for overthrowing the existing order by resort to political strikes, sabotage and civil war.[165]

In essence, the United Nations brought about a "solidarity" against these Soviet actions and "greatly decreased the possibility of Soviet domination by their preferred method of indirect aggression."[166]   As Dulles explained in his 1950 book, *War or Peace*, this exposure at the United Nations helped end an attitude of "neutrality" in the "East-West struggle," as states realized that the conflict was not merely a great power rivalry.[167]

Throughout his writings Dulles also mentioned a number of *specific* successes that had been achieved by the United Nations.   In *War or Peace*, for instance, he mentioned Iran, Greece, Israel, Indonesia, and the Italian Colonies as areas where the General Assembly had played an important role in helping to resolve conflict.[168] He also listed a number of other subjects that were being dealt with effectively by the United Nations, such as human rights, decolonization, and other activities of the Economic and Social Council.   In light of these accomplishments, and with the expectation of more successes, Dulles believed that the United States should continue participating in the United Nations and seek its continued improvement.

Of course, Dulles did recognize that the organization was still far from perfect, but, as a second conclusion, he realized that simple "mechanical solutions" to the problems of the United Nations were not possible at the time.   For example, he consistently opposed efforts to jettison the United Nations and establish a "more perfect" world government.   In 1947, he observed that "[i]t is certain that Soviet leaders would never accept a form of world government which vested the decisive power in a representative popular system.   Equally, it is certain that free societies would not subject themselves to a form of world government where the decisive power was vested in dictators."[169] Consequently, it was "impossible now to establish world government."[170]   He also opposed efforts to do away with the veto over substantive issues.   This would be impractical, he implied, since the USSR would oppose any effort to abolish the veto.[171]   Moreover, the United States needed the veto; the time could come when America would need it to protect its "interests."[172]

Instead of these simple "mechanical methods" of improving the organization, Dulles emphasized the need for gradual evolution. Echoing previous statements, he explained:

> The United Nations represents not a *final stage* in the development of world order, but only a primitive stage.

> Therefore its primary task is to create the conditions which
> will make possible a more highly developed organization.
> That requires developing a consensus of moral judgment
> and stimulating it into becoming an effective influence in
> the world community.[173]

Nevertheless, in *War or Peace* in 1950, Dulles did make a few
suggestions for minor revisions that he believed could be effected at
the time.   First, he believed that universality of the organization
could be greatly increased if both the United States and the Soviet
Union would cease opposing each other's recommendations for the
admission of new members.[174]   All governments that were in control
of a particular territory, regardless of whether they were considered
"good" or "bad," should be admitted.[175]   Second, he believed that if
the Assembly were to continue with the task of forming world public
opinion, the voting structure should more reasonably reflect the
political power of the world.   He explained that he "would not abolish
. . . an Assembly vote which, like that of our Senate, reflects the
sovereign equality of all nations and gives them all an equal vote."[176]
He did, however, believe that "there might be introduced, in addition,
a system of 'weighted' voting so that the result would indicate,
roughly, a verdict in terms also of ability to play a part in world
affairs."[177]   Thus, "it should be provided that decisions on important
matters would require a simple majority, rather than two-thirds,
under each of the two voting procedures."[178]   Third, Dulles believed
that even though the veto should not be eliminated for substantive
issues, it would be possible to reach an informal agreement that
matters such as the appointment of the secretary-general, the
admission of new members, and "preliminary steps" under Chapter VI
of the charter be interpreted as being "procedural," and thus exempt
from the veto.[179]   Fourth, Dulles felt that the duties of the Interim
Committee could be expanded so that the regular sessions of the
General Assembly would not be so long that major statesmen would
be unable to attend.[180]   Fifth, although Dulles had previously believed
the time was not yet ripe for the calling of a General Conference to
discussion revisions of the charter,[181] by 1950 he felt that such a
conference could be beneficial.   Although some of his suggested changes
could occur without such a conference, others would require charter
revision.[182]

    As can be seen from these first two conclusions, Dulles strove
to maintain and, albeit gradually, to improve the universal
organization.   It was vital, he believed, to have all states, even the
Soviet Union, subject to the moral authority of the United Nations.
But, as a third broad conclusion, he had come to believe that within
this universal framework it was possible to establish a series of less
than universal organizations.   These organizations would be collective
self-defense arrangements that were permitted under Article 51 of the
charter and would serve as a substitute for the collective security

system of Chapter VII. He explained that the desire for security "cannot now be satisfied on a universal basis. It can, however, be measurably satisfied through the organization for collective self-defense of groups of nations that have common views as regards the fundamental values that are worth defending."[183] He singled out the Rio Treaty, the Brussels Pact, and NATO as successful arrangements on such bases. These organizations could be closer-knit and could provide a greater opportunity for common defense and cooperation. (As noted earlier, Dulles also believed a regional approach to international human rights might prove beneficial. Not surprisingly, he remained a strong advocate of a Western European federation.[184])

NOTES

1. U.N. Charter, art. 79.

2. Ibid., arts. 83–85.

3. Ibid., art. 79.

4. "Minutes of Informal Mtg., U.S. Group on Trusteeship," Jan. 13, 1946, *1 Foreign Relations of the United States*, 1946, at 555 5. "Memorandum of Telephone Conversation, by the Director of the Office of Special Political Affairs," Nov. 1, 1946, *1 Foreign Relations of the United States*, 1946, 669.

6. 1 U.N. GAOR C.4, 16th Mtg., U.N. Doc. A/C.4/49 (1946), 76.

7. "Memorandum of Conversation [with Andrei Gromyko], by Mr. Charles W. Yost of the U.S. Delegation," Nov. 7, 1946, *1 Foreign Relations of the United States*, 1946, 677.

8. "Memorandum [of Conversation] by Mr. John Foster Dulles of the U.S. Delegation," Nov. 30, 1946, *1 Foreign Relations of the United States*, 1946, 690.

9. Ibid., 692.

10. Ibid.

11. Editorial Note, *1 Foreign Relations of the United States*, 1946, 708.

12. Dulles, "Rough Draft of a Speech before the Committee of Direction of the Commission on a Just and Durable Peace," Jan. 16, 1946, *JFD Papers*, at 1.

13. Ibid., 1–2.

14. Ibid.

15. Ibid.

16. "Memorandum by Mr. John Foster Dulles of the U.S. Delegation to the Secretary of State," Oct. 9, 1946, *1 Foreign Relations of the United States*, 1946, 637.

17. Ibid.

18. Ibid.

19. 1 U.N. GAOR (16th Mtg.), U.N. Doc. A/C. 4/49, 74–75; "Editorial Note," *1 Foreign Relations of the United States*, 1946, 675.

20. Dulles, "My Distinctive Contribution to U.S. Foreign Policy, as Manifested through the United Nations General Assembly . . .," Dec. 5, 1945, *JFD Papers*, 1.

21. Ibid., 1-2.

22. U.N. Charter, arts. 75-85.

23. "Editorial Note," *1 Foreign Relations of the United States*, 1946, 550.

24. Quoted in ibid.

25. "Memorandum of Telephone Conversation, by the Director of the Office of Special Political Affairs (Hiss)," *1 Foreign Relations of the United States*, 1946, 669.

26. "Memorandum by Eric Stein of the United States Delegation Staff of Advisors," Oct. 21, 1947, *1 Foreign Relations of the United States*, 1947, 296.

27. "Editorial Note," *1 Foreign Relations of the United States*, 1947, 296-298.

28. 1 U.N. GAOR (106th Plen. Mtg., 1947), 658.

29. Ibid.

30. Ibid.

31. Ibid., 658-59.

32. Ibid., 659.

33. Ibid., 661.

34. Ibid.

35. Pruessen, *John Foster Dulles*, 425.

36. 3(2) U.N. GAOR (238th mtg. 1st Comm.), 6.

37. Dulles, "My Distinctive Contribution to U.S. Foreign Policy," 5.

38. Pruessen, *John Foster Dulles*, 425 (footnote omitted).

39. Ibid.

40. Quoted in ibid.

41. Ibid.

42. Dulles, "My Distinctive Contribution to U.S. Foreign Policy," 3.

43. "Minutes of a Meeting with Members of the United Kingdom Delegation," Sept. 24, 1947, in *1 Foreign Relations of the United States*, 1947, 190.

44. Dulles, "Draft Speech," Oct. 9, 1947, *JFD Papers*, 10.

45. Ibid.

46. Ibid.

47. Ibid.

48. Ibid.

49. Ibid., 11.

50. Ibid.

51. Ibid. at 11-12.

52. "Editorial Note," *1 Foreign Relations of the United States*, 1947, 220; "United States Working Paper," Nov. 10, 1947, *1 Foreign Relations of the United States*, 1947, 222.

53. "Minutes of a Meeting with Members of the United Kingdom Delegation," Sept. 24, 1947, *1 Foreign Relations of the United States, 1947,* 191.

54. Ibid.

55. "Memorandum of Conversation, by Mr. John Foster Dulles," Oct. 2, 1947, *1 Foreign Relations of the United States, 1947,* 83.

56. Ibid.

57. "Minutes of a Meeting with Members of the United Kingdom Delegation," Oct. 7, 1947, *1 Foreign Relations of the United States, 1947,* 208.

58. "Memorandum by Mr. Eric Stein of the U.S. Delegation Staff of Advisors," Oct. 21, 1947, *1 Foreign Relations of the United States, 1947,* 212-213.

59. Ibid., 213.

60. Ibid.

61. Ibid., 213-214.

62. See, for example, 2 U.N. GAOR (78th mtg. 1st Comm.), 1947, 172-176; 2 U.N. GAOR (110th plen. mtg.), 1947, 755-781.

63. 2 U.N. GAOR (110th plen. mtg.), 760.

64. Ibid.

65. Ibid., 761.

66. Ibid.

67. Ibid.

68. Ibid.

69. Ibid., 762.

70. Ronald Pruessen emphasizes this development in Dulles's thought. See Pruessen, *John Foster Dulles,* 404-431.

71. "Editorial Note," *1 Foreign Relations of the United States, 1947,* 26; "Minutes of a Meeting with Members of the United Kingdom Delegation," Sept. 24, 1947, *1 Foreign Relations of the United States,* 192. Ironically, Dulles believed the committee could discuss the veto as one of its first issues. See "Memorandum of Conversation, by Mr. John Foster Dulles of the U.S. Delegation," Nov. 15, 1947, *1 Foreign Relations of the United States,* 1947, 224.

72. "Summary of Statement by John Foster Dulles to the Plenary Meeting of the Federal Council [of Churches]," undated (probably March 1946), *JFD Papers,* 7.

73. Dulles (?), "Memorandum: Human Rights as a Strategic Moral Rallying Point," 1947, *JFD Papers,* 1.

74. Ibid.

75. Ibid.

76. Ibid., 1-2.

77. Ibid., 2.

78. Ibid.

79. Ibid.

80. Ibid.

81. Ibid.

82. Ibid.

83. JFD Letter to Mrs. Franklin D. Roosevelt, June 15, 1948, *JFD Papers*, 2.

84. Ibid., 2-3.

85. I am indebted to Professor Inis L. Claude, Jr. for this interpretation of the approach to human rights.

86. "Minutes of 4th Mtg., U.S. Delegation," Sept. 24, 1948, *1(1) Foreign Relations of the United States*, 1948, 291.

87. "Minutes at 5th Mtg., U.S. Delegation," Sept. 25, 1948, *1(1) Foreign Relations of the United States*, 1948, 292.

88. Letter from JFD to Senator Bricker, Dec. 11, 1948, *JFD Papers*.

89. Dulles, "Report on the Paris Session of the United Nations General Assembly," Dec. 22, 1948, *JFD Papers*, 1.

90. Ibid.

91. Ibid.

92. Ibid.

93. Dulles, "Statement in First Committee," State Department Press Release No. 326/Rev. 1, Nov. 17, 1947, *JFD Papers*, 1.

94. Ibid., 2.

95. "Statement to the Federal Council," 6.

96. Dulles, "Draft of 8/16/49," *JFD Papers*, at 4.

97. Ibid.

98. "Minutes of 21st Mtg., U.S. Delegation," Nov. 15, 1946, *1 Foreign Relations of the United States*, 1946, 542.

99. Ibid., 542-543.

100. Dulles, "Statement in First Committee," 1.

101. Ibid.

102. Ibid.

103. Ibid.

104. Dulles, "Statement of Sept. 9, 1949," *JFD Papers*.

105. Ibid.

106. Dulles, "Is the United Nations Inadequate?," February 1949, *JFD Papers*, 3.

107. Ibid., 2.

108. Ibid.

109. Ibid., 3.

110. Quoted in "Speech by Mr. Dulles," 3(1) U.N. GAOR, (167th plen. mtg.), 1948, 642.

111. Ibid. (footnote omitted).

112. Ibid.

113. Truman's Speech to Congress, Mar. 12, 1947, reprinted in N. Graebner, *Cold War Diplomacy: American Foreign Policy 1945-1975*, 188-189.

114. Quoted in "Speech by Mr. Dulles," 642.

115. Dulles, "Statement on the Occasion at the Consideration of the Greek Problem by Committee I," Press Release #48, Oct. 26, 1948, *JFD Papers*, 1.

116. Ibid.

117. Ibid.
118. Ibid.
119. Ibid.
120. Ibid., 1-2.
121. Ibid., 2.
122. Ibid.
123. Ibid.
124. Ibid., 3.
125. Ibid.
126. Ibid., 3-4.
127. Ibid., 4.
128. Ibid.
129. 3(1) U.N. GAOR (167th plen. mtg.), 1948, 641-645.
130. Dulles, "My Distinctive Contribution to U.S. Foreign Policy, 2-3.
131. Ibid., 3.
132. 5 U.N. SCOR (474th mtg.), U.N. Doc. S/1511, 1950.
133. "Letter from Mr. John Foster Dulles of the United States Delegation to the Permanent Representation of France at the United Nations," Sept. 28, 1950, 2 Foreign Relations of the United States, 1950, 346.
134. U.N. Charter, art. 11, para. 2.
135. 2 Foreign Relations of the United States, 1950, 346-347.
136. Ibid., 347.
137. Ibid.
138. Ibid., 348.
139. "Memorandum of Conversation, by Mr. Harding F. Bancroft," U.S. Delegation Advisory Staff, Sept. 26, 1950, 2 Foreign Relations of the United States, 1950, 345.
140. Ibid.
141. Ibid.
142. "Editorial Note," 2 Foreign Relations of the United States, 1950, 359-361.
143. 5 U.N. GAOR C.1 (354th mtg.), U.N. Doc. A/C.1/SR.354, 1950, 63.
144. Ibid.
145. Dulles, "Statement in Committee One, on the Item, Uniting for Peace," Oct. 13, 1950, U.N. Press Release, No. 1009, JFD Papers, 6.
146. Ibid.
147. Ibid.
148. Ibid.
149. Ibid., 6-7.
150. 5 U.N. GAOR (299th plen. mtg.), 1950, 294.
151. Ibid.
152. Ibid.
153. Ibid., 295.
154. Ibid.

155. Ibid.

156. Ibid.

157. "Statement of Mr. Vyshinsky," 5 U.N. GAOR (299th plen. mtg.), 1950, 294.

158. See, for example, Dulles, "What Shall We Do With the U.N.?," 1041.

159. Dulles, *War or Peace*, 38.

160. Dulles, "The Future of the United Nations," Sept. 28, 1948, *JFD Papers*, 1.

161. Dulles, *War or Peace*, 65-66.

162. Dulles, "The Future of the United Nations," 1.

163. Ibid., 2.

164. Dulles, "Reputation and Performance in World Affairs," Apr. 12, 1949, *JFD Papers*, 1.

165. Ibid., 4.

166. Ibid.

167. Dulles, *War or Peace*, 71-73.

168. Ibid., 42-65.

169. Dulles, "What Shall We Do With The U.N.?," 1042.

170. Ibid.

171. See "Structure of the United Nations and the Relations of the United States to the United Nations," Hearings Before the Committee on Foreign Affairs, House of Representatives, 80th Cong., 2nd Sess., May 12, 1948, 279-289.

172. Dulles, *War or Peace*, 194-196.

173. Ibid., 40.

174. Ibid., 188-191.

175. Ibid., 190.

176. Ibid., 192.

177. Ibid.

178. Ibid.

179. Ibid., 194-196.

180. Ibid., at 197-198.

181. "Structure of the United Nations," 301.

182. Dulles, *War or Peace*, 207-210.

183. Dulles, "Reputation and Performance in World Affairs," 4.

184. Dulles, *War or Peace*, 211-223; Dulles, "European Unity," Nov. 18, 1948, *JFD Papers*.

9

The International Court of Justice

As noted earlier, Dulles was a strong advocate of U.S. adherence to the Statute of the Permanent Court of International Justice (PCIJ). Once the International Court of Justice was established as the successor to the PCIJ, he continued to support United States participation in the World Court--but with several caveats. On July 10, 1946, he submitted a memorandum to the Senate Foreign Relations Committee Subcommittee, which was considering a resolution on U.S. acceptance of the court's compulsory jurisdiction. In this memorandum, he urged U.S. acceptance, explaining:

> The United States, since its formation, has led in promoting a regime of law and justice as between nations. In order to continue that leadership, we should now accept the jurisdiction of the International Court of Justice. If the United States, which has the material power to impose its will widely in the world, agrees instead to submit to the impartial adjudication of its legal controversies, that will inaugurate a new and profoundly significant international advance. Conversely, failure to take that step would be interpreted as an election on our part to rely on power rather than reason.[1]

The United States could thus demonstrate its desire not to take advantage of its great power status, but to act in accordance with law. Consequently, he believed the United States should now declare its adoption of the compulsory jurisdiction of the Court.

Dulles did, however, believe that there were "certain matters which [could] usefully be clarified."[2] First, he was concerned about the effect advisory opinions could have on states who had accepted the court's compulsory jurisdiction, and believed that "[t]he compulsory jurisdiction should presumably be limited to disputes which are actual 'cases' between states, as distinct from disputes in relation to which advisory opinions may be sought."[3] He felt that the statute provisions were substantially vague as to whether states would be submitting to compulsory jurisdiction for advisory opinions and thus recommended a clarification if the United States did not want to be so bound.

Second, Dulles believed that the declaration should clearly spell out that submission to the compulsory jurisdiction was being made on condition of reciprocity. He explained that "[o]ftentimes . . . disputes arise, particularly under multilateral conventions, [which] give rise to the same issue as against more than one other nation."[4] Consequently, "[s]ince the Court statute [the provision on reciprocity] uses the singular 'any other state,' it might be desirable to make clear that there is no compulsory obligation to submit to the Court merely because one of several parties to such a dispute is similarly bound, the others not having bound themselves to become parties before the Court and, consequently, not being subject to the Charter provision (art. 94) requiring members to comply with decisions of the Court in cases to which they are party."[5] In other words, Dulles feared that it would be unfair if two parties to a multilateral treaty were obligated to submit to the court's jurisdiction, while others intimately involved in the same dispute were not.

A third concern related to the use of international law by the court as a guide to resolving disputes. Dulles had no difficulty with the court's using treaties or conventions, but believed that if the issue were not covered by those written documents "there should be prior agreement as to what are the applicable principles of international law."[6] He explained:

> Article 38 of the Statute goes on to recognize as international law not merely international conventions, but "international custom," "general principles of law recognized by civilized nations" and "the teachings of the most highly qualified publicists of the various nations." If the applicable rule of international law is so uncertain that resort must be had to *alleged custom, teachings*, etc., then the Court can scarcely avoid indulging in a large amount of judicial legislation or political expediency. The United States can properly refrain from subjecting itself to that.[7]

He went on to add that "[t]he suggested safeguard is the more appropriate because a majority of the judges of the Court are drawn from countries which are not 'common law' countries, but which depend almost wholly on written laws and decrees. Therefore, such judges can hardly be expected to be adept in the proper use of common law methods."[8] Once again, Dulles demonstrated a basic lack of faith in customary international law.9

Fourth, Dulles felt that the "[c]ompulsory jurisdiction of the Court should not extend to matters which are essentially within the domestic jurisdiction of the United States."[10] Noting Article 2(7) of the U.N. Charter, Dulles argued that "[t]he Declaration under the Statute should preserve, and not seem to waive, that limitation."[11] Interestingly enough, the resolution under consideration *did* contain a provision that "disputes with regard to matters which are essentially within the domestic jurisdiction of the United States" would be excluded from compulsory jurisdiction.[12] It was thus not clear whether or not Dulles believed that this provision was sufficient. (Just a few years before, he had opposed efforts explicitly to exclude domestic jurisdiction issues from the Court's jurisdiction. Perhaps his work on Article 2(7) at San Francisco, on which he underwent a change of opinion, had influenced his position on this issue.)

A fifth concern of Dulles was that the "[c]ompulsory jurisdiction of the Court should not extend to disputes, the solution of which may be entrusted to other tribunals."[13] This exemption had also been dealt with explicitly in the proposal before the subcommittee, as had Dulles's sixth concern--that "[c]ompulsory jurisdiction, initially, be for a limited period, say five years, with a right thereafter to terminate on reasonable notice, say six months."[14] On this last point he explained that "[t]he Court and its personnel are new. Its judicial temperament and ability are still to be tested. If the United States accepts compulsory jurisdiction for a trial period, that will not merely serve, negatively, to protect the United States; it will, affirmatively, provide an incentive to assure that the composition and functioning of the Court will increasingly inspire confidence in its high judicial quality."[15]

Although Dulles did not appear personally before the Senate subcommittee, his memo had a great influence on the committee and subsequently on the Senate. The relatively short committee report (eleven pages) spent over two pages responding point-by-point to Dulles's memorandum. On the first point, the question of advisory opinions, the committee believed that the compulsory jurisdiction could not be interpreted to apply to advisory opinions, and rejected Dulles's suggestion.[16] But on his second point, the issue of reciprocity, the committee suggested that an additional reservation could be added that would exclude from compulsory jurisdiction disputes arising under multilateral conventions.[17] This suggestion was formally proposed by Senator Vandenberg on the floor and adopted by the full Senate, becoming known as the "Vandenberg Reservation."[18] The committee rejected Dulles's third suggestion that the United States include a reservation calling for a separate agreement on principles of international law before each case. This, they believed, would require a rewriting of the charter.[19] Nevertheless, Dulles's suggestion was picked up by Senator Millikin and formally proposed to the Senate. It was, however, rejected 49 to 11.[20] Dulles's fourth point, regarding domestic jurisdiction, may have been the impetus behind the so-called Connally Reservation that exempted from compulsory jurisdiction issues within the domestic jurisdiction of the United States "as determined by the United States." Although it is difficult to determine with certainty whether Dulles's memorandum motivated Senator Connally, Preuss seems to indicate that Connally indeed picked up Dulles's point.[21] Dulles's precise attitude to the Connally Reservation, however, remains unclear. No response was made to Dulles's fifth and sixth points, presumably because they were addressed by the initial resolution. In any case, Dulles's brief memo was taken very seriously by the senators, a fact no doubt indicative of his prestige among policy makers.

From the preceding discussion of Dulles's activities during this period of his life, a great deal of continuity with the earlier period can be seen. Although tempered by a realization that the new international organization would need to be more rudimentary than he had originally thought, he remained a strong supporter of international organization for a number of specific tasks: the promotion of decolonization, the development of international law, the performance of economic and social tasks, the peaceful resolution of international disputes, the formation of world public opinion and moral norms, and so on. If one could, however, single out two major differences in his thoughts and actions during this later period, they would be his attitude toward the Soviet Union[22] and his tendency to support, in one form or another, the concept of collective security.

Generally speaking, Dulles did not quite foresee, or at least did not articulate, the problems with the Soviets that developed once the United Nations came into existence. Although he had not anticipated harmonious great power relations, the extent of "Soviet obstructionism" seemed to surprise him. As he struggled in 1945 at San Francisco and in the succeeding years, he seemed to become more aware of the problem that the Soviets presented for world organization. The Soviets, he came to believe, subscribed to a radically different conception of the nature of human beings. This dictated their behavior on foreign policy issues, and, of course, at the United Nations. With at least two drastically different philosophical orientations at the United Nations (and Dulles seemed aware that there were more), true international cooperation on important matters would be a slow and arduous task.

Secondly, Dulles's behavior between 1945 and 1952 is interesting due to the emphasis that he seemed to place on collective security or its substitutes. In the previous chapters, it was seen that during the early period of his thought, he emphasized peaceful change first and foremost, and *then* a host of other functional activities of international organization. In fact, he felt that there was entirely too much emphasis on enforcing world order, without sufficient concern for establishing an order worthy of enforcement. After 1945, Dulles did not abandon his beliefs about peaceful change (although he did seem to demonstrate some ambivalance) nor did he change his beliefs about the possibilities of the functional approach to peace; he still seemed to think that there was too much emphasis on the Security Council as opposed to the General Assembly. Nevertheless, he did have to deal, not so much as a theorist but as a practitioner, with actual aggression of both a direct and an indirect nature. With the council unable to respond, Dulles, often at the behest of his colleagues, sought to devise other means for promoting the goal of collective security. This he attempted to do in two ways. First, he endeavored to secure more power for the General Assembly through the establishment of the Interim Committee and the adoption of the "Uniting for Peace Resolution." Second, and simultaneous with his efforts to boost the power of the assembly, Dulles advocated and supported the formation of regional defense organizations. Where the universal organization could not prevent and repress aggression, perhaps a smaller, tighter, regional arrangement acting within the charter framework could.

NOTES

1. "Memorandum of John Foster Dulles Concerning Acceptance by the United States of Compulsory Jurisdiction of the International Court of Justice," in Compulsory Jurisdiction, International Court of Justice, Hearings Before a Subcommittee of the Committee on Foreign Relations, United States Senate, 79th Cong., 2nd Sess., July 11, 1946, 43.

2. Ibid., 44.

3. Ibid.

4. Ibid.

5. Ibid.

6. Ibid.

7. Ibid. (emphasis added).

8. Ibid., 44–45.

9. See Lawrence Preuss, "The International Court of Justice, The Senate, and Matters of Domestic Jurisdiction," *American Journal of International Law*, 40, 1946, 720, 721 n. 4.

10. "Memorandum of John Foster Dulles Concerning Compulsory Jurisdiction," 45.

11. Ibid.

12. S. Res. 196, 79th Cong., 1st Sess., International Court of Justice, Hearings, 1.

13. "Memorandum of John Foster Dulles Concerning Compulsory Jurisdiction," 45.

14. Ibid.

15. Ibid.

16. Report of the Committee on Foreign Relations, No. 1835, House of Representatives, 79th Cong., 2nd Sess., July 25, 1946, 6.

17. Ibid., 6-7.

18. See Preuss, "The International Court of Justice," 720-721.

19. Report of the Committee on Foreign Relations, No. 1835, 7.

20. Preuss, "The International Court of Justice," 720, 721 n. 5.

21. Ibid.

22. On this point, I draw heavily on Pruessen's analysis. See Pruessen, *John Foster Dulles*, 410-431.

PART THREE

THE WASHINGTON YEARS
(1952–1959)

10

Collective Defense:
The Fight Against Aggression

Between 1945 and 1950, Dulles was deeply involved with international organization. In 1952, as he moved away from the day-to-day workings of international organization, he entered a position where his decisions were *the* major influences on United States policy toward international organization. The following chapters will examine Dulles's involvement with international organization in the final eight years of his life, during most of which he served as secretary of state. The analysis will focus on his thoughts and action on collective defense, economic and social issues, the international legal, system and peaceful change. This thematic approach will facilitate the examination of the similarities and dissimilarities between his earlier activities in these areas and those during this later period.

As noted in previous chapters, Dulles had become convinced of the need for international organization to respond to potential and actual aggressors. Having seen the failure of "true" collective security with the inability of the Security Council to act, he realized that the General Assembly and regional defense organizations were the most appropriate institutions to combat aggression. In a 1952 article published in *Life* magazine, "A Policy of Boldness," he reiterated the need for the non-Communist states to organize and fight aggression, believing that a would-be aggressor could be deterred if the "free world" could "develop the will and organize the means to retaliate instantly against open aggression by Red armies."[1] During his tenure as secretary of state, he was confronted with several cases of aggression or potential aggression. This chapter will examine his response to several of these instances, emphasizing the role that international organization played in his actions.

GUATEMALA

In the early years of the Eisenhower administration, the State Department became particularly concerned about communist subversion in Latin America and desired a strong regional stance against it. At the 10th Inter-American Conference in March of 1954, the United States proposed the adoption of a resolution condemning communist intervention in the Americas and calling upon members to unite in combating such intervention. This resolution was not immediately well received by all the Latin countries and Dulles was called upon to travel to Caracas to persuade the other foreign ministers. Eventually, an anti-communist resolution was adopted by a vote of 17-1, with Guatemala dissenting, and Mexico and Argentina abstaining.[2] It was the lone dissenter that was to present problems.

Guatemala had been experiencing a series of domestic political problems in the late 1940s and early 1950s. In 1953, following the election of Jacabo Arbenz Guzman, communist forces began gaining power in the country. By 1954, the situation had worsened and efforts were allegedly being made to "export" the revolution to nearby countries.[3] Soon, Honduras and Nicaragua requested U. S. assistance, presumably to secure their countries against potential interference. On May 17, 1984, it was revealed that the Arbenz regime had received shipments of Czechoslovakian arms.[4] In response to these problems, the United States authorized a small shipment of arms to Nicaragua and Honduras, and began "stopping suspicious foreign-flag vessels on the high seas off Guatemala to examine cargo."[5] In addition, the United States requested a convocation of the Organization of American States to discuss the matter. On June 18, an exiled Guatemalan colonel, Carlos Castillo Armas, moved a group of rebel forces into Guatemala to challenge Arbenz.[6] When Castillo lost two of his bombers, the United States decided to aid in replacing them by sending them to "the country which had originally supplied this equipment to Castillo Armas' forces."[7] That country would then give them to Castillo. Eventually, Castillo's forces triumphed, and he became president.

Dulles's involvement in the Guatemalan crisis is very interesting. According to Louis Gerson, this conflict was not one which "received his entire personal attention . . . and it is difficult to say therefore that he had a 'policy' toward" it.[8] Nevertheless, he was present at a number of meetings with the president at which this matter was discussed, and implicitly approved of actions taken by the State Department. He furthermore explicitly supported the effort to intercept foreign ships and defended such action in part on the basis of an Article 51 right of the United States to defend itself. As the notes of a meeting with the president indicated, Dulles argued: "What is going on in Guatemala, since the Russians never furnish arms to a country without bad motive, is a direct threat to the security of the U.S. (via Panama Canal)."[9] He also believed that the Caracas

Resolution and the requests by Nicaragua and Honduras for arms gave legitimacy to U.S. actions. At the request of the president to obtain specific requests from "some of Guatemala's neighbors who were threatened by Guatemalan aggression"[10] for the quarantine, Dulles solicited, and apparently received, requests from El Salvador, Honduras, Mexico and Nicaragua.[11]

From the perspective of international organization, Dulles, and Eisenhower's emphasis on regional organization was clearly visible. In light of Eisenhower's desire to obtain as much collective support as possible, the issue was taken to the Organization of American States (OAS). Guatemala, however, sought to bring the matter directly to the Security Council, presumably to avoid the unfavorable hearing the case would receive at the OAS. The United States strongly opposed this move, and Dulles later called it "an effort to disrupt the inter-American system," arguing that Guatemala had taken its action "without first referring the matter to the American regional organization as is called for by both the United Nations Charter itself and by the treaty creating the American Organization."[12] A move by the council formally to refer the problem to the OAS was vetoed by the Soviet Union, but subsequently, the council simply "decided not to take up the Guatemalan matter."[13] The OAS then authorized the Inter-American Peace Committee to investigate the matter, "but the change of government had made further action unnecessary."[14]

These statements and actions by Dulles demonstrated once again a preference for regional organizations, but they went even further. Previously, he had spoken about the United Nations Security Council being the *first* resort for the resolution of problems relating to a threat to the peace, a breach of the peace, or an act of aggression. In the Guatemalan case, however, he was convinced that the Security Council, with the presence of Guatemala's "friend," the Soviet Union, would be unable to resolve the problem favorably. Consequently, he supported efforts to *start* with the OAS, where the U.S. position clearly enjoyed majority support. Interestingly enough, Dulles's statement that the charter *required* states to take recourse to regional arrangements *first* is not entirely correct. Article 52(2) does provide that states "should make every effort" to resolve a conflict on the regional level first, but Article 35 still gives states the right to bring a matter to the Security Council.[15] It is also interesting to note that Dulles relied on Article 51 to justify U. S. support for the Guatemalan rebels. Actually, Article 51 provides for the right of individual or collective self-defense in the event of "an armed attack." While a literal interpretation of "armed attack" is rejected by many international legal scholars, most would agree that there has to be at least the indication that an attack is imminent. Receiving arms from Czechoslovakia, while perhaps not desirable from a policy standpoint, does not seem to indicate that an attack on the United States (even the Canal Zone) was imminent. Dulles was perhaps a bit too loose in his interpretation of Article 51.

INDOCHINA

Indochina--Vietnam, Cambodia, and Laos--was yet another area confronted with indirect aggression. In the early 1950s there had not yet been any overt attacks from China or the Soviet Union against the French colonies, but there was outside support for an ever-increasing group of indigenous rebels, the Viet Minh. Very early in the Eisenhower administration, Dulles asserted the importance of ending this "aggression," telling the Senate Foreign Relations and House Foreign Affairs Committees that "Communist aggression in Indochina represents one of the most serious present threats to the free world."[16]

While he supported certain unilateral actions, Dulles generally preferred a collective response to the situation in Indochina, either through international agencies or through *ad hoc* groups of states. In the spring of 1953, when Viet Minh forces moved into northern Laos, he tried very hard to persuade the French to take the matter to the United Nations Security Council. He explained that "the conflict in Indochina [had] not yet fully received the status of an international war or an international act of aggression."[17] But bringing the issue to the Security Council "would give the conflict more international standing and would make it more readily a subject for international negotiation and settlement, which it is not today."[18] The French, however, balked at this suggestion, fearing that U.N. consideration would invite a discussion of the entire French colonial issue. Dulles, on the other hand, believed that "the danger of this in the Security Council might not be as great as in the General Assembly and that it would probably be possible to find out in advance what the result would be in the Security Council, recognizing that Soviet Russia would, presumably, interpose a veto."[19] When Thailand, concerned about its own security, did propose taking the matter to the Security Council, Dulles once again tried to persuade the French to accept such action:

[I] told the French Ambassador that it seemed to me that Thailand was wise in presenting this case to the Security Council and working for action to provide observers under a subcommittee of the Peace Observation Commission. I told the Ambassador that the whole purpose of that part of the "Uniting for Peace" resolution of 1950 was to take timely action which in itself would serve to deter aggression and, if aggression occurred, would enable U.N. observers to report the facts to the U.N. I told the Ambassador that it seemed to me that the time to take action was precisely during this lull when there is an opportunity to get observers in the field before anything happens and not wait until aggression has actually occurred.[20]

But the French Ambassador remained unconvinced, and Dulles, in deference to France, asked the Thais to delay submitting the issue to the council.[21]

As the situation began to worsen in late 1953 and early 1954, the United States continued to advocate strongly some kind of collective approach to Indochina. In January of 1954, the National Security Council adopted a policy statement favoring U.N. or other collective efforts if they became necessary.[22] As the French, fighting desperately against Viet Minh forces at the village of Dien Bien Phu, continued to request U.S. intervention, Dulles made it clear that his preference was to combat aggression through a joint effort. On March 29, 1954, he explained that "[u]nder the conditions of today, the imposition on Southeast Asia of the political system of Communist Russia and its Chinese Communist ally, by whatever means, would be a grave threat to the whole free community."[23] Consequently, "[t]he United States feels that that possibility should not be passively accepted but should be met by *united action*."[24] Two days later he presented a draft congressional resolution to the president that provided, in part, that "peace and order may be restored and this aggression ended if it is known that the United States is prepared, in pursuance of a decision or recommendation of the United Nations, or by united action with other free nations or in the exercise of the inherent right of individual or collective self defense recognized by Article 51 of the United Nations Charter, to restrain and retaliate against such armed attack."[25]

But while the United Nations action *per se* remained *one* possible means of world action, Dulles had become convinced that the emphasis should be on another form of collective action. On April 2, he explained "that the question of United Nations intervention had been considered in a preliminary way and, although he did not want to rule it out entirely, there were a good many difficulties in this course of action."[26] He explained that "[t]hese included not only the veto in the Security Council but the question of whether a two-thirds majority could be obtained in the General Assembly."[27] Instead, "what he had in mind . . . was some kind of a collective organization of free world countries which shared common interests in Southeast Asia. These would include the United States, Great Britain, France, Australia, New Zealand, the Philippines (the last three with which we have security pacts), the Associated States, and Thailand."[28] In sum, "[t]he general idea would be for these states to band together in some kind of common defense of Southeast Asia."[29] Even though "regional," as opposed to universal, action seemed to hold out the greatest possibility of success, Dulles intended that this action be within the Article 51 framework of the

U.N. Charter.   Of course, in *addition* to this regional action, the United Nations could still be involved.   Dulles "thought in terms of invoking the Uniting for Peace Resolution with the idea of sending observation teams to the border" and "also had in mind that we could call on others to make contributions to broaden the base as much as possible."[30]   (But France continued to oppose reference to the United Nations.)

In the weeks preceding the 1954 Geneva Conference on the Far East, Dulles attempted to set up a coalition to act in Indochina.   He met with the Ambassadors of Viet Nam, Cambodia, Laos, Thailand, New Zealand, the Philippines, Great Britain, and France in an effort to obtain their commitment to a united venture.[31]   He believed it imperative that these states join together before the Geneva Conference, presumably as a demonstration of strength that could prevent an unfavorable settlement.   Several of the delegations that Dulles contacted indicated their willingness to join in collective action, but the British, while not ruling out the establishment of some *general* Southeast Asian collective defense organization, were reluctant to participate in any immediate action against the Viet Minh.   As the French military position at Dien Bien Phu worsened, the French became increasingly convinced that without outside assistance, there would be no use continuing to fight.[32]   But the United States remained steadfastly unwilling to enter into the war unless Great Britain would join in collective action.   On May 7, Dien Bien Phu fell to Viet Minh forces, leaving the French demoralized and anxious to reach a settlement at Geneva to extricate them.   A little more than a month later, the French government collapsed and the new Premier, Mendes, resolved to "end the war within four weeks . . . or resign."[33]

By the end of May, Thailand had renewed its desire to take the matter to the United Nations.   With U.N. assistance, the Thais drafted an appeal to the Security Council, alleging that their security had been threatened and requesting the council to send "observers to Thailand under the Peace Observation Commission."[34]   Dulles strongly supported this approach; he seemed to believe that since an Article 51 "united action" had not been implemented, an appeal to the U.N. could provide collective legitimization for U.S. actions.   He told Dag Hammarskjold, who feared U.N. action would produce a chilling effect at Geneva, that

> "success" at Geneva seemed to me to involve something more than merely getting an agreement but involved getting the right kind of agreement.   That, I thought, would be impossible unless French had some alternative to complete surrender and U.S. was trying to provide that. One of the preconditions to any contingent U.S. action would be some participation in area by U.N.   Also it was important from standpoint of getting MSA [Mutual Security

Assistance] appropriations. We had followed the course which seemed to us least likely to involve Geneva. I did not see how the Russians could very well make this reason for breaking off at Geneva if only reason why U.N. talks covered Indochina was because Russians themselves brought that element in.[35]

In mid-June, under U.S. pressure, nine members of the Security Council voted in favor of a Thai resolution calling for observers to be sent to Thailand. There was one abstention and one negative vote. Unfortunately, the negative vote was the Soviet Union, who "contended during the debate that the Thai request was in fact an attempt by the United States to deepen the conflict in Indochina and to prepare the way for armed intervention of the United Nations."[36] In July the Thais requested the assembly to consider the matter; the request, however, was withdrawn in August, after an armistice was reached at Geneva.[37]

Even though the Geneva Settlement seemed to resolve the immediate conflict, Dulles continued to believe that a formal NATO-style regional organization was necessary in Southeast Asia to prevent further aggression. On August 17, he told the president that even though a Southeast Asia collective defense treaty "would involve committing the prestige of the United States in an area where we had little control and where the situation was by no means promising," "failure to agree [with the Treaty] would mark a total abandonment of the area without a struggle."[38] Eisenhower concurred, and Dulles went about establishing such an organization. After negotiating with the concerned states for several weeks, he signed the Southeast Asia Collective Defense Treaty at Manila on September 8, 1954. This agreement, also signed by Australia, France, New Zealand, Pakistan, the Philipines, Thailand and the United Kingdom, formally established SEATO, the Southeast Asian Treaty Organization. Under the "Manila Pact, each Party agreed in the event of aggression against any other Party to act to meet the common danger in a manner consistent with its constitutional process."[39] In addition, the parties signed a protocol in which they pledged "to guarantee . . . the territory of Cambodia, Laos, and non-Communist Vietnam against aggression."[40] Dulles later explained in a speech before the United Nations General Assembly on September 23, 1954, that "[t]he Manila Pact constitutes significant action taken under the Charter of the United Nations, which recog-nizes the inherent right of individual and collective self-defense."[41]

THE OFF-SHORE ISLANDS: QUEMOY AND MATSU

While the Manila Conference was being held, another problem was occurring in Asia. In early September of 1954, the People's

Republic of China (PRC) began shelling the Nationalist-held island of Quemoy. The United States had previously committed itself to defend the island of Formosa and the Pescadores chain, also occupied by the Nationalists, but had resolved not to become involved in the dispute over Quemoy, the Matsus, and the other off-shore islands. Now the United States had to reevaluate its policy.[42] Even though the islands were not of any major military importance, they possessed a great deal of symbolic significance for the Chinese; losing the islands could represent a capitulation to the PRC.[43] Unfortunately, there was division within the U.S. government about how to deal with the problem.

On September 12, Eisenhower convened a meeting at his "summer" White House in Denver. At that meeting, Admiral Arthur W. Radford, Chairman of the Joint Chiefs of Staff, argued in favor of U.S. action to hold the islands. According to Eisenhower, Radford, "Admiral Carney [Chief of Naval Operations] and General Twining [Air Force Chief of Staff] therefore urged that the United States commit itself to defend the islands and help the Chinese Nationalists bomb the mainland."[44] The president, however, did not agree with the cause of action, fearing that such a move would open a Pandora's box.[45] Dulles, on the other hand, presented a position with which the president agreed. Eisenhower recounted:

> Secretary Dulles observed that the problem involved complex and conflicting considerations. The Chinese Communist, he said, were probing; unless we stopped them, we faced disaster in the Far East. But, he added, if we drew a line and committed ourselves to defend Quemoy and Matsu, we might find ourselves, without allies, in a war against Red China. He therefore suggested an alternative: "We should take the off-shore question to the United Nations Security Council with the view of getting there an injunction to maintain the status quo and institute a cease fire in the Formosa Strait. Whether Russia vetoes or accepts such a plan," he said, "the United States will gain."[46]

In essence, Dulles did not want the United Nations to take action against an aggressor, but rather to call on both sides to cease and desist; as Eisenhower put it, "Foster wanted a Security Council recommendation that military activity both against the islands and in their defense be suspended."[47] Hence, at this stage, Dulles was explicitly rejecting collective security as the proper role for the United Nations. Undoubtedly he realized that a collective security action would never be undertaken because of the veto and allied opposition to defending the islands.

In an effort to carry out this plan, Dulles met with New Zealand officials to suggest that their country submit this proposal to the United Nations. They agreed to do so, but Chiang Kaishek indicated his opposition to the proposal. He feared that this would be "the first step toward letting it [the Security Council] decide who owned Formosa and which China had a right to United Nations representation."[48] Dulles wrote Chiang and tried to persaude him to accept the proposal, "assuring him that the United States would never agree to submit to the United Nations the question of Chiang's right to rule Formosa."[49] At the end of January, New Zealand brought the matter to the attention of the Security Council. The Nationalists continued to oppose the New Zealand approach, believing that calling for a cease-fire did not properly acknowledge PRC aggression. The Soviets, on the other hand, responded by introducing their own draft resolution on "[a]cts of aggression by the United States of America against the People's Republic of China in the area of Taiwan and other islands of China."[50] The council then began considering both questions. Eventually, it extended an invitation to the People's Republic of China to participate in the discussions of the matter. Chou En Lai refused and, in light of this refusal, on February 14, 1955, the Council essentially decided to stop considering the New Zealand proposal.[51]

But the United States had not waited for U.N. action. In November of 1954 the PRC had begun shelling other offshore islands. In December Dulles and the Nationalist Chinese Foreign Minister signed a mutual defense treaty,[52] in which the signatories promised to "maintain and develop their individual and collective capacity to resist armed attack and Communist subversion activities."[53] Both sides also pledged not to use force in the area without consulting the other.[54] With the continued attacks on the offshore islands, including the Tachens, U.S. government officials tended to fall into two camps: some called for the abandonment of all the islands, while others advocated strong action against the PRC. Dulles proposed an alternative, telling Eisenhower that "[i]t is unlikely . . . that any of the offshore islands can be defended without largescale American help. But we all agree that we cannot permit the Communists to seize *all* the offshore islands."[55] Thus, he explained, "I believe we must modify our policy: we should assist in the evacuation of the Tachens, but as we do so we should declare that we will assist in holding Quemoy and possibly the Matsus, as long as the Chinese Communists profess their intention to attack Formosa."[56] Dulles and Eisenhower specifically wanted it to be clear that the United States *would* defend Formosa. Explained Eisenhower, "I believed [and so did Dulles] the Korean War had resulted, partially at least, from the mistaken Communist notion that under no circumstances would the United States move to the assistance of the Korean Republic. I resolved that this time no uncertainty about our commitment to defend Formosa should invite a major Chinese Communist attack."[57] Subsequently, on January 29, Eisenhower signed the so-called Formosa Resolution, which authorized the president to use force to protect Formosa, the Pescadores and "related positions and territories of that area now in friendly hands."[58]   In sum, the United States resolved to protect Quemoy and the Matsus if it appeared that an attack on the islands was merely a precursor to an attack on Formosa itself. In April, U.S. officials were dispatched to meet with Chiang to see if some face-saving evacuation of the islands might be possible; Chiang, however, remained steadfast in his determination to keep the islands.[59]   Fortunately, at the end of the month, Chou En Lai, who was at the Bandung Conference, indicated his willingness to discuss the problem with the United States; by May 22 the attacks had ceased.[60]

THE SUEZ CRISIS

Gamel Abdel Nassar, the Egyptian leader, was struggling to industrialize his country. In an effort to play a "neutralist" role in the cold war, Nassar was flirting with both Eastern and Western sources of aid.[61]   In September of 1955, he concluded an arms agreement with Czechoslovakia and Western statesmen began to be troubled about Soviet penetration.[62]   Britain, in an effort to counter communist moves, asked the United States to help finance a loan for the construction of a dam at Aswan.[63]   Initially, the United States favored such assistance and made a formal offer on December 17, 1955,[64] but over the course of the next several months, Egypt's behavior indicated an unwillingness to finalize the U.S. offer and by June of 1956, the United States had begun to view the issue as "dead".[65]   According to Michael Guhin, among the concerns of the United States were "Egypt's financial conditions and continuous flirtation with the Soviet Union, plus growing congressional opposition to the Aswan Dam project in particular and aid for Egypt in general . . . [and the fact that] Egypt had made no effort to cooperate with Sudan, and there persisted the problem of Sudanese rights to Nile waters."[66]   Even though Egypt was told on July 13, 1956 by the United States that the loan question could not be resolved in the short run,[67] the Egyptian Ambassador to the United States arrived in Washington several days with the announced purpose of accepting the December 17 offer. Dulles believed this was a deliberate attempt to force the hand of the United States.[68]   When the ambassador did meet with Dulles on July 19, the secretary told him that the United States had rescinded its formal offer,[69] calling Egyptian action "blackmail."[70]   Some days later Nassar nationalized the Suez Canal, an act for which he had been preparing.

The reactions of the Western states to Nassar's act were quite different.[72]   Britain and France were both angered, and determined to act swiftly to prevent the nationalization from succeeding.   The United States, however, was not as intensely worried.[73]   Eisenhower was not pleased with Nassar's move, but, according to Louis Gerson, "the President doubted that the Suez Canal was the right issue for military action."[74] Instead of immediately recalling Dulles, who was in Peru at the time of nationalization, the president sent Robert Murphy, deputy secretary of state, to London to meet with Britain and France. But as British and French consternation grew, Dulles was called from Latin America and flew to London. Following Eisenhower's policy, Dulles endeavored to prevent military action and suggested that a conference of concerned states be held in August.[75] Dulles felt that the matter should not be taken to the United Nations.[76]

Formal efforts soon began to reach some specific settlement of the dispute. From August 16 to August 23, twenty-two states met in London to frame an arrangement for regulating the canal. The states formulated "a majority proposal for an 'international system,' a Suez Canal Board, which would operate the waterway, safeguard Egyptian interests, and adhere to the Convention" of 1888, which guaranteed freedom of navigation and to which Egypt was a party.[77] But when representatives from the London Conference met with Nassar, he rejected the proposal. Dulles countered this rejection by proposing the establishment of a Suez Canal Users Association (SCUA): "The Association would employ pilots, coordinate traffic, collect transit dues, and enlist Egyptian cooperation. Should Egypt refuse, and interrupt traffic, the Association would invoke the requirements of the Convention,"[78] presumably acting forcibly to ensure free passage through the canal. In mid-September of 1956, another conference was convened in London to establish SCUA formally.

But even as this effort was underway, unbeknown to the United States, France and Great Britain had decided to take the matter to the United Nations. On October 13, a Security Council resolution calling for free transit through the canal was vetoed by the Soviet Union.[79] For a couple of weeks tensions seemed to ease, but then, on October 29, Israel launched an attack on Egypt. Britain and France, after calling for an Israel disengagement, began their own attack on Egypt.

From the perspective of collective defense, the most significant aspect of Dulles's actions during the Suez Crisis was his response to the British-French-Israeli attack on Egypt in October of 1956. Before examining this, however, it is interesting to explore the reasoning behind his reluctance to take a potentially explosive situation to the United Nations directly after the nationalization of the canal in July.

On August 7, the ambassador from El Salvador questioned Dulles about his desire not to involve the United Nations. The ambassador was concerned about the "prestige of the United Nations" and "the question of this possible resort to arms without referring the case to the United Nations."[80] Dulles replied:

Well, I wouldn't conceal the fact that I would have a real concern as to the future prestige and authority of the United Nations if events moved her into serious hostilities and the United Nations was fully ignored, and that has been very much a factor in my own mind and has been part of the motivation of my own course of action here in the United States policy in this situation.[81]

He seemed to indicate that if there were an actual breach of the peace or act of aggression, the United Nations should become involved, but that at the present stage it was still a dispute that the parties should attempt to settle themselves. He explained:

The United Nations Charter, as you recall, refers to the fact that in the event of a dispute and so forth the nations shall, first of all, try to seek a solution by conciliation, negotiation, and conference and what not, and other peaceful means of their own choosing. And it is because the Charter puts the obligation upon the members to try, first of all, to find a peaceful solution that I urged so strongly at London that the British and French should certainly, first of all, try this method.[82]

In other words, Dulles believed that the issue was still one that fell into the realm of Chapter VI of the charter, which deals with the pacific settlement of disputes, rather than Chapter VII of the charter, which deals with threats to the peace, breaches of the peace, and acts of aggression.

Dulles later elaborated on other reasons why the matter was not taken to the United Nations. One reason the August proposal for a Suez Canal board was not taken to the United Nations after its formulation was that "it was not the kind of proposal which fitted in with the procedure and powers of the United Nations, either the Security Council or much less the Assembly, which in any event can only make recommendations."[83] He explained that the August proposal was a very detailed attempt to resolve permanently the crisis in which the delegates "proposed to Egypt the making of a new treaty."[84] Unfortunately, "however meritorious our proposal may have been the United Nations has not the authority to require a nation to make a new treaty."[85] He explained:

As I read the Charter, that perhaps goes beyond what is within the competence of the Security Council. It can require existing treaties to be lived up to. It can call on the parties to adopt provisional measures; but I do not believe that the Security Council, much less the Assembly, has the authority to compel what we hoped would come about by voluntary agreement at our last meeting, namely, the conclusion of a new treaty which would redefine the rights of the parties and which would deal in perpetuity with this problem.[86]

It was beyond the powers of the United Nations to impose a very specific settlement on Egypt.

Even though Nassar had rejected this proposal, Dulles felt that another attempt to formulate an arrangement among the parties should also be made before going to the United Nations. He actually believed that the September meeting was formulating the problem so that if it failed a second time, the issue would then be well prepared for U.N. consideration. This was true for two reasons. First, the meeting in September would consolidate the position of the concerned states for the United Nations: "We present a group which if it is cohesive and holds together would give the United Nations something to deal with vis-a-vis Egypt. If we break apart and fall asunder, then I do not readily see how the problem can be solved by the United Nations."[87] Second, unlike the August proposal, which required a specific treaty, the September proposal was to be more of a temporary solution. Explained Dulles, "[w]hat we are suggesting here is a mechanism for the kind of a provisional solution which is precisely the kind that the United Nations could seize hold of, whereas it could not have seized hold of the proposal which we made at the time of our August meetings."[88] Such a proposal "is within the competence of the Security Council as I read the Charter, notably under Article 36 as to procedural ways of dealing with practical problems and Article 40 dealing with provisional measures."[89] In addition, during the proceedings at the Second Suez Canal Conference in September, Dulles expressed a concern for the complexity of taking the matter to the United Nations; it was, at that point, a logistical problem as well.[90]

As noted earlier, before the proposal of the Second Conference could be put into practice, Great Britain and France took the matter to the United Nations themselves--without consulting Dulles. The latter feared that this move would discourage membership in the Suez Canal Users Association. He even speculated that the effort to take the issue to the United Nations might have been motivated by certain elements who wished a vetoed resolution so that the states could then use force, claiming the United Nations had failed.[91] In any case, the United Nations took up the matter in October, and although there were low points, it actually seemed to be encouraging movement toward peaceful settlement. Before any settlement could be reached, however, Israeli troops moved into Egypt.

When the Israeli attack occurred, Eisenhower and Dulles felt it incumbent on them not to support Israeli aggression. Eisenhower was especially concerned about fulfilling the pledge the United States had made in the Tripartite Resolution of 1950, in which the United States, Great Britain and France had promised to aid the victim of aggression in any Arab-Israeli conflict.[92] Immediately, the United States took the matter to the Security Council, in order, Eisenhower explained, to get there before the Soviet Union.[93]   In the Security Council, the United States introduced a resolution calling upon "Israel immediately to withdraw its armed forces behind the established armistice lines."[94]   The proposed resolution called upon all members of the United Nations

(a) to refrain from the use of force or threat of force in the area in any manner inconsistent with the purposes of the United Nations;
(b) to assist the United Nations in ensuring the integrity of the armistice agreements;
(c) to refrain from giving any military economic or financial assistance to Israel so long as it has not complied with this resolution.[95]

This latter provision constituted what Ambassador Lodge called "a minimum sanction"[96] against Israel. The vote on a slightly modified version of the original resolution was seven to two, with two abstentions, but since France and Great Britain were the dissenters, the resolution failed.[97]

While all this was taking place, France and Great Britain had issued an ultimatum to Egypt and Israel calling for a cessation of hostilities, and threatening to move their troops into the area if this did not occur. This action, the United States believed, had the potential to exacerbate the conflict. Eisenhower sent the British and French a message expressing his "deep concern at the prospect of this drastic action even at the very time when the matter is under consideration as it is today by the United Nations Security Council."[98] He added, "It is my sincere belief that peaceful processes can and should prevail to secure a solution which will restore the armistice condition as between Israel and Egypt and also justly settle the controversy with Egypt about the Suez Canal."[99]   Despite this appeal, on the following day, France and Great Britain officially entered the war against Egypt.

On November 1, the General Assembly took up consideration of the crisis, which had been referred to it by the Security Council under the "Uniting for Peace" Resolution. Eisenhower directed Dulles to formulate "an announcement of our suspension of all military and some governmental economic aid to Israel,"[100] and to draft "a moderate resolution for submission to the General Assembly in an effort to block a resolution--certain to be an objectionable one--by the Soviet Union."[101]   But while part of Eisenhower and Dulles's motivation seemed to be to prevent the Soviets from appearing as the champions against aggression, Dulles seemed truly concerned that aggression not be condoned as a means of change. According to Herman Finer, Dulles was not heartbroken about the possible demise of Nassar, but could not agree with the method. He allegedly told Abba Eban:

> I'm torn. . . . *Yet*: can we accept this good end when it is achieved by means that violate the Charter? Look here, we could improve our position in the world if we used force, say in Korea, or Quemoy, or in Germany. But if we did that, the United Nations would collapse. So I am forced to turn back to support international law and the Charter. I have to work on the basis that the long-term interests of the United States and the world are superior to the considerations of self-benefit. Another thing: if the intruders do not evacuate and go back behind the armistice frontier, Secretary General Hammarskjold would resign![102]

Dulles echoed these concerns when he presented the U.S. resolution to the General Assembly. "I doubt," he began, "that any delegate ever spoke from this forum with as heavy a heart as I have brought here tonight."[103]   After a recitation of the facts surrounding the crisis, he recognized that the aggression was far from unprovoked. He explained, "We are not blind . . . to the fact that what has happened in the last two or three days comes out of a murky background."[104] However, he continued, "we have come to the conclusion that these provocations, serious as they are, cannot justify the resort to armed force which has occurred within the last two and three days, and which is going on tonight."[105] He recognized that "the United Nations perhaps had not done all that it should have done,"[106] but argued that this could not justify a right of self-help:

> [I]f we were to agree that the existence of injustices in the world, which this Organization so far has been unable to cure, means that the principle of renunciation of force is no longer respected, and that there exists the right wherever a nation feels itself subject to injustice to resort to force to try to correct that injustice, then . . . we would have, I fear, torn the Charter into shreds and the world would again be a world of anarchy.[107]

Dulles then recounted all the means that had been undertaken to settle the Suez dispute peacefully, but concluded that "there seemed to be peaceful processes that were at work which, as I say, had not yet, it seemed to us at least, run their course."[108] While recognizing that force could be used under certain circumstances (self-defense, for example), the United States believed "that under the circumstances which I described, the resort to force, the violent armed attack by three of our members upon a fourth cannot be treated as other than a grave error, inconsistent with the principles and purposes of the Charter, and one which if persisted in would gravely undermine our Charter and undermine this organization."[109]

With this conclusion, Dulles recommended a course of action for the General Assembly. While the assembly could not take binding action, he argued, it could make recommendations, which, if they reflected "the moral judgment of the world community, of world opinion, will, I think, be influential upon the present situation."[110] He then presented the U.S. resolution, which essentially called for a return to the *status quo ante*. It took note of Israeli, British, and French actions against Egypt, and urged all parties to consent to a cease-fire, to remove their troops to the armistice lines, to stop further action against Egypt, and not to bring new forces into the crisis.[111]   While Dulles recognized that this resolution essentially emphasized only a return to the situation preceded the hostilities, he felt that the fighting must be stopped before further corrective action could be taken.   Early on the morning of November 2, the U.S. Resolution was adopted by a vote of sixty-four to five, with six abstentions.[112]

This resolution is very interesting in light of Dulles's desire to prevent the use of aggression. Like the proposed resolution in the offshore islands dispute, it was not a "collective security" resolution. While the proposed Security Council resolution had called for mild sanctions against Israel, the assembly resolution simply called for a cease-fire and a withdrawal. It did not, as could have been the case under the "Uniting for Peace" Resolution, recommend any collective action against the aggressors. This was most likely due to the realization that no collective action would be practical against two of the permanent members of the Security Council. The resolution did, nevertheless, seek to end aggression and uphold Article 2(4), even if it did not recommend sanctions.

THE HUNGARIAN INVASION

The day after British and French troops joined the invasion of Egypt, Premier Imre Nagy proclaimed the neutrality of Hungary and requested aid from the United Nations in maintaining its neutrality. But before the United Nations could discuss the matter, Dulles was hospitalized for emergency surgery. He was, therefore, unable to participate in the decision making on the Hungarian issue. It may nevertheless be useful to examine briefly the U.S. reaction to the problem, with the understanding that Dulles later expressed support for the United States position.

After Hungary's appeal, the Security Council began dealing with the problem. On November 4, an American resolution that called "upon the Russian government at once to withdraw its forces from Hungary" was vetoed by the Soviet Union.[113]   (There were still troops on Hungarian soil.)   With the situation worsening from the

Soviet perspective, they then sent more troops into the country in an attack calculated to crush the renegade Nagy regime. On the afternoon of the 4th, the General Assembly adopted by a vote of fifty to eight a United States resolution calling for a Soviet withdrawal.[114] Needless to say, there was no recommendation that any collective action be undertaken. Dulles did, however, later express the idea that if the United Nations had not been considering the Suez Crisis, it might have been able to adopt a stronger resolution. He told Andrew Berding:

> Coming at the same time as the Soviets' brutal repression of the uprising in Hungary, it [the Suez Crisis] served to distract much world attention from that development. The United Nations, I am convinced, would have taken a stronger stand on Hungary had it not been for the Suez incident. I would dearly have loved to focus the eye of the world public opinion uniquely on what was happening in Hungary.[115]

Presumably, Dulles believed that if world opinion could have indeed been channeled against Soviet actions, it might have had some effect on the Soviets.

Neither Eisenhower nor Dulles seriously contemplated other action against the Soviets. Hungary was not easily accessible, and no cooperation from Great Britain or France could be anticipated. Moreover, any actions would likely precipitate a major war.[116] After Dulles had recovered from his operation, he commented on the prospects for United States actions in Hungary:

> This would be madness. The only way we can save Hungary at this time would be through all-out nuclear war. Does anyone in his senses want us to start a nuclear war over Hungary? As for sending American divisions into Hungary, they would be wiped out by superior Soviet ground forces. Geography is against us. And in either event what happens to Hungary? Obviously it would be devastated from one end to the other and the Hungarians would be the greatest sufferers.[117]

In sum, while the United States did take the matter to the United Nations, it did not consider any collective action to repel the aggressor. The Soviet Union was simply too powerful, the allies too divided, and Hungary too isolated. Any potential action would not end aggression but only escalate the conflict. Once again, with a great power involved, collective security could not work, a fact that the founders of the United Nations no doubt had had in mind when they established the veto provision.

THE INTERVENTION IN LEBANON

In the wake of the Suez Crisis of 1956, "the Middle East remained highly unstable."[118] Fearing the possibility of communist adventurism in the area, the United States promulgated the so-called Eisenhower Doctrine. This doctrine, which was affirmed by congressional resolution, authorized the president, as Eisenhower explained, "to undertake programs of military assistance and cooperation with any nation desiring them, such programs to include United States military aid when requested, against armed aggression from any nation controlled by international Communism."[119]   In 1958, this doctrine was put to the test.

In spring of 1958, Lebanese President Camille Chamoun's government began to be challenged by domestic strife. In mid-May, Chamoun asked Eisenhower how the United States would respond to a request for assistance. Both Dulles and Eisenhower, while recognizing the difficulties such military assistance could cause, believed that intervention should be provided if requested. Explained Eisenhower, "[b]ehind everything was our deepseated conviction that the Communists were principally responsible for the trouble."[120] Eisenhower had Dulles explain to Chamoun that the United States would intervene if asked, provided that "certain conditions" were met. These included Eisenhower's desire that "the request should have the concurrence of some other Arab nation" and the recognition that "the mission of the United States troops in Lebanon would be twofold: protection of the life and property of Americans, and assistance to the legal Lebanese government."[121] Eisenhower also stressed that such intervention should be regarded as a "last resort."[122] Initially, the United States did not anticipate bringing the matter to the Security Council, "assuming that it would be better for the Lebanese to submit their own statement to the Security Council."[123] As it turned out, the problems seemed to remain below a level requiring U.S. action.

At the request of Lebanon, the Security Council did begin considering allegations of Egyptian and Syrian involvement on the side of the rebels. On June 10, the council adopted a resolution authorizing the Secretary-General to dispatch a "military observation team"[124] to the country. This observation group was sent to Lebanon, with Hammarskjold as its leader. On July 4, the team issued a report that seemed to indicate that the "vast majority" of rebels were themselves Lebanese.[125]   (But as Townsend Hoopes explained, "[t]his report may have been literally true, but it was misleading in the sense that it implied the absence of outside support from Egypt and Syria. Later evidence showed that the U.N. team had been able to work in the mountainous frontier area only during daylight hours and had thus missed a considerable flow of arms and saboteurs crossing into Lebanon after dark.")[126]

On July 14, King Faisal was removed from power in Iraq and

killed. CIA Director Allen Dulles told the president that he believed this coup had been brought about by "pro-Nassar elements of the Iraqi army."[127] Allen's brother felt, in Eisenhower's words, "we lacked hard evidence implicating Nassar [himself]."[128] In any case, on July 14, the administration decided it was time to move in to Lebanon and, at Chamoun's request, U.S. Marine and Army units landed.

The next day, the United States called an emergency meeting of the Security Council. At the United Nations, Ambassador Henry Cabot Lodge explained the scope of U.S. actions in Lebanon. He told the council that U.S. "presence is designed for the sole purpose of helping the Government of Lebanon at its request in its efforts to stabilize the situation, brought on by the threats from outside, until such time as the United Nations can take 'the steps necessary to protect the independence and political integrity of Lebanon.'"[129] The following day, in an effort to allow U.N. forces to replace U.S. troops, the United States introduced a resolution requesting, among other things that the secretary-general "consult the Government of Lebanon and other Member States as appropriate with a view to making arrangements for additional measures, including the contribution and use of contingents, as may be necessary to protect the territorial integrity and independence of Lebanon and to ensure that there is no illegal infiltration of personnel or supply of arms or other materiel across the Lebanese borders."[130] The resolution also called for a cessation of all unlawful aid to the rebels,[131] but this resolution as well as a less forceful one presented by Japan were both vetoed by the Soviets.

As the U.S. troops remained in Lebanon, Khrushchev claimed that American actions amounted to aggression, and continued to call for a great-power summit to resolve the matter. Eisenhower and Dulles strongly preferred that the matter continue to be discussed at the United Nations Security Council. The president even suggested that the council itself could become a "summit" meeting if the various heads of state chose to attend. Dulles saw such a meeting as an opportunity to expose Soviet-backed indirect aggression and refute charges alleging American aggression. In response to a reporter's question, he explained:

> It would be a conference which would, as I said before, dispel the fiction that there is armed aggression going on by the United States or by the United Kingdom [Britain had intervened to assist the regime in Jordan] and which would, I hope, take steps so that through the United Nations or some international machinery there can be eliminated the indirect aggression which was the cause of the United States and the United Kingdom going in.[132]

He specifically hoped that efforts could be made to counter

concretely the growing problem of indirect aggression, which he believed needed to be controlled before any economic progress could be made in the area.[133] In his press conference, Dulles spoke about the possibility of the United Nations investigating propaganda broadcasts and reporting on such broadcasts to determine when they reached the level of aggression.[134] He also referred to the possibility of "a standing group of the United Nations which could go to any place which felt itself endangered by this type of indirect aggression and throw a kind of mantle of security around it."[135] He added: "If that were done in Lebanon, perhaps in Jordan, that would perhaps establish a precedent."[136]

Dulles was also working at the regional level to strengthen the commitment of states in the area to fight aggression. In late July he attended a ministerial meeting of the Baghdad Pact countries--Iran, Pakistan, Turkey, and Great Britain; Iraq had withdrawn--which was held in London. These countries, with the United States joining in, adopted a declaration, in which "the United States, in the interest of world peace, and pursuant to existing Congressional authorization, agrees to co-operate with the nations making this Declaration for their security and defense, and will promptly enter into agreements designed to give effect to this co-operation."[137]

Even as the situation began, in Eisenhower's words, "to stabilize," the Soviets called an emergency meeting of the General Assembly, rejecting the notion of a great power summit at the Security Council.[138] On August 13, Eisenhower addressed the Assembly, presenting a six-point peace plan, allegedly formulated by Dulles,[139] that called for, among other things, the establishment of a standing "United Nations peace force"[140] that could be used in situations of indirect aggression. The proposal also called for the organization of an institution that would foster economic development in the area.[141] Eventually, the Arab states proposed a resolution that seemed to fulfill most of the United States' desires. Speaking before the assembly, Dulles told the delegates that he felt this resolution generally reflected American concerns. One concern, he explained, was a "need to reaffirm, not only in terms of words but of deeds, the principle of our Charter and of prior General Assembly resolutions that each member should respect the freedom, independence, and integrity of other states and scrupulously avoid what might foment civil strife within another state."[142] This, Dulles felt, was dealt with in the Arab resolution. He also praised the fact that the preamble to the resolution called for cooperation under the auspices of the Arab League, explaining that the United States welcomed "the strengthening everywhere of ties which are designed to keep peace and harmony as between the members and which equally accept the overriding provisions of the United Nations Charter dealing with relations of states with each other."[143] The secretary was also pleased with provisions in the resolution calling upon the secretary-general to assist in devising means for troop withdrawal in Lebanon and Jordan.[144] The resolution was adopted, and by October 25, 1958, U.S. troops had left Lebanon.

AN EVALUATION

From Dulles's actions during these crises, and in the light of other comments, several general conclusions can be drawn. First, he demonstrated a strong desire to deter aggression and uphold the basic principle of Article 2(4) of the United Nations Charter. The free world, Dulles felt, had to make it clear that they would not be willing to tolerate the aggressive use of force by any state and had to express their willingness to fight such aggression if it occurred. In October of 1956, he explained that "[o]ne of the great advances of our time is recognition that one of the ways to prevent war is to deter it by having the will and the capacity to use force to punish an aggressor."[145] He believed that the Korean war had resulted because the United States and others had given the impression that they would not defend the South.[146] This sort of war of "miscalculation" could be avoided if states made it clear that they would respond to aggression. This was especially important in the case of the "indirect" aggression that was being perpetrated by the communist regimes. But even when U.S. allies were involved in initiating the aggression, it was necessary for the United States to stand against the aggressors. Hence, in the Suez Crisis, Dulles came to the United Nations not to praise Great Britain, France, and Israel, but to condemn them. In a November 1958 speech, Dulles told his audience that "[t]he United States has consistently supported this principle [Article 2(4)] even when to do so risked war or the alienation of friend."[147] He contended that "[t]he Truman Doctrine for Greece and Turkey; the Berlin Airlift; the Korean War; the Suez Crisis; the Eisenhower Doctrine for the Middle East; the support given to Lebanon; the stand against Communist armed aggression in the Taiwan (Formosa) area--all testify to the dedication of the United States to the principle that force should not be used for aggrandizement or to resolve disputes."[148] Consequently, whenever the United States used force or contemplated using force, Dulles emphasized that it was in the exercise of the Article 51 right of individual or collective self-defense against aggression (as in Guatemala, Taiwan, Indochina) or at the invitation of a lawful government (as in Lebanon).

A second conclusion that can be drawn from Dulles's actions in these cases is that he had a collectivist tendency. In all the cases discussed above, Dulles and Eisenhower wished to refrain as much as possible from major unilateral action, especially unilateral use of force. One reason the United States did not intervene in Indochina was that it had been impossible to set up a collective force. Similarly, the inability to take *collective* action in Hungary was at least one factor that influenced U.S. policy. Much of the reluctance to act unilaterally was probably due not to limited U.S. capabilities, but rather to a belief that collective action had more international legitimacy. As seen above, it was often felt that congressional authorization for using force abroad could be obtained much more easily if other states, either as part of a formal international organization or on an *ad hoc* basis, would join the United States.

Third, Dulles had an ambivalent feeling about the ability of the United Nations to deal with aggression, and seemed to place more hope in regional arrangements. Although he generally supported referring crises to the United Nations, believing that some good could be accomplished by exposing aggression at that forum, he seemed to believe that actual collective security actions were not possible. Concrete actions seemed more plausible on the regional level. In the case of Guatemala, he desired to keep the matter at a regional level, presumably wishing to avoid adverse Soviet actions at the universal level. Similarly, he wished the Suez nationalization to be handled by the parties concerned before taking the matter to the United Nations.

Because of these attitudes toward regional organization, Dulles made efforts to work through existing organizations and sought to create new regional agencies. He praised the Organization of American States and, as noted above, worked with that organization in the Guatemala crisis. Following the Indochina Conference, he negotiated the Manila Pact establishing SEATO, and during the Lebanon crisis, he obtained a cooperative declaration from the Baghdad Pact. In addition to these actions, Dulles remained concerned about the plight of Europe and placed strong pressure on the French to adopt the European Defense Community Treaty. When the French Assembly failed to do this, he continued to push for other forms of European unity. Only under some such arrangement, he believed, could West Germany be integrated into the western defensive structure and the age-old French-Germany rivalry be overcome.

NOTES

1. Dulles, "A Policy of Boldness," 146, 151.
2. See "Memorandum by the Assistant Secretary of State for Inter-American Affairs (Cabot) to the Acting Secretary of State," Feb. 10, 1954, *4 Foreign Relations of the United States*, 1952-1954, 279; "Memorandum of Discussion at the 189 Mtg. of the National Security Council," Mar. 18, 1954, *4 Foreign Relations of the United States*, 1952-1954, 304.
3. D. Eisenhower, *Mandate for Change, 1953-1956*, 424. This chapter draws heavily on the facts presented in Eisenhower's book.
4. Ibid.

5. Ibid.

6. Ibid., 425.

7. "Editorial Note," *4 Foreign Relations of the United States,* 1952–1954, 1177.

8. L. Gerson, *John Foster Dulles,* 312.

9. "Memorandum of Conversation, by the Special Assistant to the President (Cutler)," May 22, 1954, *4 Foreign Relations of the United States,* 1952–1954, 1123.

10. "Memorandum of Conversation with the President, by the Secretary of State," May 22, 1954, *4 Foreign Relations of the United States,* 1952–1954, 1123.

11. "The Secretary of State to the Embassy in El Salvador," May 22, 1954, *4 Foreign Relations of the United States,* 1952–1954, 1125 n. 1.

12. "Address by the Honorable John Foster Dulles," Jan. 30, 1954, Press Release No. 357, in *JFD Papers,* 3.

13. Ibid.

14. Eisenhower, *Mandate for Change,* 426.

15. U.N. Charter, arts. 35 and 52.

16. Quoted in "Editorial Note," *13(1) Foreign Relations of the United States,* 1952–1954, 542.

17. U.S. Minutes of U.S.-U.K.-French mtg., Apr. 15, 1953, *13(1) Foreign Relations of the United States,* 1952–1954, 505.

18. Ibid.

19. "Memorandum of Conversation with the Secretary of State," Apr. 27, 1953, *13(1) Foreign Relations of the United States,* 1952–1954, 513.

20. "Memorandum of Conversation, by the Secretary of State," Jan. 1, 1953, *13(1) Foreign Relations of the United States,* 1952–1954, 588.

21. "The Secretary of State to the Embassy in Thailand," Jan. 1, 1953, *13(1) Foreign Relations of the United States,* 1952–1954, 589.

22. See "Report to the National Security Council by the Executive Secretary (Lay)," Jan. 16, 1954, *13(1) Foreign Relations of the United States,* 1952–1954, 971.

23. Quoted in "Editorial Note," *13(1) Foreign Relations of the United States,* 1952–1954, 1182.

24. Ibid. (emphasis added).

25. "Draft Prepared in the Department of State," Apr. 2, 1954, *13(1) Foreign Relations of the United States,* 1952–1954, 1212.

26. "Memorandum of Conversation by the Deputy Assistant Secretary of State for Far Eastern Affairs (Drumright)," Apr. 2, 1954, *13(1) Foreign Relations of the United States,* 1952–1954, 1216.

27. Ibid.

28. Ibid.

29. Ibid.

30. "Memorandum of Conversation, by the Deputy Assistant Secretary of State for European Affairs (Drumright)," Apr. 4, 1954, *13(1) Foreign Relations of the United States*, 1952-1954, 1235.

31. See, for example, "The Secretary of State to the Embassy in New Zealand," Apr. 7, 1954, *13(1) Foreign Relations of the United States*, 1952-1954, 1284.

32. See "Memorandum of Conversation by the Assistant Secretary of State for European Affairs (Merchant)," Apr. 16, 1954, *13(1) Foreign Relations of the United States*, 1952-1954, 1836.

33. Gerson, *John Foster Dulles*, 179.

34. "Editorial Note," *13(2) Foreign Relations of the United States*, 1952-1954, 1635.

35. Dulles-Hammarskjold Meeting, Jun. 2, 1954: The Secretary of State to the U.S. Delegation, *16 Foreign Relations of the United States*, 1952-1954, 1012.

36. "Editorial Note," *13(2) Foreign Relations of the United States*, 1952-1954, 1636.

37. Ibid.

38. "Memorandum of Conversation with the President," Aug. 17, 1954, *13(2) Foreign Relations of the United States*, 1952-1954, 1953.

39. "Editorial Note," *13(2) Foreign Relations of the United States*, 1952-1954, 2012.

40. Ibid.

41. Dulles, "Address Before the United Nations General Assembly," Sept. 23, 1954, Press Release 1960, *JFD Papers*, 4.

42. Eisenhower, *Mandate for Change*, 463. This section draws heavily on Eisenhower's book.

43. Ibid.

44. Ibid., 464.

45. Ibid.

46. Ibid.

47. Ibid.

48. Ibid.

49. Ibid., 465.

50. "Letter dated 30 January 1955 from the Representative of the Union of Soviet Socialist Republics to the President of the Security Council Concerning the Question of Acts of Aggression by the United States of America Against the People's Republic of China in the Area of Taiwan (Formosa) and Other Islands of China," U.N. Doc. S/3355, 1955.

51. See "Report of the Security Council to the General Assembly," 10 U.N. GAOR Supp. (No. 2), U.N. Doc. A/2935, 1955.

52. Eisenhower, *Mandate for Change*, 465.

53. Quoted in ibid., 465.

54. Ibid., 466.

55. Quoted in ibid, 467.

56. Ibid.

57. Ibid.

58. Quoted in ibid., 459.

59. See Eisenhower, *Mandate for Change*, 481.

60. Ibid., 482.

61. See M. Guhin, *John Foster Dulles: A Statesman and His Times*, 264.

62. Ibid., 265.

63. Ibid.

64. H. Finer, *Dulles Over Suez: The Theory and Practice of His Diplomacy*, xiii.

65. Guhin, *John Foster Dulles*, 269.

66. Ibid.

67. Ibid., 270.

68. Gerson, *John Foster Dulles*, 280.

69. Guhin, *John Foster Dulles*, 271.

70. Gerson, *John Foster Dulles*, 280.

71. Ibid., 282.

72. Guhin, *John Foster Dulles*, 277.

73. Gerson, *John Foster Dulles*, 283.

74. Ibid.

75. Ibid., 289-90.

76. Ibid., 290.

77. Ibid., 291. On the convention, see Finer, *Dulles Over Suez*, 17.

78. Gerson, *John Foster Dulles*, 292.

79. Ibid., 293-294.

80. "Report for Secretary Dulles to Latin American Ambassadors," Aug. 7, 1956, *JFD Papers*, 13.

81. Ibid., 13.

82. Ibid., 13-14.

83. "Extemporaneous Remarks by Secretary of State John Foster Dulles at Second Plenary Session of Suez Canal Conference," Sept. 19, 1956, *JFD Papers*, 1.

84. Ibid.

85. Ibid.

86. Ibid.

87. Ibid., 2.

88. Ibid.

89. Ibid., 3.

90. Second Suez Canal Conference, 5th Plen. Sess., Sept. 21, 1956, Verbatim Record, in *JFD Papers*, at 30-31.

91. See "Memorandum of Conversation," Sept. 27, 1956, in *JFD Papers* at 2-3.

92. See D. Eisenhower, *Waging Peace, 1956-61*, 73.

93. Ibid.

94. See U.N. Doc. S/3710, Oct. 30, 1956, reprinted in 35 Dep't St. Bull., 1956, 750.

95. Ibid.

96. Introduction of U.S. Draft Resolution, U.S./U.N. Press

Release 1485, Oct. 30, 1956, reprinted in 35 Dep't St. Bull., 1956, 750.

97. U.S. Proposal in the Security Council, reprinted in 35 Dep't St. Bull., 1956, 750, n. 1.

98. Eisenhower, *Waging Peace*, 77.

99. Ibid., 77-78.

100. Ibid., 83.

101. Ibid.

102. Quoted in Finer, *Dulles Over Suez*, 392.

103. "Statement by John Foster Dulles, at the Plenary Session of the Special Emergency Session of the U.N. General Assembly, on the Palestine Question," Nov. 1, 1956, Department of State Press Release No. 566, in *JFD Papers*, 1.

104. Ibid., 2.

105. Ibid.

106. Ibid.

107. Ibid., 3.

108. Ibid., 5.

109. Ibid.

110. Ibid.

111. Quoted in ibid., 5-6.

112. Eisenhower, *Waging Peace*, 84.

113. Ibid., 86.

114. Ibid., 88.

115. A. Berding, *Dulles on Diplomacy*, 111.

116. Eisenhower, *Waging Peace*, 88-89.

117. Berding, *Dulles on Diplomacy*, 115-116.

118. Eisenhower, *Waging Peace*, 266.

119. Ibid., 167.

120. Ibid.

121. Ibid.

122. Ibid.

123. Ibid.

124. Ibid., 168.

125. T. Hoopes, *The Devil and John Foster Dulles*, 434.

126. Ibid.

127. Eisenhower, *Waging Peace*, 270.

128. Ibid., 271.

129. "Statement of Ambassador Henry Cabot Lodge of July 15," U.S./U.N. Press Release 1956, reprinted in 39 Dep't St. Bull., 1958, 186.

130. U.N. Doc. S/4050/Rev. 1, reprinted in 39 Dep't St. Bull., 1958, 198.

131. Ibid.

132. Secretary Dulles News Conference of July 31, 39 Dep't St. Bull., 1958, 266, 268.

133. Ibid.

134. Ibid., 270-271.

135. Ibid., 272.

136. Ibid.

137. "Text of Declaration," State Department Press Release 431, July 29, 1958, reprinted in 39 Dep't St. Bull., 1958, 272, 273.

138. Eisenhower, *Waging Peace*, 285.

139. Townsend Hoopes makes this contention. See Hoopes, *The Devil and John Foster Dulles*, 438.

140. Eisenhower, *Waging Peace*, 287.

141. Ibid.

142. "Statement of Secretary Dulles," U.S./U.N. Press Release 1983, Aug. 21, 1958, reprinted in 39 Dep't St. Bull., 1958, 409.

143. Ibid.

144. Ibid.

145. "Address by John Foster Dulles," Oct. 6, 1956, Dep't. of State Press Release No. 525, in *JFD Papers*, 2.

146. Michael Guhin emphasizes this element of Dulles's thought. See Guhin, *John Foster Dulles*, 149-153.

147. "Address by John Foster Dulles Before the National Council of Churches of Christ," World Order Study Conference, Nov. 18, 1958, *JFD Papers*, 11.

148. Ibid.

11

Economic and Social Issues

During his tenure as secretary of state, Dulles was unable to be involved to any great extent in economic and social activities of international organization. In light of his earlier involvement with these issues, however, it is important to examine his actions in two different areas related to these issues: human rights and economic issues.

HUMAN RIGHTS

As noted previously, Dulles had tended to favor nonbinding instruments on human rights, but had come to have doubts about the plausibility of universal covenants. After he became secretary, he encountered domestic problems that led him to decide that the United States should not move forward with the formulation of international covenants on human rights and should not ratify the Genocide Convention, which Truman had submitted to the Senate.

During the 1950s many American legislators had become greatly troubled by U.N. efforts to draft a covenant on human rights and other similar legal instruments. It was feared that if these international agreements were adopted, they would grant the United Nations or other international agencies the right to intervene in matters that had traditionally been regarded as falling within the domestic jurisdiction of the United States. Indeed, some individuals, notably Senator John Bricker, believed that a human rights covenant could actually abridge the rights guaranteed by the U.S. Constitution.[1] In light of these feelings, Senator Bricker and his colleagues introduced several proposals to amend the constitution to prevent the easy adoption of objectionable covenants.

While Dulles strongly opposed the various versions of the "Bricker Amendment" because of the potentially damaging effect they could have on the president's ability to conclude international agreements, he began reassessing the official position of the United States on U.N. human rights covenants and the promotion of human rights by the United Nations. On February 19, 1953, he considered a joint memorandum by Legal Advisor Herman Phleger and Assistant Secretary of State for United Nations Affairs John Hickerson that contained various alternatives for U.S. policy toward human rights.[2] After reviewing this memorandum, Dulles decided to accept a Phleger-Hickerson alternative that represented a change in U.S. policy. Under the proposal, the United States would "move away from active support of the covenants" and "urge that the United Nations give attention and emphasis to means other than the Covenants for making progress toward the goals set forth in the Declaration on Human Rights."[3] Two days later, the policy seemed to have been generally accepted by the president.[4]

On April 3, Dulles sent a letter to the U.S. Representative on the U.N. Human Rights Commission, providing a public explanation of the new American position. In this letter, the Secretary reaffirmed the general United States commitment to human rights, but then explained that "the opening of a new session of the Commission on Human Rights appears an appropriate occasion for a fresh appraisal of the methods through which we may realize the human rights goals of the United Nations. These goals have a high place in the Charter as drafted at San Francisco and were articulated in greater detail in the Universal Declaration of Human Rights."[5] Since then, he continued, efforts had been made to develop covenants on human rights, but "[w]e have found that such drafts as Covenants as had a reasonable chance of acceptance in some respects established standards lower than those now observed in a number of countries."[6] Consequently, he explained,

> While the adoption of the Covenants would not compromise higher standards already in force, it seems wiser to press ahead in the United Nations for the achievement of the standards set forth in the Universal Declaration of Human Rights through ways other than the proposed Covenant on Human Rights. This is particularly important in view of the likelihood that the Covenants will not be as widely accepted. Nor can we overlook the fact that the areas where human rights are being persistently and flagrantly violated are those where the Covenants would most likely be ignored.[7]

With these factors, Dulles argued, "there is a grave question whether the completion, signing and ratification of the Covenants at the time is the most desirable method of contributing to human betterment particularly in areas of greatest need."[8] "Furthermore," he continued, "experience to date strongly suggests that even if it be assumed that this is a proper area for treaty action, a wider general acceptance of human rights goals must be attained before it seems useful to codify standards of human rights as binding international legal obligations in the Covenants."[9]

On the advice of his advisors, Dulles decided that while the U.S. representative would continue to attend meetings of the Human Rights Commission on the Covenant, she should make other substantive proposals, such as calling for "comprehensive annual reports" from states on "human rights development," and should "study of significant aspects" of human rights throughout the world.[10] The programs, it was hoped, would demonstrate the continuing devotion of the United States to promoting human rights through the United Nations.

With the new human rights policy being implemented at the United Nations, Dulles was able to counter some of the fears of the "Brickerites." On April 6, he told the Senate Judiciary Committee that "[d]uring recent years there developed a tendency to consider treaty making [a] as way to effectuate reforms, particularly in relation to social matters, and to impose upon our Republic conceptions regarding human rights which many felt were alien to our traditional concepts."[11] This trend, he believed, was what motivated advocates of the Bricker Amendment. Now, Dulles continued, "[t]here has been a reversal of the trend toward trying to use the treaty-making power to effect internal changes."[12] The administration was "committed to the exercise of the treaty-making power only within traditional limits."[13] Lest this be misunderstood, he explained that "[b]y 'traditional' I do not mean that [*sic*] to imply that the boundary between domestic and international concerns is rigid and fixed for all time. I do mean that treaties are contracts with foreign governments designed to promote the interests of our nation by securing action by others in a way deemed advantageous to us;" he did "not believe that treaties should, or lawfully can, be used as a device to circumvent the constitutional procedures established in relation to what are essentially matters of domestic concern."[14] Dulles then explained that the administration did "not intend to become a party to any such [Human Rights] covenant or present it as a treaty for consideration by the Senate," nor did it "intend to sign the Convention on Political Rights of Women."[15] He also told a Judiciary subcommittee that the United States would refrain from pressing for the adoption of the Genocide Convention.[16]

To someone unfamiliar with Dulles's earlier thought on human rights, the change in U.S. human rights policy might appear to be a simple political compromise--the United States would refrain from pressing for the drafting and adoption of various covenants in an effort to appease the advocates of the Bricker Amendment. Given the general development of Dulles's view on human rights, however, this interpretation does not tell the entire story. Clearly, Dulles was engaging in a tactical political move to attempt to avoid what he felt would be a grave crippling of the power of the executive to conduct foreign affairs. But he did not suddenly subsume his view on human rights to those considerations. As noted earlier, as Dulles became involved in the United Nations, he had become convinced that a truly universal covenant on human rights would be virtually impossible at that time. There were not yet enough shared moral beliefs to undergird such legal documents. His decision as secretary of state to change United States policy, while perhaps motivated by domestic considerations, was itself largely a consistent evolution of his own thought on the matter.

ECONOMIC ISSUES

During his years as secretary of state, Dulles did not speak about economic activities of international organization as much as he had during other periods of his life, yet, several elements from his speeches indicate a continuing concern for these areas. First, he seemed to continue to accept the general tenets of the functionalist thesis. In an address delivered on April 25, 1956, he recognized economic problems as a basic cause of war, contending that it was important to look behind the personalities of World War II "to the economic conditions that brought Hitler and the Japanese warlords into power in the early 1930's."[17] While economic conditions had improved since the war, it was important that the relationship of economic prosperity to peace not be forgotten. He told his audience that "[a]ny serious interruption of international trade could readily again bring reckless men to power in hard-hit countries, demanding for their country the resources and markets needed for economic well-being."[18] "This," he felt, "could precipitate World War III."[19] Further in support of the functionalist approach, Dulles suggested that a free flow of goods and people could help facilitate peace. Noting the need for peaceful change, he explained that "the need for change of boundaries becomes less if boundaries are not barriers to the reasonable flow of trade and movement of persons and ideas."[20] Implicit in this statement was a belief that national sovereignty would lose some of its importance if international cooperation made borders less restrictive.

Second, Dulles continued to support both multilateral and unilateral programs for economic development. In 1955, he praised the work of the Economic and Social Council in this task, explaining that through the council "much is being done to improve the economic and social conditions of the less developed areas of the world."[21] On November 18, 1958, he reaffirmed the need to provide aid for the less developed countries, especially to prevent them from "falling prey" to communism. He explained numerous projects that the United States had undertaken or would undertake, such as "educational exchanges," "health programs," and "agricultural assistance."[22] In short, it was a matter of U.S. foreign policy to encourage economic development and a number of specific actions were being taken.

NOTES

1. "A Proposal to Amend the Constitution of the United States, Statement by Senator John W. Bricker on the Floor of the U.S. Senate," Feb. 7, 1952, *JFD Papers*, 3.
2. "Memorandum by the Legal Advisor (Phleger) and the Assistant Secretary of State for United Nations Affairs (Hickerson) to the Secretary of State," Feb. 18, 1953, *3 Foreign Relations of the United States*, 1952–1954, 1549.
3. Ibid., 1552.
4. "Memorandum of the Secretary of State," Feb. 20, 1953, *3 Foreign Relations of the United States*, 1952–1954, 1585, n. 2.
5. "The Secretary of State to the United States Representative on the Commission on Human Rights (Lord)," Apr. 3, 1953, *3 Foreign Relations of the United States*, 1953–1954, 1564, 1565.
6. Ibid., 1565–1566.
7. Ibid., 1566.
8. Ibid.
9. Ibid.
10. "The Secretary of State to the Embassy in the United Kingdom," Apr. 6, 1953, *3 Foreign Relations of the United States*, 1952–1954, 1567.
11. "Statement by John Foster Dulles, Before the Judiciary Committee of the United States Senate," Apr. 6, 1953, Dep't of State Press Release No. 174, *JFD Papers*, 2.
12. Ibid.
13. Ibid.
14. Ibid.
15. Ibid.
16. "Memorandum by the Assistant Secretary of State for the United Nations Afairs (Hickerson) to the Secretary of State," Feb. 9, 1953, *3 Foreign Relations of the United States*, 1952–1954, 1542, 1546 n. 4.
17. "Address by John Foster Dulles before the Fifteenth Annual Meeting of the American Society of International Law," Apr. 25, 1956, *JFD Papers*, 11.
18. Ibid.
19. Ibid.
20. Ibid.
21. "Address by John Foster Dulles at the Tenth Anniversary Meeting of the U.N.," June 24, 1955, *JFD Papers*, 1.

22. "Address by John Foster Dulles before the National Council of Churches of Christ, World Order Study Conference," Nov. 18, 1958, *JFD Papers*, 4.

12

The International Legal System

When Dulles assumed the helm at the State Department, he remained concerned about the international legal system and its relationship to international organization. This chapter will explore several aspects of his thoughts and actions relating to international law. First, it will examine Dulles's views on the status of the international legal system. Second, it will explore his activities associated with the development of international law. Finally, it will discuss the role that international legal considerations played in the secretary's foreign policy.

THE STATUS OF THE INTERNATIONAL LEGAL SYSTEM

As noted above, during much of Dulles's life, he believed that the international legal system was very poorly developed, and only late in life did he seem to recognize the normative significance of certain new developments. Once he became secretary of state, he continued to express concerns about the inadequacies of international law. This was especially true at the beginning of his tenure. In a letter dated July 1, 1953, to Special Assistant to the President C. D. Jackson, Dulles reiterated his earlier concerns. He told Jackson that "[l]ack of law is a serious defect" and claimed that "[a]t the San Francisco Conference of 1945, when the Charter was drawn up, I was responsible for getting in the clause requiring the Assembly to develop international law."[1] Unfortunately, "very little has been done [to develop international law], because in fact most of the member states are not willing to subject themselves to law as developed and applied by an international body."[2] The major culprit, he believed, was the Soviet Union. He told Jackson that "[l]aw in the sense that we use the word is a codification of moral principles. In the Soviet world, there is no such concept, because they deny the existence of moral law."[3] Previously, on September 27, 1952, he had elaborated on this concept, explaining that the Soviets "believe that international law, and the treaties which make it, are like their own national law, merely devices to get advantages over their class enemies--among whom we rank as Enemy Number One. They do not themselves feel subject to any moral sanctions or restraint by virtue of their own engagements."[4]

In addition to his belief in the "lack" of international law, he also believed that there was inadequate enforcement of existing international law and a failure of states to avail themselves of the international judicial process. In an address before the American Society of International Law on April 25, 1956, he explained how the General Assembly through the "Uniting for Peace" Resolution and regional agencies became substitutes for a Security Council that was unable to act. He also pointed out that the International Court of Justice (ICJ) had not been sufficiently utilized. He explained that "despite much lip service to that [the judicial] process, most nations prefer to seek the settlement of their dispute by diplomatic means or perhaps they prefer to keep the disputes open for political reasons."[5] After reviewing the caseload of the ICJ as compared to that of the PCIJ, he concluded that it was "significant that with all the disputes which exist in the world, there are only two contentious cases now on the docket of the International Court of Justice. It is demonstrated that nations are reluctant to settle serious disputes and the basis of rules of law."[6]

But even though Dulles continued to believe that international law was not wholly adequate, he did at times acknowledge certain positive developments in the legal system. First, despite his earlier reluctance to recognize the normative nature of the United Nations Charter, by April of 1956 he had come to believe that "[t]he Charter itself establishes some basic international law."[7] This was largely accomplished in "Article 2 which deals with sovereign equality; the settlement of international disputes by peaceful means; and the renunciation of the threat or use of force."[8] In other words, these "principles" of the charter were, in fact, legal obligations. (Indeed, it has already been seen how he came to feel that Article 2(4) created a legal obligation.) Furthermore, "Chapter XI dealing with non-self-governing territories also contains an important enunciation of legal principles."[9] Second, even though much remained to be done, he believed that "[t]here has occurred a healthy growth in the multilateral, law-making type of treaty."[10] Third, he seemed pleased by the progress in the area of customary international law. He explained:

There is also a body of world opinion which, when it is crystallized and brought to bear on a particular situation, plays a role equivalent to our "common law." There has been a gratifying progress in developing this kind of community judgment and the gatherings of the nations at the General Assembly of the United Nations greatly promoted this result. There, international conduct is judged, sanctioned formally but more often informally; and even the most powerful nations feel it expedient to be able to represent their conduct as conforming to this body of world opinion.[11]

In sum, by the mid-1950s Dulles was able to acknowledge politically that there was a certain amount of international law embodied in the charter, treaties, and perhaps custom. As noted earlier, he had begun to recognize the normative significance of Article 2(4) during his involvement with the U.S. delegation to the United Nations. His acceptance of other aspects of the charter as law seems to represent the continuation of a trend begun during this earlier time.

THE DEVELOPMENT OF THE INTERNATIONAL LEGAL SYSTEM

Notwithstanding the positive developments in international law, there was still a great deal of room for improvement. Dulles supported several concrete efforts to improve the international legal system. First, he continued to believe that an attempt should be made to revise the United Nations Charter. In 1953 he expressed United States support for the convening of a general review conference. In August of that year he told the American Bar Association that the "Charter of the United provides that the 1955 General Assembly will have on its agenda a proposal to call a general conference to review the present Charter," and explained that he had "already announced that the United States will then vote in favor of holding such a review conference."[12] He hoped that this conference could deal with a number of specific issues. For instance, he believed that the conference could "reconsider the present 'veto' power in relation to the admission of new members, particularly if that veto power continued to be abused."[13]

The Soviet Union, Dulles believed, had repeatedly used the veto to prevent legitimate states from being admitted to the United Nations. Hence, "the membership of the United Nations falls far short of representing the totality of those nations which are peace-loving, which are able and willing to carry out the obligations of the Charter and which are indispensable parties to many critical international problems."[14] (Dulles did, interestingly enough, point out that "[n]one of these is in the category of Communist China, which has been found by the United Nations to be guilty of aggression"[15] and whose admission the United States opposed.) Dulles also believed the conference could deal with the problem of nuclear weapons. The charter, he felt, did not and could not have addressed itself to nuclear weapons, and was thus "a pre-atomic age charter."[16]   He explained that "epochal developments in the atomic and disarmament fields may make it desirable to give this Organization a greater authority in these matters."[17]   Unfortunately, although the General Assembly considered the question of calling a conference, it did not set a date.[18]

Second, Dulles continued to advocate the further development of other aspects of international law. While he seemed to support efforts to expand conventional international law, he tended to prefer the development of customary international law. He told the American Society of International Law that "[i]n view . . . of the difficulty of gaining multilateral acceptance of formal codification of international law, we shall have to place much reliance upon unwritten law."[19]   This would require "constant education of public opinion, so that it will reflect a sound judgment about international conduct."[20]   He also suggested that there needed "to be improvement of the processes of the United Nations General Assembly, so that when it acts in a quasilegislative or judicial capacity, it will comply with such high standards as evoked [sic] the Anglo-Saxon concept of the King's conscience which the Equity Chancellor was to apply."[21]

In addition to advocating the development of general international law, which had been a consistent theme in Dulles's thought, he also suggested the development of less than universal law. He explained that "[t]here can also be a useful development of law among the free world nations as a whole and also among those groups of free nations as naturally draw together."[22]   As an example, he contended that the "Organization of American States has already done much to develop a body of American law and precedent which helps to keep peace and order in the new world."[23]   His support for "regional" law seems to be the logical conclusion of his advocacy of Article 51 organizations and the promotion of human rights on a less than universal basis. Indeed, in the conclusion to his April 1956 speech, he argued that "[w]here universality may not be practical, we can find in regional and collective defense associations an area where notable progress can be made."[24]   "These associations," he explained, "can serve as important stepping stones toward a universal order. They can, as between their own members, develop such principles of conduct as we have referred to and they can make force into a sanction for these principles, thus making it serve the community."[25]   Dulles thus reiterated a theme present in his early thought: regional arrangements by promoting law and order on a less than universal basis could eventually lead to a cohesive world organization.

Under Dulles's administration, a number of efforts were undertaken to give practical effect to the development of international law. For instance, negotiations were begun to establish legal regimes for outer space, the Arctic, and Antarctica. In speaking of these areas, the secretary of state even seemed to foresee the development of a new legal doctrine akin to the "common heritage of mankind" notion that has played a predominant role in international negotiations in subsequent years. On November 18, 1958, he explained that "[w]hat we have said about the Arctic, the Antarctic, atomic power and outer space suggests a new principle. As change opens up new areas of world-wide concern, where *national* control has not yet entrenched itself, let us seek the maximum possible *international* status."[26]   In addition to these activities, the First United Nations Conference on the Law of the Sea (UNCLOS I) convened in 1958 and produced four conventions that sought both to codify existing international law and progressively develop it. The United States played a major role in this conference, and subsequently ratified three of the four conventions. While Dulles was not directly involved in the law-of-the-sea negotiations, his general policy to promote the development of international law no doubt set the tone for U.S. participation in the conference. (It is interesting to note that even though Dulles emphasized the development of customary international law, these formal codification efforts were also undertaken.)

Third, Dulles also seemed, at least late in life, to support increased use of international adjudication. In one of the last speeches he made on international law, he explained that there was "a serious need for all of us to develop a respect for law as a basis for stability and confidence."[27]   He therefore believed that "[t]hose nations which do have common standards should, by their conduct and example, advance the rule of law by submitting their disputes to the International Court of Justice, or to some other international tribunal upon which they can agree."[28]   The United States, he told his audience, was "closely examining the question of our own relationship to the International Court of Justice with the view of seeing whether ways and means can be found to assure a greater use of that Court by ourselves, and, through our example, by others."[29]

Despite Dulles's periodic skepticism about the possibiity of making any improvements in the international legal system, he maintained his optimism. At times, he even felt that the Soviet Union would come around. In his speech before the American Society of International Law in 1956, he indicated that notwithstanding the Soviet conception of law, there was "some glimmering of hope in this respect."[30]   In light of some development in the Soviet Union, he felt that "despite the Communist doctrinal rejection of our concept of law, there may be emerging a *de facto* acceptance of law as a protection of the individual against the capricious will of those in authority."[31] And he also believed that it was "a fact that, on the international plane, the Soviet rulers, if only grudgingly and as a matter of expediency, take some account of the opinion of mankind. And these, as we have observed, can form a body of common or unwritten international law."[32] He echoed this belief in November of 1958,[33] but in January of 1959 he was once again troubled by Soviet intransigence.[34] Nevertheless, he felt that efforts to promote a functioning legal system should continue.

In general, these beliefs about the improvement of the international legal system are perfectly consistent with Dulles's earlier views. During his tenure in office, however, there was a major change. As noted earlier, he had often spoken about the development of a body of law that would be applicable directly to individuals. Once in office, however, he seemed to reject this notion. This was probably precipitated by the debate over the Bricker Amendment. As has been seen, the "Brickerites" were greatly troubled that international law, in the form of human rights instruments, would produce effects on matters that were within domestic jurisdiction. Dulles opposed the Bricker Amendment, but seemed persuaded that international law should not affect anything but states. As noted earlier, while acknowledging "that the boundary between domestic and international concerns is [not] rigid and fixed for all time," he told the Senate Judiciary Committee "that treaties are contracts with *foreign governments* designed to promote the interests of our nation by securing action by others in a way deemed advantageous to us."[35] He was even more explicit in a letter to the President on proposed International Labour Organisation conventions. He told Eisenhower, "[you] hit the nail on the head when you question 'the propriety of this nation making itself a party to an international treaty which would purport to govern the internal affairs of any nation.'"[36] Dulles explained:

> That is precisely the line which has been taken by Root, Hughes, and other authorities. They point out that while the United States treaty power is not limited explicitly, it is limited implicitly in the sense that treaties should only deal with the normal subject of treaty making, namely, the advancement of the interests of the United States and its citizens by contract with other nations. It was never conceived that the treaty power would be used for the purpose of protecting the citizens of a country from their own government or to enable other governments to protect United States citizens from their government. These, as you say, are internal affairs, not properly subject to the treaty-making power.[37]

Interestingly enough, such a rejection of this type of law was based on the fact that it was inconsistent with the principles of constitutional law. As noted previously, while at the United Nations, Dulles had wondered how it would be possible to create transnational law. Now he seemed to be saying that given the nature of the treaty-making power, it would not be possible at all.

INTERNATIONAL LAW AND FOREIGN POLICY

It is often very difficult to determine with precision the role of international law in the decision-making process of a statesman. In the case of John Foster Dulles, however, it does seem clear that legal principles played a rather important role. This can be seen in several different respects. First, in all cases where the United States used, or contemplated the use of, force, Dulles justified its use on *jus ad bellum* principles found in the United Nations Charter. As noted, in the cases of Guatemala, Indochina, and Taiwan, Dulles justified U.S. actions on the basis of Article 51. In all these cases, he believed that a threat or actual use of force, in violation of Article 2(4), gave rise to the inherent right of individual or collective self-defense. In the case of the Lebanese intervention in 1958, he emphasized the difference between U.S. action there and the British-French-Israeli action in the Suez crisis, by pointing out that U.S. troops were invited by a lawful government. Thus, U.S. activities did not constitute the use of force against the political independence or territorial integrity of that state.

Second, Dulles always explained regional defense organizations in terms of their permissibility under the United Nations Charter. He repeatedly emphasized that such organizations were not intended to derogate from the Charter framework for conflict management but rather were legitimate arrangements in conformity with Article 51: They were established to provide backup systems to enforce, on a less than universal level, the charter proscription of aggression.

Third, and perhaps most important, legal norms seemed to have had a great deal of influence on Dulles's actions during the Suez Crisis. This was true in two respects: Dulles's desire to avoid the use of force in a manner contrary to the charter, and his desire that the canal be regulated in accordance with principles of international law and justice. On the first point, much has already been said. In 1959, Dulles explained that the U.S. "attitude toward the use of armed force is a matter of principle and not merely an anti-Communist policy."[38] "This," he felt, "is shown by the fact that the United States has made clear, even to its good friends, that we are opposed to the use of force in the settlement of international problems."[39] He explained that "it seemed to us, in the fall of 1956, that the entire peace concept of the United Nations was at stake and . . . that if Article 2(4) of the Charter, involving the renunciation of the use of force, were to become a dead letter, the world would revert to chaos."[40] In consequence, the United States took a stand contrary to that of its friends, the United Nations supported the United States, and "[t]he United Kingdom, France and Israel responded. The invading forces were withdrawn. Tolerable solutions were found through peaceful means."[41]

But the desire of the United States during the Suez Canal was not merely the avoidance of force. On September 26, Dulles explained that "[t]he purpose of the United States in relation to the Suez situation is precisely that set out in the First Article of the Charter of the United Nations, namely, to seek a settlement by peaceful means, *and in conformity with the principles of justice and international law.*"[42]   There needed to be peace, but there also needed to be fidelity to principles of international law and justice. At Williams College, on October 6, 1956, he explained:

> There has been strong worldwide sentiment against using force to right this situation. That is natural and proper. But those who are concerned about peace ought to be equally concerned about justice. Is it just, or even tolerable, that those great nations which have rights under the 1888 treaty and whose economies depend upon the use of the canal should accept an exclusive control of this international waterway by a government which professes to be bitterly hostile?[43]

Indeed, Dulles struggled throughout the summer of 1956 to create a legal regime that would reaffirm the rights of parties under the 1888 Convention. Even after the invasion, he emphasized the need for "not merely a peaceful solution, but a just solution."[44]

In conclusion, Secretary of State Dulles took the legal norms that he had come to recognize very seriously. During the Suez Crisis, law appears to have been a major motivating factor in his policy-making. In other areas, he used law to justify decisions, and, even in those cases, it probably had a restraining influence. If United States military actions were not easily justified, or if collective defense arrangements were not permitted by the Charter, Dulles may very well have adopted another policy. In 1959 he said, "we are seeking to establish world order based on the assumption that the collective life of nations ought to be governed by law--law as formulated in the Charter of the United Nations and other international treaties, and law as enunciated by international courts."[45]   Given Dulles's actions, he seemed to have meant this sincerely.

NOTES

1. Letter from JFD to C. D. Jackson, July 1, 1953, *Eisenhower-JFD Papers*, 1.
2. Ibid.
3. Ibid.
4. Dulles, "Principle Versus Expediency in Foreign Policy," Sept. 26, 1952, *JFD Papers*, 4-5.

5. "Address by John Foster Dulles before the Fiftieth Annual Meeting of the American Society of International Law," April 25, 1956, Dep't of State Press Release No. 216, *JFD Papers*, 6.

6. Ibid.

7. Ibid. at 4.

8. Ibid.

9. Ibid.

10. Ibid., 8.

11. Ibid.

12. "Address by John Foster Dulles before the American Bar Association," Aug. 26, 1953, *JFD Papers*, 7.

13. Dulles, "The United Nations--Entering the Second Decade," Sept. 22, 1955, *JFD Papers*, 1.

14. Dulles, "Partnership for Peace," Sept. 23, 1954, U.S./U.N. Press Release No. 1460, *JFD Papers*, 7.

15. Ibid.

16. Dulles, "The United Nations--Entering the Second Decade," 2.

17. Ibid.

18. See L. Goodrich, E. Hambro, and A. Simons, *Charter of the United Nations*, 646-647.

19. "Address by John Foster Dulles before the Fiftieth Annual Meeting of the American Society of International Law," 9.

20. Ibid.

21. Ibid.

22. Ibid.

23. Ibid.

24. Ibid., 14.

25. Ibid.

26. "Address by John Foster Dulles before the National Council of Churches of Christ," 7.

27. "Address by John Foster Dulles before the New York State Bar Association Award Dinner," Jan. 31, 1959, Dep't of State Press Release No. 86, *JFD Papers*, 8.

28. Ibid.

29. Ibid., 9.

30. Dulles, "Address before the Fiftieth Annual Meeting of the Annual Society of International Law," 9.

31. Ibid.

32. Ibid.

33. Dulles, "Address before the National Council of Churches of Christ."

34. Dulles, "Address before the New York State Bar Association Award Dinner."

35. Dulles, "Statement before the Judiciary Committee of the U.S. Senate," Apr. 6, 1953, Dep't of State Press Release No. 174, *JFD Papers*, 2.

36. Letter from JFD to the President, Apr. 27, 1956, *Eisenhower-JFD Papers.*

37. Ibid.

38. Dulles, "Address before the New York State Bar Association Award Dinner," 6.

39. Ibid.

40. Ibid.

41. Ibid.

42. "Secretary Dulles' News Conference," September 26, 1956, Dep't of State Press Release No. 508, *JFD Papers*, at 1.

43. Dulles, "Peace with Justice," Oct. 6, 1956, Dep't of State Press Release No. 525, *JFD Papers*, 5.

44. "Statement by John Foster Dulles at the Plenary Session of the Special Emergency Session of the United Nations General Assembly," Nov. 1, 1956, Dep't of State Press Release No. 566, *JFD Papers*, 2.

45. Dulles, "Address before the New York State Bar Association Award Dinner," 9.

13

Peaceful Change and Other Issues

During the early period of Dulles's life, he believed that the promotion of peaceful change should be the major function of international organization. As he became more involved in the United Nations, he tended, in his words and deeds, to give more emphasis to the collective defense function. Nevertheless, during his time in office, he did not ignore the importance of pursuing peaceful change through international organization. In 1955, on the tenth anniversary of the United Nations, Dulles stressed the need for the international system to enter a "decade for peaceful change."[1] This chapter will examine several themes that ran through Dulles's activities on peaceful change during this period, and will conclude with an exploration of some other issues on which Dulles worked.

PEACEFUL CHANGE

When Dulles was writing *War, Peace, and Change* during the late 1930s, he was mostly concerned with establishing a new *mechanism* to secure peaceful change. In the 1950s, however, he was less concerned with establishing a new mechanism than with making the existing mechanism function. On April 25, 1956, he explained that Article 14 of the charter had been adopted in order to give the United Nations a role in promoting peaceful change. While this article only gave the assembly the power to *"recommend* change," which was "considerably less than the power to *enact* change," "the power to recommend, when exercised in a responsible way by a great majority of the nations of the world, is a considerable power and many Assembly recommendations have been transformed into fact."[2] Even though, as will be seen, he had questions about the success of peaceful change in the postwar era, he did not seem to believe that the answer was to establish additional methods for peaceful change. Instead, states should use the charter method. He explained that it was "of the utmost importance that nations be responsive to informed world opinion and that the 'peaceful adjustment' article of the United Nations Charter (Article 14) should be put to better use."[3] Indeed, he continuously advocated the formulation of public sentiment through the United Nations so that pressure could be put on countries to institute change.

It should be noted, however, that Dulles had noticed a somewhat disturbing trend within the General Assembly. He explained "that debates in the General Assembly in relation to resolutions calling for change tend to be emotional, and votes are sometimes cast not on the basis of impartial study and judgment of the fact, but rather on the basis of the political alignment of the members, and sometimes on the basis of what one might refer to as international 'logrolling.'"[4] Consequently, he contended, "[s]ometimes Assembly debate is counterproductive and makes change less likely because it arouses nationalistic sentiments. Indeed, it sometimes seems that world opinion is more powerful when it is sensed than when the United Nations tries to formulate it in an Assembly resolution."[5] He concluded, "[t]here are vast potentialites in Article 14, but the potentialities are not yet sufficiently well developed so that peaceful change is a well ordered function of the Assembly."[6] Still, what was needed was not a new instrumentality, but the development of the current one so that it could reach its potential.

A second theme in Dulles's consideration of peaceful change was his belief that the decolonization process was, generally speaking, a paradigm example of peaceful change. He explained in 1956:

> World opinion bears particularly upon the conduct of those peoples who, in the words of our Declaration of Independence, feel they owe a decent respect to the opinions of mankind. It is largely through this force, which found expression in Chapter XI of the Charter, that here has occurred the greatest peaceful evolution that history has ever known. During the eleven years since World War II ended and the United Nations charter came into force, over 650 million people have gained a new political independence, now represented by 18 new sovereign nations. Other non-self-governing peoples are at the threshold of independence.[7]

He concluded that it was "highly encouraging that these vast changes should have come about peacefully. It demonstrates dramatically that a very large measure of peaceful change is possible."[8]   But Dulles was not unreservedly happy about this example of peaceful change. It was important, he felt, that the change proceed in an orderly and balanced manner in order to prevent territories from falling into communist hands.[9]

A third element in Dulles's comments on peaceful change was his ambivalence about the prospect for peaceful change within the Soviet bloc. He felt change was necessary in the "captive nations" and strongly advocated, especially during the campaign of 1952, a policy of "liberation" to promote peaceful change within the communist orbit. At times he seemed to be very hopeful of change within these countries. In a speech delivered on October 10, 1955, he explained that "[t]here are some skeptics who doubt that change can be brought about peacefully," but, he felt, "[h]istory does not justify this conclusion."[10] He elaborated: "The recent liberation of Austria came about primarily because world opinion insistently demanded it as a step which represented elemental justice. In the same way world opinion will act as a compulsion on the Soviet Union to relax its grip upon East Germany and to permit the unification of Germany."[11] He even felt "that world opinion will compel the restoration of national independence to the captive states of Eastern Europe."[12] At other times, however, he was not so optimistic. On April 25, 1956, he explained that "we must record the fact that those changes [decolonization] only took place within the free nations and that elsewhere there has been an obstinate resistance to moral pressure for change toward independence and self-government."[13] Hence, he concluded that "[t]here is not, in the world as a whole, any adequate assurance of peaceful change."[14] In 1959, he explained that "we have found no effective means of persuading or inducing the countries of that [Soviet] bloc to accept the principles of justice and law and peaceful change."[15] Perhaps he had generally become less hopeful about Soviet bloc liberation during his last years but, in this 1959 speech he continued to argue that pressure should be applied to the Soviets.

A fourth aspect of Dulles's thought on peaceful change, especially later in his life, was a belief that change *per se* was not necessarily good. He had tended in his early writings to emphasize the need *for* change, rather than merely a legitimate mechanism to *consider* change and grant it if it was felt to be justified. Later in his life, however, Dulles seemed to be more concerned about placing some caveats on change. First, a desire for change had to be balanced by the need for stability. In 1959, he argued that "[p]erhaps . . . the pendulum is swinging too far in the direction of change. . . . A measure of stability is an essential ingredient of peace and order."[16] "Change," he explained, "even political and social change--should not be so impetuous as to paralyze forward planning or to wreak unnecessary injury upon established rights. While law is and should be subject to an orderly process of change, as required by justice, it should be a shield and a protector of those who rely in good faith on international engagements."[17] Second, change also had to be balanced by a need for justice. In his 1959 speech, he praised efforts by the "free world" to promote "a remarkable amount of 'peaceful change' to conform to concepts of justice, and morality."[18] Indeed, in that speech he tended to link law, justice and change together. Third, and perhaps because of these two elements, Dulles believed that a certain type of change should always be resisted-- accommodation to the Soviet system. In 1958, he explained that "[t]here are some who seem to feel that because International Communism is a powerful and stubborn force, we should give way before it."[19]   "Nothing," he contended, "could be more dangerous than to operate on the theory that if hostile and evil forces do not readily change it is always we who must change to accommodate them. . . . Communism is stubborn for the wrong; let us be steadfast for the right. . . .   A capacity to change is indispensable. Equally indispensable is the capacity to hold fast that which is good."[20] Thus, he argued, "while we seek to adapt our policies to the inevitability of change, we resist aspects of change which counter the enduring principles of moral law."[21] (Of course, he did feel the West should establish positive alternatives to the Soviet system and not just promulgate a negative policy.)[22]

A fifth element in Dulles's thinking about change was that he seemed to suggest, contrary to earlier statements, that the prerequisite for peaceful change was a strong collective security system or one of its substitutes. In 1957, he spoke of the need for peaceful change, explaining:

Two decades ago I wrote that world peace depended, not on preserving the *status quo*, but on finding ways of peaceful change. Today, this requirement is more than ever imperative. Our foreign policy accepts change as the law of life. We seek to assure that change will be benign, and not destructive, so that it will promote not merely survival but freedom and well-being.[23]

But, he added, "[a] first requirement is that the door be firmly closed to change by violent aggression."[24] He then proceeded to describe efforts that had been undertaken to secure collective defense. These statements seem to be confirmed by his general emphasis on the collective defense function of international organization discussed above.

In light of Dulles's previous work on peaceful change, his comments during this period are most interesting. While he continued to support peaceful change, he had come to realize that it was important that change be qualified by factors such as justice, stability, and law. He even began to feel that collective defense was the prerequisite to peaceful change. (In the earlier period of his thought he had explicitly criticized those who emphasized on collective defense.) Perhaps most interesting is his attitude toward the Soviet Union. In *War, Peace and Change*, he explained that Japan, Italy, and even Nazi Germany, had had legitimate claims for change that should have been met before they became bellicose. The Soviet Union, however, seemed to fall into a different category. Japan, Italy, and Germany were dynamic forces that, he felt, could have been accommodated early in the post-World War I period. This would have prevented their belligerency. Perhaps he believed that the Soviet Union was not a dynamic force; in fact, it seemed decidedly against dynamism since it was striving to suppress and eliminate dynamic elements within its own society and the societies of Soviet bloc nations. "Change" through accommodation would bring about an international community in which there could be no further change. Moreover, he believed that the Soviet Union was "evil." While he had previously rejected the notion of labeling a state "evil," the nature of communist ideology, as he saw it--materialistic, atheistic, anti-democratic, and anti-individualistic--was contrary to all that he understood as just and moral. Since change, as he had come to believe, had to be qualified by norms of justice and law, tolerance of the Soviet desire for the forcible imposition of communism would be inexcusable.

OTHER ISSUES: DECOLONIZATION AND ARMS CONTROL

In addition to the major issues discussed above, Dulles also dealt with a number of other areas in which international organization could be involved. These include two areas discussed previously, decolonization and disarmament. Although Dulles's views on these areas have been touched on in connection with other issues, it may be useful to summarize them before proceeding.

The general approach of the Eisenhower Administration to the colonial problem, outlined by Dulles in numerous addresses, contained two basic tenets. First, despite all indications to the contrary, the United States remained strongly committed to promoting self-government for all colonial territories. On November 18, 1953,[25] Dulles explained that "[t]here is no slightest wavering in our conviction that the orderly transition from colonial to self-governing status should be carried resolutely to a completion."[26] On numerous occasions he praised the Trusteeship Council and Chapter XI of the charter as institutions that aided in the function of this movement to self-determination. Moreover, this dedication to decolonization played a major role in U.S. policy in Indochina. One of the conditions for American support of the French "was the stipulation that there must be assurance that the French will, in fact, make good on their July 3, 1953, declaration of intention to grant complete independence" to Vietnam, Laos and Cambodia.[27] Even following the Geneva Conference, while he was attempting to negotiate the SEATO agreement, Dulles formulated the Pacific Charter in which "the eight nations--Asian and non-Asian--which met at Manila proclaimed in ringing terms the principle of self-determination, self-government, and independence."[28]

The second element in Dulles's decolonization policy was a belief that because the colonial territories were easy prey for Soviet subversion, the progress to self-government needed to proceed in an orderly and well-balanced manner. The Soviets, he believed, were attempting to stimulate nationalism and then move in before the fledgling countries could get established.[29]   Self-government, he seemed to feel, should be accorded only when the territories were prepared for it, lest they fall into a far worse type of colonization.[30]

Even though Dulles is not normally associated with arms control initiatives, throughout his tenure as secretary of state he remained convinced that some measures needed to be be taken to check the development of these new weapons of destruction.[31] During his administration, he supported several efforts aimed at international regulation of nuclear weapons and control of atomic energy. Following Eisenhower's lead, he favored the establishment of the International Atomic Energy Agency to regulate the production of fissionable materials.[32]   He also worked with and took part in the negotiations of the United Nations Subcommittee on Disarmament and favored action under the United Nations to prohibit nonpeaceful activities in Antarctica[33] and outer space.[34]   Additionally, he supported the establishment of "a system of international inspection of the Arctic area that would reduce the danger of surprise attack over that polar region, and the danger of miscalculation."[35]

NOTES

1. Dulles, "The United Nations--Entering the Second Decade," 14.

2. "Address by John Foster Dulles before the Fiftieth Annual Meeting of the American Society of International Law," Apr. 25, 1956, Dep't of State Press Release No. 216, *JFD Papers*, 5.

3. Ibid., 10.

4. Ibid., 5.

5. Ibid.

6. Ibid., 6.

7. Ibid.

8. Ibid.

9. See, for example, "Address by John Foster Dulles before the National Council of Churches of Christ," 3-5.

10. Dulles, "Confident of Our Future," Oct. 10, 1955, Dep't of State Press Release No. 597, reprinted in Dep't of St. Bull., 1955, 639, 642.

11. Ibid.

12. Ibid.

13. "Address by John Foster Dulles before the Fiftieth Annual Meeting of the American Society of International Law," 6.

14. Ibid.

15. "Address by John Foster Dulles before the New York State Bar Association Award Dinner," 7.

16. Ibid., 7.

17. Ibid., 8.

18. Ibid., 7.

19. "Address by John Foster Dulles before the National Council of Churches of Christ," 8.

20. Ibid.

21. Ibid.

22. Ibid.

23. Dulles, "Dynamic Peace," April 21, 1957, Dep't of State Press Release No. 229, reprinted in Dep't. St. Bull., 1957, 715.

24. Ibid.

25. See "Editorial Note," *3 Foreign Relations of the United States*, 1952-1954, 1166-1167.

26. Dulles, "The Moral Initiative," Nov. 18, 1953, reprinted in Dep't of St. Bull, 1983, 741, 742.

27. Dulles, "International Unity," June 10, 1954, Dep't of State Press Release No. 316, *JFD Papers*, 7.

28. "Address by John Foster Dulles before the United Nations General Assembly," Sept. 23, 1954, U.S./U.N. Press Release 1960, *JFD Papers*, 4.

29. Dulles, "The Moral Initiative," 742-743.

30. Ibid., 743.

31. See A. Berding, *Dulles on Diplomacy*, 89.

32. "Address by John Foster Dulles before the United Nations General Assembly," 5.

33. See "Address by John Foster Dulles before the National Council of Churches of Christ," World Order Conference, Nov. 18, 1958, *JFD Papers*, 6.

34. Ibid., 7.

35. Ibid., 4.

PART FOUR

CONCLUSION

14

Dulles and International Organization: An Appraisal

For over a quarter of a century, scholars have been examining the role of John Foster Dulles in international affairs. The preceding analysis has attempted to contribute to this effort by exploring an often neglected aspect of his life--his involvement with international organization. Several observations can be derived from this study.

First, it is clear that from the early 1920s until his death in 1959, Dulles was devoted to promoting world order through international organization. In the early period of his life, he published numerous works which explored the problems caused by the lack of international mechanisms for peaceful change and the pacific settlement of disputes. During World War II, he became intensely involved in the planning of a new world organization, first as chairman of the Commission on a Just and Durable Peace, and later as an advisor to the U.S. delegation to the San Francisco Conference. After San Francisco, he continued his work with international organization by serving as a member of the U.S. delegation to the United Nations General Assembly. Once he became secretary of state, he continued to take international organization seriously, and made participation in international organization a major tenet of U.S. foreign policy.

Second, there was a large degree of continuity between the early and later phases of Dulles's thought. For instance, despite periods of pessimism, he was rather consistent in his belief that international organization should attempt to develop international law. Even though during most of the early period of his life he doubted that there was much international law, he nevertheless felt that an effort should be made to formulate it. This desire to develop international law continued after he became actively involved in international organization. There was also a great deal of consistency in his belief in "moral force." In his early period, Dulles came to believe that international organization could exert influence on states by unifying world public opinion. After 1945, he continued to believe that moral force could play an important role in international affairs and felt that the United Nations General Assembly could be especially useful in developing moral force. Furthermore, there was also a marked continuity in Dulles's discussions of a host of other issues, such as functionalism, arms control, and European integration, and in his development of the concept of peaceful change. While he clearly redefined the relationship of peaceful change to other roles of international organization during the later years of his life, he never came to believe in an iron-clad *status quo* and continued to support changes in the international system. In fact, his much criticized policy of "liberation" was a reflection of his desire for peaceful change.

Third, despite these continuities in Dulles's thought, it is clear that it underwent a great deal of change. This can undoubtedly be attributed to a number of factors, but two seem to be most important: a change in the role that he played in international affairs, and a change in his conception of the international system.

In 1945, Dulles experienced an important role change. Prior to that date, he had been a theorist about and an advocate for international organization: His official involvement with international organization had been minimal. While he was never unrealistically optimistic about the possibilities of international organization, Dulles did tend to be more optimistic during the earlier period of his thought. As he began to be involved in the day-to-day negotiations at San Francisco and New York, however, he began to see international organization differently. As he was exposed to the concrete problems of international organization, he came to recognize, as Ronald Pruessen has explained, that the United Nations could be only a rudimentary organization, perhaps even more rudimentary than he had originally envisioned. In this new role of participant, Dulles may have also begun to recognize that at times the national goals of the United States were perhaps best *not* entrusted to international organization. This may explain, for instance, why he became concerned about preventing the interference of international organization in the domestic jurisdiction of the United States. It may also be why he became skeptical about the benefits of developing international law that would apply to individuals rather than states.

But perhaps the most important reason why Dulles's views on international organization changed was that his conception of the nature of the international system underwent a radical change. This change occurred as he began to perceive the Soviet Union as a fundamentally different force in international relations. Prior to the mid-1940s, Dulles believed that there were three major problems with the international system. First, there was no adequate means to accommodate properly the competing needs of the dynamic and static elements of the world. Second, states were pursuing economic policies without regard for the adverse affects that these policies were having on the rest of the world. Third, the world was suffering from grave spiritual inadequacies. These problems, Dulles felt, led to war. Without timely peaceful change, the dynamic states--Germany, Italy, and Japan--were forced to pursue change through the use of force. Poor economic conditions provided circumstances under which dictators gained power in these three states and in Russia, and although the revolutions in Germany and Russia may have begun because of depressed economies, they quickly became atheistic and devoted to overturning the old world order, presenting a major moral and political problem.

During this early period, Dulles did not seem to regard the Soviet Union as fundamentally different from other states. Although, as Pruessen has argued, Dulles may have regarded communism as a grave threat, he did not see the Soviet Union as being synonymous with communism.[1] Instead, it simply seemed to be another great power.[2] He placed it in the same category as Germany and even compared them both with revolutionary France of the late eighteenth century. As noted earlier, Dulles explained: "Just as the French Revolution, which grew out of economic distress, became atheistic, so the German and Russian are atheistic."[3] Indeed, he even seemed to condone a certain amount of Russian expansion. As late as 1945, he argued that "[s]ome expansions and contractions of zones of national influence are reprehensible and some may be desirable"; "the expansion of the U.S.S.R. from the low ebb to which Russia fell under the Tsars"[4] was among the desirable changes. Moreover, while he believed that spiritual inadequacies existed in the Soviet Union, he also felt that they were present in the United States, whose efforts to discourage change and to promote hatred of the enemy were immoral and un-Christian.

During 1945 and 1946, however, Dulles's perception of the nature of the Soviet Union underwent a dramatic change. He began to see the country as an "evil" nation, bent on imposing totalitarian police states upon helpless peoples throughout the world. Indeed, he castigated the Soviets in terms that he had declined to use for Nazi Germany. The Soviet Union was not just another great power; it was something drastically different.[5] He told a group of churchmen in September of 1946 that "[w]e seem to be witnessing a challenge to established civilization--the kind of thing which occurs only once in centuries."[6] He then went on to compare the Soviet challenge to the world to the Islamic challenge to Christianity in the tenth century. In essence, even though he continued to recognize a number of problems in the international system, there now seemed to be one overriding problem, the Soviet Union.[7]

Exactly why this change in Dulles's perception of the Soviets took place remains unclear,[8] and the reason lies largely beyond the scope of this study. Nevertheless, several factors can be suggested.

First, starting in 1945, Dulles had begun working with Soviet negotiators at the United Nations and elsewhere, and was quickly becoming exposed to Soviet intransigence firsthand.[9]   Second, he apparently began intensively studying Soviet ideology as reflected in the writings of Stalin and others.[10] This doctrine, he felt, went a long way toward explaining the Soviet-backed subversive activities that he was seeing in the world. Third, as Pruessen explains, the atmosphere around Dulles was becoming decidely anti-Soviet. Not only were U.S. leaders in general beginning to see the Soviets in a new light, but those close to him, such as Arthur Vandenberg and Allen Dulles, were becoming quite critical of the Soviet Union.[11] Fourth, he was beginning to perceive Soviet aggression and other activities that seemed to constitute a threat to the international organization that he had worked so hard to establish.[12]   But whatever the precise reasons may have been, by the end of 1946 it was clear that Dulles's understanding of the international system had changed.

With this new awareness of the threat of Soviet communism, he saw the tasks of international organization differently than before. Instead of peaceful change, collective security or one of its substitutes became the primary function of international organization. As a delegate to the United Nations, Dulles understood the inability of the Security Council to act and worked to utilize the General Assembly and regional organizations to prevent aggression. As secretary of state, while continuing to support the U.N. actions in this area, he tended to place more practical value on the collective defense activities of regional organizations. He praised existing organizations, such as NATO and the OAS, and worked to establish SEATO. These organizations, he believed, could function in accordance with article 51 of the charter to provide the effective deterrent to aggression that the universal organization could not.

In conjunction with this new concentration on collective defense, Dulles also began to acknowledge the existence of international legal norms, especially those relating to the use of force. He came to believe that Article 2(4) of the charter needed to be respected and upheld if the U.N. system were to survive. Indeed, this attitude, which came rather late in his life, was no doubt one reason why he earned the reputation of being a "legalist." Furthermore, while he continued to consider the promotion of peaceful change an important function of international organization, he now made it clear that change had to be limited by principles of justice, stability, and law.

In short, Dulles had undergone a "conversion." But the most remarkable aspect of this conversion was its apparent completeness. Even though his "discovery"[13] of the Soviets may have been the factor that initially led him to modify his views on international organization, he did not then see international organization solely as an anti-Soviet instrument. Once he accepted the need for strong collective defense mechanisms and fidelity to international law, he accepted it across the board. Thus, he could oppose three important allies of the United States during the Suez crisis because he believed that it was necessary to uphold the charter prohibition of aggressive use of force no matter who the culprit may have been.

A fourth observation that can be made about Dulles was that he seemed to recognize a change in the nature of international *conflict* and the need for international organization to respond accordingly. Two elements seemed to alter the nature of conflict: the development of nuclear weapons and the use of indirect aggression. The United Nations Charter, he repeatedly explained, was formulated before the destructive potential of nuclear weapons was known. The charter was thus a "pre-atomic" document that failed to address the problems raised by these new weapons of mass destruction. Because of this, he supported efforts to revise the charter, presumably to provide a greater role for the United Nations in the regulation of nuclear weapons and atomic energy. Indirect aggression also seemed to be a new element in international conflict. Prior to 1945, most major conflicts had resulted from overt aggression. The army of one state would march across the border of another state. Following World War II, however, fewer wars were of that nature. Instead of overt aggression, one state would commit aggression against another state through methods of subversion, by supporting, both financially and militarily, rebels within another state--indirect aggression.[14] Beginning with his work at the United Nations in the late 1940s, Dulles came to recognize the problem of indirect aggression. It too, he believed, constituted a threat against the political independence and territorial integrity of states, and was therefore a violation of Article 2(4). He seemed to feel that indirect aggression consisted not only of physical aid to rebels, but also of such actions as propaganda broadcasting, when it reached a certain level. International organization, he believed, needed to respond to this problem, and during the Lebanese crisis he even suggested the establishment of a United Nations "standing group" that could investigate allegations of indirect aggression.

In conclusion, even though this study has examined only one aspect of Dulles's life and can not be considered the definitive study of the man, it has revealed one very important fact--John Foster Dulles was a complex individual. Too often historians and political scientists have painted Dulles as a one-dimensional man. For instance, Barbara Tuchman, in her 1984 book *The March of Folly*, has said:

> The Republicans also brought to office a domineering policy-maker in foreign affairs, John Foster Dulles, a man devoted to the offensive by training and temperament. If Truman and Acheson adopted cold war rhetoric even to

excess, it was at least partly in reaction to being accused of belonging to the "party of treason," as McCarthy called the Democrats, and to the peculiar national frenzy over the "loss" of China. Dulles, the new Secretary of State, was a cold war extremist *naturally*, a drum-beater with the instincts of a bully, deliberately combative because that was the way he believed foreign relations should be conducted.[15]

Tuchman here implies that while Truman's and Acheson's cold war approach can be attributed to political factors, Dulles's cold-war attitudes lay in his very nature. The findings of this study do not support this interpretation. It may be true that Dulles always possessed certain personality traits and beliefs that allowed him to develop into the strong anti-communist that he was in the 1950s.[16] But the Dulles of the 1920s, 1930s, and early 1940s was not a cold warrior. His emphasis during this period was on peaceful change and accommodation, not "holding the line" or "going to the brink." To portray Dulles as a cold warrior by nature fails to acknowledge the thoughts and actions of most of his life. It ignores a number of fascinating elements of his early thought--his concern with change, his functionalist approach, his support for arms control, and his initial tendency to deny the existence of international law. It fails to recognize that many of the elements from his early thought continued to be present, in one form or another, during his later period and may have had some influence on his policy decisions. Finally, the portrait of Dulles as cold warrior ignores the most fundamental aspect of his thought; it was suscepible to change. Just like the international system that he described in his writings and speeches, Dulles's ideas were dynamic. They changed as his role in international affairs changed and as his perception of the international system changed. Sometimes these changes were slow; at other times they were more abrupt. To fail to recognize them, however, is to ignore both the complexity and subtlety of his thought, and to leave history with a cardboard image of John Foster Dulles.

NOTES

1. Pruessen, *John Foster Dulles*, 168-178. This chapter draws heavily on Preussen's discussion of the change in Dulles.

2. Ibid., 272.

3. Dulles, "The Church's Role in Developing the Bases of a Just and Durable Peace," May 28, 1941, *JFD Papers*, 12.

4. Dulles, "The General Assembly," 1, 3.

5. See Pruessen, *John Foster Dulles*, 287-288.

6. Dulles Address, Sept. 8, 1946, quoted in Pruessen, *John Foster Dulles*, 286.

7. Ibid., 290.

8. This is Pruessen's contention. See ibid., 287–297.

9. Hoopes suggests this factor (*The Devil and John Foster Dulles*, 62–63).

10. Ibid., 63–67.

11. Pruessen, *John Foster Dulles*, 293–294.

12. This factor is partially derived from Pruessen's discussion (ibid., 289–290).

13. Hoopes titles his chapter "Discovering the Russians." See Hoopes, *The Devil and John Foster Dulles*, 62.

14. See J. Moore, "Toward an Applied Theory for the Regulation of Intervention," in J. Moore, ed., *Law and Civil War in the Modern World* (Baltimore: John Hopkins University Press, 1974), 3.

15. Tuchman, *The March of Folly*, 252.

16. See, for example, Pruessen, *John Foster Dulles*, 291–293.

Selected Bibliography

PRIMARY SOURCES

The John Foster Dulles Papers. Princeton, N. J.: Princeton University. (Cited as *JFD Papers*.)

The Eisenhower Papers. Princeton, N.J.: Princeton University. (These are copies of the Eisenhower Papers that are housed in the Dulles Collection. They are cited as *Eisenhower-JFD Papers*.)

National Archives. Materials relating to John Foster Dulles and U.S. Foreign Policy (1919-1922). Washington, D. C.

United Nations. *General Assembly, Official Records* 1946-1950.

United Nations. *United Nations Conference on International Organization*. Documents. 1945.

United States. *The Charter of the U.N.: Hearings Before the Senate Committee on Foreign Relations*. 79th Cong., 1st Sess. Washington, D. C., 1945.

United States. *Department of State Bulletin*. Washington, D. C., 1953-1959.

United States. *Foreign Relations of the United States*, Washington, D. C., 1945-1954.

United States. *International Court of Justice, Hearings Before a Subcommittee of the Committee on Foreign Relations, United States Senate*. 79th Cong., 2nd Sess. Washington, D. C., 1946.

United States. *Structure of the United Nations and the Relation of the United States to the United Nations, Hearings Before the Committee on Foreign Affairs, House of Representatives*. 80th Cong., 2nd Sess. Washington, D. C., 1948.

BOOKS BY DULLES

Dulles, John Foster. *War, Peace and Change.* New York: Harper and Brothers, 1939.
_____. *War or Peace.* New York: Macmillan, 1950.

OTHER BOOKS

Beal, John Robinson. *John Foster Dulles.* New York: Harper & Row, 1959.
Berding, Andrew H. *Dulles on Diplomacy.* Princeton: D. Van Nostrand Co., 1965.
Claude, Inis L., Jr. *Power and International Relations.* New York: Random House, 1962.
_____. *Swords Into Plowshares*, 4th ed. New York: Random House, 1971.
Comfort, Mildred Houghton. *John Foster Dulles: Peacemaker.* Minneapolis: T. S. Denison, 1960.
Drummond, Roscoe, and Gaston Coblentz. *Duel at the Brink: John Foster Dulles's Command of American Power.* London: Weidenfeld & Nicolson, 1960.
Dulles, Eleanor Lansing. *John Foster Dulles: The Last Year.* New York: Harcourt Brace Jovanovich, 1963.
Eisenhower, Dwight D. *Mandate for Change: 1953-1956.* Garden City: Doubleday, 1963.
_____. *Waging Peace, 1956-61.* Garden City: Doubleday, 1965.
Finer, Herman. *Dulles Over Suez: The Theory and Practice of His Diplomacy.* Chicago: Quadrangle, 1964.
Gerson, Louis L. *John Foster Dulles.* New York: Cooper Square, 1967.
Goodrich, Leland M., Edvard Hambro, and Anne Patricia Simons. *Charter of the United Nations: Commentary and Documents.* New York: Columbia University Press, 1969.
Graebner, Norman A. *Cold War Diplomacy: American Foreign Policy 1945-1975.* 2nd. ed. New York: D. Van Nostrand Co., 1977.
Guhin, Michael A. *John Foster Dulles: A Statesman and His Times.* New York and London: Columbia University Press, 1972.
Heller, Deane, and David Heller. *John Foster Dulles: Soldier for Peace.* New York: Holt, Rinehart & Winston, 1960.
Hoopes, Townsend. *The Devil and John Foster Dulles.* Boston: Little, Brown and Co., 1973.
Keynes, John Maynard. *A Revision of the Treaty.* London: Macmillan, 1922.
Mitrany, David. *A Working Peace System.* Chicago: Quadrangle, 1966.
Pruessen, Ronald W. *John Foster Dulles: The Road to Power.* New

York: The Free Press, 1982.

Rakowska-Harmstone, Teresa, and Andrew Gyorgy. *Communism in Eastern Europe.* Bloomington and London: Indiana University Press, 1979.

Russell, Ruth B., and Jeanette E. Muther. *A History of the United Nations Charter: The Role of the United States 1940-1945.* Washington, D.C.: Brookings, 1958.

Toulouse, Mark G. *The Transformation of John Foster Dulles.* Macon, Georgia: Mercer University Press, 1985.

Tuchman, Barbara W. *The March of Folly: From Troy to Vietnam.* New York: Alfred A. Knopf, 1984.

Vandenberg, Arthur H., Jr., ed. *The Private Papers of Senator Vandenberg.* Westport, Conn.: Greenwood Press, 1974.

Van Dusen, Henry P., ed. *The Spiritual Legacy of John Foster Dulles.* Philadelphia: Westminister Press, 1960.

ARTICLES BY DULLES

Dulles, John Foster. "The Aftermath of the World War," *International Conciliation*, No. 369, April 1941, pp. 265-271.

_____. "The Allied Debts," *Foreign Affairs*, October 1922, pp. 117-132.

_____. "Conceptions and Misconceptions Regarding Intervention," *Annals of the American Academy of Political and Social Science*, July 1929, pp. 102-104.

_____. "A First Balance Sheet of the United Nations," *International Conciliation*, No. 420, April 1946, pp. 117-182.

_____. "Our Foreign Loan Policy," *Foreign Affairs*, October 1926, pp. 33-48.

_____. "The Future of the United Nations," *International Conciliation*, No. 445, November 1948, pp. 579-590.

_____. "The General Assembly," *Foreign Affairs*, October 1945, pp. 1-11.

_____. "Ideas are not Enough," *International Conciliation*, No. 409, March 1945, pp. 131-141.

_____. "Peaceful Change, *International Conciliation*, No. 369, April 1941, pp. 493- 498.

_____. "Policy for Security and Peace," *Foreign Affairs*, April 1954, pp. 363-364.

_____. "A Policy of Boldness," *Life*, May 17, 1952, pp. 146-160.

_____. "The Road to Peace," *The Atlantic Monthly*, October 1935, pp. 492-499.

_____. "Should Economic Sanctions Be Applied in International Disputes?," *Annals of the American Academy of Political and Social Science*, July 1932, pp. 103-108.

_____. "What Shall We Do with the U.N.?," *The Christian Century*, September 3, 1947, pp. 1041-1042.

OTHER ARTICLES

Claude, Inis L., Jr. "The OAS, the UN and the United States." Reprinted in Joseph S. Nye, Jr., ed., *International Regionalism.* Boston: Little, Brown & Co., 1968, pp. 3-21.
Kovrig, Bennette. "Hungary." In Teresa Rakowska-Harmstone and Andrew   Gyorgy,   ed.,   *Communism   in   Eastern   Europe.* Bloomington & London: Indiana University Press, 1979, pp. 71-99.
Preuss, Lawrence. "The International Court of Justice, The Senate, and Matters of Domestic Jurisdiction," *American Journal of International Law*, October 1946, pp. 720-736.

Index

About the Author

ANTHONY CLARK AREND is an Assistant Professor of Government at Georgetown University. He is the editor of and a contributor to *The United States and the Compulsory Jurisdiction of the International Court of Justice* and a coeditor of and contributor to *The Falklands War: Lessons for Strategy, Diplomacy, and International Law.* His articles have been published in the *Virginia Journal of International Law.*